# CALIFORNIA History–Social Science

# myWorld
## INTERACTIVE

3

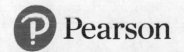
# Pearson

Boston, Massachusetts    Chandler, Arizona
Glenview, Illinois    New York, New York

Pearson would like to extend a special thank you to all of the California teachers who helped guide the development of this program. We gratefully acknowledge your efforts to realize the possibilities of elementary Social Studies teaching and learning. Together, we will prepare California students for college, careers, and civic life.

**Cover:** Clock Tower of the Novato City Hall, Novato, California, USA
Credit: Dee Jolie / Alamy Stock Photo

Excerpts from the History-Social Science Content Standards for California Public Schools Grades K–5. Copyright © California Department of Education.

Credits appear on pages R65–R67, which constitute an extension of this copyright page.

ISBN-13: 978-0-328-95167-3
ISBN-10: 0-328-95167-6
12  20

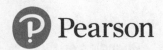

# Program Authors

**Dr. Linda B. Bennett**
Faculty, Social Studies Education
College of Education
University of Missouri
Columbia, MO

**Dr. James B. Kracht**
Professor Emeritus
Departments of Geography and
　Teaching, Learning, and Culture
Texas A&M University
College Station, TX

# Reviewers and Consultants

## Program Consultants

**ELL Consultant**
**Jim Cummins Ph.D.**

Professor Emeritus,
Department of
　Curriculum, Teaching,
　and Learning
University of Toronto
Toronto, Canada

**Differentiated Instruction**
**Consultant**

**Kathy Tuchman Glass**
President of Glass
　Educational Consulting
Woodside, CA

**Reading Consultant**
**Elfrieda H. Hiebert Ph.D.**

Founder, President and
　CEO, TextProject, Inc.
University of California
　Santa Cruz

**Inquiry and C3 Consultant**

**Dr. Kathy Swan**
Professor of Curriculum
　and Instruction
University of Kentucky
Lexington, KY

## Academic Reviewers

**Paul Apodaca, Ph.D.**

Associate Professor,
　American Studies
Chapman University
Orange, CA

**Warren J. Blumenfeld, Ed.D.**

Former Associate
　Professor, Iowa State
　University, School
　of Education
South Hadley, MA

**Dr. Albert M. Camarillo**

Professor of History,
　Emeritus
Stanford University
Palo Alto, CA

**Steven Hackel, Ph.D.**

Professor, History
Department of History
University of California
　at Riverside
Riverside, CA

**Xiaojian Zhao**

Professor, Department
　of Asian American
　Studies
University of California,
　Santa Barbara
Santa Barbara, CA

## Teacher Reviewers

**Stephanie Fortunato**
Teacher
Inglewood USD
Inglewood, CA

**Mercedes Kirk**
First grade teacher
Folsom Cordova USD
Folsom, CA

**Janet Mulder**
Educational Consultant
San Diego, CA

**Doris Sterling**
Teacher
Sacramento City USD
Sacramento, CA

**Kristin Sullens**
Teacher, Grade 4
Chula Vista ESD
San Diego, CA

## Program Partner

***Campaign for the Civic Mission of Schools*** is a coalition of
over 70 national civic learning, education, civic engagement,
and business groups committed to improving the quality and
quantity of civic learning in American schools.

CAMPAIGN FOR THE CIVIC MISSION OF SCHOOLS

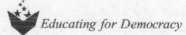

*Educating for Democracy*

# Celebrating California and the Nation

**HSS** 3.1, 3.1.1, 3.3.1, 3.4.3, 3.4.4 **Analysis** HI.2

# Geography Skills Handbook

**HSS** 3.1 **Analysis** CST.4, CST.5, HI.2

# Writing Workshop

**HSS** 3.1.2 **Analysis** HI.2

# Using Primary and Secondary Sources

**HSS** 3.2, 3.2.3, 3.3.1, 3.3.3 **Analysis** RE.1, RE.2

# Chapter 1
# California's Geography and Resources

GO ONLINE FOR DIGITAL RESOURCES

 **ETEXT**

 **VIDEO**

- **Field Trip Video**
  Where Two Deserts Meet

 **AUDIO**

**Rap About It!** lyrics and music

**INTERACTIVITY**

- **Big Question Activity**
  How do we interact with our environment?
- **Quest Interactivities**
  Quest Kick Off
  Quest Connections
  Quest Findings
- **Lesson Interactivities**
  Lesson Introduction
  Lesson Review
- **Digital Skill Practice**
  Compare and Contrast
  Analyze Images

 **GAMES**

Vocabulary Practice

 **ASSESSMENT**

Lesson Quizzes and Chapter Tests

**The BIG Question** How do we interact with our environment?

# Chapter 2
# American Indians of California

GO ONLINE FOR
DIGITAL RESOURCES

ETEXT

VIDEO

- **Field Trip Video**
California's First
Communities

AUDIO

**Rap About It!** lyrics
and music

INTERACTIVITY

- **Big Question
Activity**
How did the first
people in my
community live?
- **Quest
Interactivities**
Quest Kick Off
Quest Connections
Quest Findings
- **Lesson
Interactivities**
Lesson Introduction
Lesson Review
- **Digital Skill
Practice**
Main Idea and
Details
Compare Points
of View

GAMES

Vocabulary Practice

ASSESSMENT

Lesson Quizzes and
Chapter Tests

**The BIG Question** How did the first people in my community live?

GO ONLINE FOR
DIGITAL RESOURCES

ETEXT

VIDEO

- **Field Trip Video**
  Golden
  Opportunities

AUDIO

**Rap About It!** lyrics
and music

INTERACTIVITY

- **Big Question
  Activity**
  How does life
  change throughout
  history?

- **Quest
  Interactivities**
  Quest Kick Off
  Quest Connections
  Quest Findings

- **Lesson
  Interactivities**
  Lesson Introduction
  Lesson Review

- **Digital Skill
  Practice**
  Cause and Effect
  Interpret Timelines

GAMES

Vocabulary Practice

ASSESSMENT

Lesson Quizzes and
Chapter Tests

**The BIG Question** How does life change
throughout history?

# Chapter 4

# Government, Landmarks, and Symbols

## GO ONLINE FOR DIGITAL RESOURCES

 ETEXT

 VIDEO

- **Field Trip Video** Touring a Government Landmark

 AUDIO

**Rap About It!** lyrics and music

 INTERACTIVITY

- **Big Question Activity** Why do we have government?
- **Quest Interactivities** Quest Kick Off Quest Connections Quest Findings
- **Lesson Interactivities** Lesson Introduction Lesson Review
- **Digital Skill Practice** Sequence Interpret Graphs

GAMES

Vocabulary Practice

ASSESSMENT

Lesson Quizzes and Chapter Tests

The **BIG** Question **Why do we have government?**

# Chapter 5

# Citizenship and Civic Engagement

GO ONLINE FOR
DIGITAL RESOURCES

 ETEXT

 VIDEO

- **Field Trip Video**
Volunteering:
Mentor, Tutor,
Friend

🔊 AUDIO

**Rap About It!** lyrics
and music

👆 INTERACTIVITY

- **Big Question
Activity**
How can I
participate?
- **Quest
Interactivities**
Quest Kick Off
Quest Connections
Quest Findings
- **Lesson
Interactivities**
Lesson Introduction
Lesson Review
- **Digital Skill
Practice**
Distinguish Fact
From Fiction
Ask and Answer
Questions

🎮 GAMES

Vocabulary Practice

☑ ASSESSMENT

Lesson Quizzes and
Chapter Tests

**The BIG Question** How can I participate?

# Chapter 6 Economics

## GO ONLINE FOR DIGITAL RESOURCES

 ETEXT

 VIDEO

- **Field Trip Video**
  Farmers Market: Meet Me at Third and Fairfax

 AUDIO

**Rap About It!** lyrics and music

👆 INTERACTIVITY

- **Big Question Activity**
  How do people get what they want and need?
- **Quest Interactivities**
  Quest Kick Off
  Quest Connections
  Quest Findings
- **Lesson Interactivities**
  Lesson Introduction
  Lesson Review
- **Digital Skill Practice**
  Summarize
  Analyze Costs and Benefits

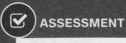 GAMES

Vocabulary Practice

☑ ASSESSMENT

Lesson Quizzes and Chapter Tests

## Quests

Ask questions, explore sources, and cite evidence to support your view!

## Maps

Where did this happen? Find out on these maps in your text.

# Charts and Graphs

Find these charts, graphs, and tables in your text. They'll help you pull it together.

# Primary Sources

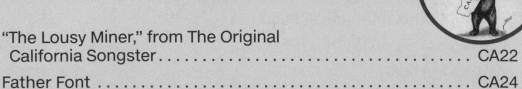

Read primary sources to hear voices from the time.

## Primary Sources continued

## People to Know

Read about the people who made history.

### Citizenship

## Biographies Online

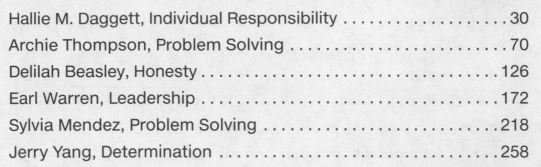

Abigail Adams

John Adams

Samuel Adams

Elsie Allen

James Armistead

Benedict Arnold

Clara Barton

Delilah Beasley

James Beckwourth

William Bradford

Chaz Bono

Sergey Brin

Jerry Brown

Edmund Burke

Juan Rodríguez
    Cabrillo

Tani Gorre Cantil-Sakauye

Christopher "Kit" Carson

César Chávez

Louise Clappe

Thomas Clifford

Christopher Columbus

Hernán Cortés

Juan Crespi

Charles Crocker

Hallie M. Daggett

Juan Bautista de Anza

Pedro Menéndez de Avilés

Samuel de Champlain

Gaspar de Portolá

Antonio Lopez de Santa Anna

María Angustias de la Guerra

Bartolomeu Dias

John Dickinson

Walt Disney

Frederick Douglass

Ralph Waldo Emerson

William Fargo

| | |
|---|---|
| Wong Chin Foo | Biddy Mason |
| Benjamin Franklin | Ferdinand Magellan |
| John C. Fremont | Louis B. Mayer |
| Eric Garcetti | Sylvia Mendez |
| John Gast | Metacom |
| Nathan Hale | Harvey Milk |
| Alexander Hamilton | James Monroe |
| John Hancock | Samuel Morse |
| Kamala D. Harris | John Muir |
| Patrick Henry | José Nicolás |
| Mark Hopkins | First Lady Pat Nixon |
| Henry Hudson | Thomas Paine |
| Dolores Huerta | Charley Parkhurst |
| Collis P. Huntington | William Penn |
| Anne Hutchinson | William Pitt |
| Daniel Inouye | James K. Polk |
| Joseph James | Prince Henry the Navigator |
| Thomas Jefferson | Edmund Randolph |
| Hiram Johnson | Ronald Reagan |
| Billie Jean King | Paul Revere |
| Martin Luther King, Jr. | Sally Ride |
| King Charles III | Jackie Robinson |
| King George III | Eleanor Roosevelt |
| Dorothea Lange | Sarah Royce |
| Lewis and Clark | Bernarda Ruiz |
| Abraham Lincoln | Sacagawea |
| Henry Wadsworth Longfellow | Haym Salomon |
| Mary Ludwig Hays | Deborah Sampson |
| Lord Dunmore | José Julio Sarria |
| Wilma Mankiller | Dalip Singh Saund |
| James Wilson Marshall | Junípero Serra |
| John Marshall | Roger Sherman |

## People to Know continued

Sir Francis Drake

John Drake Sloat

Jedediah Smith

John Smith

Leland Stanford

John Steinbeck

Levi Strauss

John A. Sutter

Mary Tape

Archie Thompson

Tisquantum

Harriet Tubman

Mariano Guadalupe Vallejo

Earl Warren

Mercy Otis Warren

George Washington

Henry Wells

Phillis Wheatley

Narcissa Whitman

Roger Williams

Sarah Winnemucca

John Winthrop

Jerry Yang

## Skills

Practice key skills in these skills lessons.

### Literacy Skills

### Critical Thinking Skills

## Skills continued

Gold found at Sutter's Mill.  Calif becoi

'48  1849  1850  1

## Map and Graph Skills

**Build Historical and Social Sciences Analysis Skills.**

## Analysis Skills

## Skills continued

## Skills Online

Analyze Cause and Effect

Analyze Costs and Benefits

Analyze Images

Ask and Answer Questions

Classify and Categorize

Compare and Contrast

Compare Viewpoints

Conduct Research

Create Charts

Deliver an Effective Presentation

Distinguish Fact and Opinion

Distinguish Fact From Fiction

Draw Conclusions

Draw Inferences

Evaluate Media Content

Generalize

Generate New Ideas

Identify Bias

Identify Main Idea and Details

Interpret Cultural Data on Maps

Interpret Economic Data on Maps

Interpret Graphs

Interpret Physical Maps

Interpret Timelines

Make Decisions

Predict Consequences

Resolve Conflict

Sequence

Solve Problems

Summarize

Use and Interpret Evidence

Use Latitude and Longitude

Use Primary and Secondary Sources

Use the Internet Safely

Work in Cooperative Teams

# Standards at a Glance

## History-Social Science Content Standards

| | |
|---|---|
| **3.1** | Students describe the physical and human geography and use maps, tables, graphs, photographs, and charts to organize information about people, places, and environments in a spatial context. |
| 3.1.1 | Identify geographical features in their local region (e.g., deserts, mountains, valleys, hills, coastal areas, oceans, lakes). |
| 3.1.2 | Trace the ways in which people have used the resources of the local region and modified the physical environment (e.g., a dam constructed upstream changed a river or coastline). |
| **3.2** | Students describe the American Indian nations in their local region long ago and in the recent past. |
| 3.2.1 | Describe national identities, religious beliefs, customs, and various folklore traditions. |
| 3.2.2 | Discuss the ways in which physical geography, including climate, influenced how the local Indian nations adapted to their natural environment (e.g., how they obtained food, clothing, tools). |
| 3.2.3 | Describe the economy and systems of government, particularly those with tribal constitutions, and their relationship to federal and state governments. |
| 3.2.4 | Discuss the interaction of new settlers with the already established Indians of the region. |
| **3.3** | Students draw from historical and community resources to organize the sequence of local historical events and describe how each period of settlement left its mark on the land. |
| 3.3.1 | Research the explorers who visited here, the newcomers who settled here, and the people who continue to come to the region, including their cultural and religious traditions and contributions. |
| 3.3.2 | Describe the economies established by settlers and their influence on the present-day economy, with emphasis on the importance of private property and entrepreneurship. |
| 3.3.3 | Trace why their community was established, how individuals and families contributed to its founding and development, and how the community has changed over time, drawing on maps, photographs, oral histories, letters, newspapers, and other primary sources. |
| **3.4** | Students understand the role of rules and laws in our daily lives and the basic structure of the U.S. government. |
| 3.4.1 | Determine the reasons for rules, laws, and the U.S. Constitution; the role of citizenship in the promotion of rules and laws; and the consequences for people who violate rules and laws. |
| 3.4.2 | Discuss the importance of public virtue and the role of citizens, including how to participate in a classroom, in the community, and in civic life. |

| | |
|---|---|
| 3.4.3 | Know the histories of important local and national landmarks, symbols, and essential documents that create a sense of community among citizens and exemplify cherished ideals (e.g., the U.S. flag, the bald eagle, the Statue of Liberty, the U.S. Constitution, the Declaration of Independence, the U.S. Capitol). |
| 3.4.4 | Understand the three branches of government, with an emphasis on local government. |
| 3.4.5 | Describe the ways in which California, the other states, and sovereign American Indian tribes contribute to the making of our nation and participate in the federal system of government. |
| 3.4.6 | Describe the lives of American heroes who took risks to secure our freedoms (e.g., Anne Hutchinson, Benjamin Franklin, Thomas Jefferson, Abraham Lincoln, Frederick Douglass, Harriet Tubman, Martin Luther King, Jr.). |
| **3.5** | Students demonstrate basic economic reasoning skills and an understanding of the economy of the local region. |
| 3.5.1 | Describe the ways in which local producers have used and are using natural resources, human resources, and capital resources to produce goods and services in the past and the present. |
| 3.5.2 | Understand that some goods are made locally, some elsewhere in the United States, and some abroad. |
| 3.5.3 | Understand that individual economic choices involve trade-offs and the evaluation of benefits and costs. |
| 3.5.4 | Discuss the relationship of students' "work" in school and their personal human capital. |

# Historical and Social Sciences Analysis Skills

## Chronological and Spatial Thinking

| | |
|---|---|
| **CST.1** | Students place key events and people of the historical era they are studying in a chronological sequence and within a spatial context; they interpret time lines. |
| **CST.2** | Students correctly apply terms related to time, including *past, present, future, decade, century,* and *generation.* |
| **CST.3** | Students explain how the present is connected to the past, identifying both similarities and differences between the two, and how some things change over time and some things stay the same. |
| **CST.4** | Students use map and globe skills to determine the absolute locations of places and interpret information available through a map's or globe's legend, scale, and symbolic representations. |
| **CST.5** | Students judge the significance of the relative location of a place (e.g., proximity to a harbor, on trade routes) and analyze how relative advantages or disadvantages can change over time. |

## Research, Evidence, and Point of View

| | |
|---|---|
| **RE.1** | Students differentiate between primary and secondary sources. |
| **RE.2** | Students pose relevant questions about events they encounter in historical documents, eyewitness accounts, oral histories, letters, diaries, artifacts, photographs, maps, artworks, and architecture. |
| **RE.3** | Students distinguish fact from fiction by comparing documentary sources on historical figures and events with fictionalized characters and events. |

## Historical Interpretation

| | |
|---|---|
| **HI.1** | Students summarize the key events of the era they are studying and explain the historical contexts of those events. |
| **HI.2** | Students identify the human and physical characteristics of the places they are studying and explain how those features form the unique character of those places. |
| **HI.3** | Students identify and interpret the multiple causes and effects of historical events. |
| **HI.4** | Students conduct cost-benefit analyses of historical and current events. |

# Welcome to Your Book!

**Your worktext is made up of chapters and lessons.**
**Each lesson starts with pages like this.**

**Look for these words as you read.**

**Words with yellow highlight are important social studies words. The sentence with the word will help you understand what the word means.**

---

## Lesson 1 · California's Geography

**INTERACTIVITY**
Participate in a class discussion to preview the content of this lesson.

**Unlock The BIG Question**
I will know about the physical features found in California.

### Vocabulary

physical geography
landform
elevation
range
valley
desert
irrigate
ecosystem

### Academic Vocabulary

feature
area
interact
common

### Jumpstart Activity

As a class, draw a simple map of your community on the board. Working one person at a time, draw a part of the map. Include your school, homes, roads, trees, parks, hills, and any bodies of water. What things are part of nature? What things are made by people?

What does the land look like where you live? Is it hilly, or flat? You might live near a body of water, like the ocean or a lake. Does the place where you live get hot during the summer? Perhaps it gets cold enough to snow in the winter.

Sierra Nevada mountains

4   Chapter 1 • California's Geography and Resources

The land, water, and other natural **features** of a place are its **physical geography**. The physical geography and features of California are what make it unique, or not like any other state. California's physical geography is made up of a variety of landforms and bodies of water. A **landform** is a natural part of Earth's surface. Mountains, deserts, and valleys are all types of landforms.

### Mountains and Hills

California is dotted with mountains and hills. A hill has a lower elevation than a mountain. **Elevation** is the height of land above sea level. The higher the elevation of a place, the cooler its temperature. A mountain's peak can rise to very high elevations.

Mountains are usually found in a **range**, or group, of other mountains. California has a number of major mountain ranges, such as the Sierra Nevada mountain range. Hills also come in groups, like the Montezuma Hills in Northern California. A hill found next to a mountain is called a *foothill*.

Montezuma Hills

**HSS** 3.1, 3.1.1 **Analysis** HI.2
**ELA** RI.3.1, RI.3.2, RI.3.4, RI.3.7, RF.3.3.b

### Academic Vocabulary

**feature** • *n.*, an important or interesting part of something

1. ☑ **Reading Check**
**Compare and Contrast** Study the landforms in the photos. **Identify** and circle two differences you see between the mountains and the hills.

Lesson 1 • California's Geography   5

**Reading Checks will help you make sure you understood what you read.**

---

## Your Turn!

### Flip through your book with a partner.

1. Find the start of another lesson.
   What do you see on the page?

This book will give you a lot of chances to figure things out. Then you can show what you have figured out and give your reasons.

The Quest Kick Off will tell you the goal of the Quest.

Watch for Quest Connections all through the chapter.

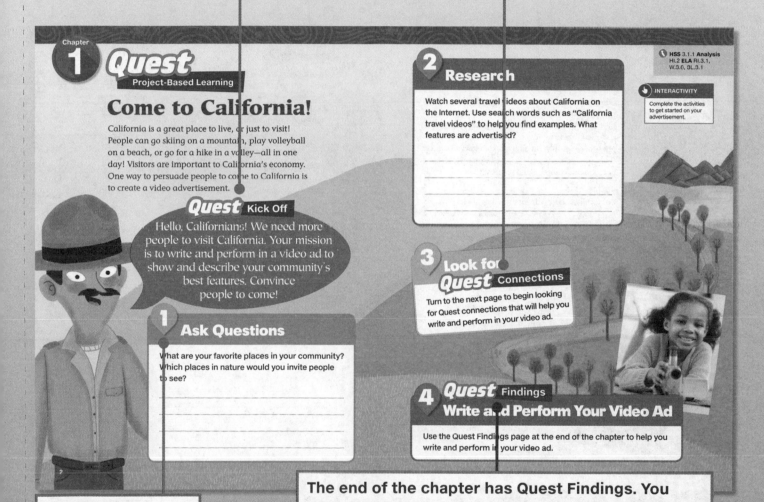

Chapter 1

**Quest**
Project-Based Learning

## Come to California!

California is a great place to live, or just to visit! People can go skiing on a mountain, play volleyball on a beach, or go for a hike in a valley—all in one day! Visitors are important to California's economy. One way to persuade people to come to California is to create a video advertisement.

**Quest Kick Off**

Hello, Californians! We need more people to visit California. Your mission is to write and perform in a video ad to show and describe your community's best features. Convince people to come!

**1 Ask Questions**

What are your favorite places in your community? Which places in nature would you invite people to see?

**2 Research**

Watch several travel videos about California on the Internet. Use search words such as "California travel videos" to help you find examples. What features are advertised?

HSS 3.1.1 Analysis HI.2 ELA RI.3.1, W.3.0, SL.3.1

INTERACTIVITY
Complete the activities to get started on your advertisement.

**3 Look for Quest Connections**

Turn to the next page to begin looking for Quest connections that will help you write and perform in your video ad.

**4 Quest Findings**
**Write and Perform Your Video Ad**

Use the Quest Findings page at the end of the chapter to help you write and perform in your video ad.

You can get started right away.

The end of the chapter has Quest Findings. You will write or have a discussion or make something. Share what you figured out with other people.

2. Find two words with yellow highlight. What page are they on?

3. Find another Reading Check. What does it ask you to do?

4. Find another Quest. What is it called?

# Learn to use important skills.

**Read the explanation. Look at all the text and pictures.**

**Practice the skill. You'll be ready to use it whenever you need it.**

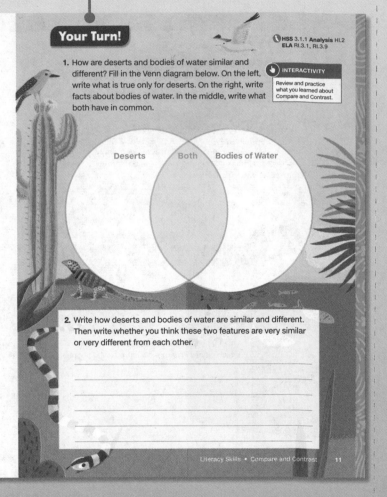

## Literacy Skills

### Compare and Contrast

When you compare two things, you find ways that they are alike. When you contrast them, you find how they are different. Comparing and contrasting is a great way to understand more about California's physical geography. Read the text below about California's deserts and bodies of water. Think about how you can compare and contrast them.

California's bodies of water are part of its physical geography. The Pacific Ocean forms California's western coast. People surf and sunbathe on its beaches. Beautiful rivers such as the American River provide visitors with a place to canoe and fish. California's rivers and lakes provide water for irrigation and personal use.

California's deserts are also part of its physical geography. People enjoy visiting deserts, but not very many people live there. The weather is often dry, and deserts lack resources to support life, such as water.

**Fun Fact**
Bighorn sheep that live in the deserts of California often go without drinking water for a week or longer in the summer.

## Your Turn!

HSS 3.1.1 Analysis HI.2
ELA RI.3.1, RI.3.9

1. How are deserts and bodies of water similar and different? Fill in the Venn diagram below. On the left, write what is true only for deserts. On the right, write facts about bodies of water. In the middle, write what both have in common.

**INTERACTIVITY**
Review and practice what you learned about Compare and Contrast.

Deserts     Both     Bodies of Water

2. Write how deserts and bodies of water are similar and different. Then write whether you think these two features are very similar or very different from each other.

_____
_____
_____
_____
_____

## Your Turn!

### Work with a partner.

1. Find another skill lesson. What skill will you learn?
   Talk about another time you might need that skill.

**Every chapter has primary source pages. You can read or look at these sources to learn right from people who were there.**

Find out what this source is about and who made it.

These questions help you think about the source.

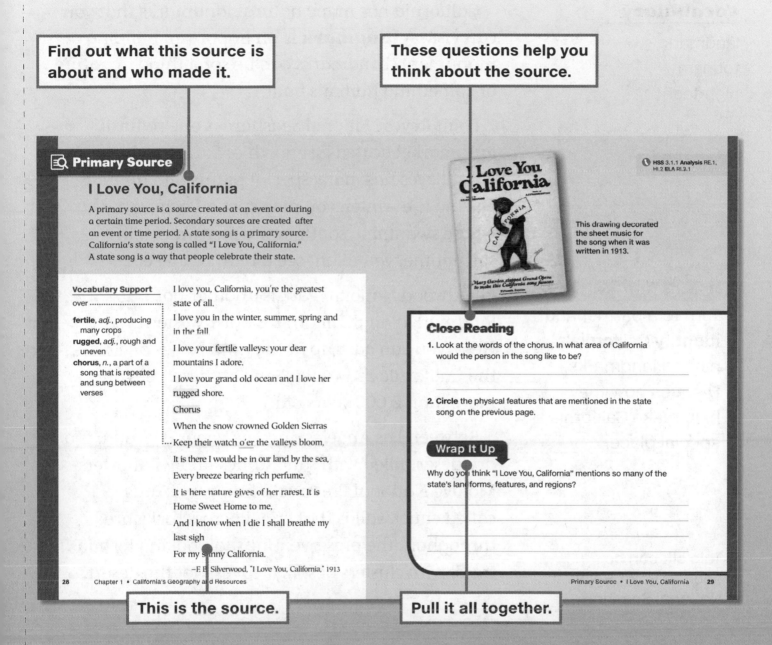

HSS 3.1.1 Analysis RE.1, HI.2 ELA RI.3.1

### I Love You, California

A primary source is a source created at an event or during a certain time period. Secondary sources are created after an event or time period. A state song is a primary source. California's state song is called "I Love You, California." A state song is a way that people celebrate their state.

This drawing decorated the sheet music for the song when it was written in 1913.

**Vocabulary Support**

over ...........

**fertile**, *adj.*, producing many crops

**rugged**, *adj.*, rough and uneven

**chorus**, *n.*, a part of a song that is repeated and sung between verses

I love you, California, you're the greatest state of all.

I love you in the winter, summer, spring and in the fall

I love your fertile valleys; your dear mountains I adore.

I love your grand old ocean and I love her rugged shore.

Chorus

When the snow crowned Golden Sierras

Keep their watch o'er the valleys bloom,

It is there I would be in our land by the sea,

Every breeze bearing rich perfume.

It is here nature gives of her rarest. It is Home Sweet Home to me,

And I know when I die I shall breathe my last sigh

For my sunny California.

—F. B. Silverwood, "I Love You, California," 1913

### Close Reading

1. Look at the words of the chorus. In what area of California would the person in the song like to be?

_____

_____

2. **Circle** the physical features that are mentioned in the state song on the previous page.

**Wrap It Up**

Why do you think "I Love You, California" mentions so many of the state's land forms, features, and regions?

_____

_____

_____

This is the source.

Pull it all together.

2. Find another primary source in your book. What is the source about?

# Celebrating California and the Nation

## Natural Landmarks of California

**Vocabulary**

landmark
tourism
high-tech

California has many natural landmarks that you can visit. A **landmark** is an important building or monument. Landmarks can be something in nature or something humans built.

Point Reyes National Seashore is one natural landmark. Located just north of San Francisco, Point Reyes has many special plants and animals. During the winter, you may spot a Pacific gray whale swimming south to warmer waters. In springtime, you might see a herd of tule elk.

Redwood National Park is another natural landmark along California's northwestern coast. Here, you can gaze up at the tallest trees on Earth, the California redwood. Some of these trees are more than 2,000 years old.

Between Los Angeles and Las Vegas, Nevada, is a dry desert filled with sand dunes and wildflowers. Mojave National Preserve is home to lizards called chuckwallas that crawl across rocky areas throughout the preserve. Unusual-looking Joshua trees, with clusters of spiky leaves, dot the desert.

**1.** ☑ **Reading Check**
Turn to a partner and **identify** California's natural landmarks. **Discuss** how they help make California a special place.

Tule elk can be seen at Point Reyes National Seashore.

# California Business and Tourism

California's economy is larger than any other state's economy. It is even larger than the economies of many countries!

Our state is a leader in tourism, farming, and technology. **Tourism** is the business of providing hotels, restaurants, and entertainment for visitors. Many people visit California's tourist attractions. These include Disneyland in southern California and Golden Gate National Recreation Area in the north. People visit beaches to swim, surf, and play volleyball. They travel to the mountains to snowboard and ski.

Southern California's beaches are a major tourist attraction.

Good soil in the Central Valley and coastal valleys makes California a leader in the growing of vegetables, fruits, and nuts. Our state grows more than three quarters of the country's nectarines, olives, walnuts, and almonds. It leads in the growing of strawberries, peaches, grapes, and avocados.

One of the world's largest technology communities is called Silicon Valley. It is located in the southern part of the San Francisco Bay area. Companies like Google and Apple make computers and other electronics and computer services. These companies are leaders in **high-tech** products. They create some of the most advanced technology in the world.

California is a leading grower of avocados.

2. ☑ **Reading Check** With a partner, **summarize** how California is a leader in tourism, farming, and technology.

# Symbols of the United States and California

## Vocabulary

White House
state seal
seal
governor

The **White House** is an important landmark and symbol for our nation. Located in Washington, D.C., the White House is where the president of the United States lives and works. The White House symbolizes leadership and freedom for Americans.

Another symbol of our country is the American flag. We may say the Pledge of Allegiance to it each morning in school. By promising our loyalty, we show that we honor and care about the United States. We also create a sense of community with other citizens.

### Primary Source

I pledge allegiance to the flag of the United States of America, and to the Republic for which it stands, one Nation under God, indivisible, with liberty and justice for all.

—Pledge of Allegiance to the Flag of the United States, Adopted by U.S. Congress, 1942

California state seal

California has important symbols, too, like the **state seal**. A **seal** is an official symbol of a place, group, or office. The state motto, *Eureka*, meaning "I have found it," is written on the state seal. This motto symbolizes the discovery of gold. California Indians have seals that honor and symbolize their culture and beliefs. For example, the tribal seal of the Bishop Paiute shows black mountains that stand for the Sierra Nevada, a mountain range in eastern California.

3. ☑ Reading Check **Identify** symbols of our state and country. **Discuss** with a partner what each one means to you.

# California State Government

Just as our country has a federal government, California has a state government. The capital of California is Sacramento, a city in the Central Valley. Sacramento is between the Sierra Nevada and the coast.

The California State Legislature works at the capitol in Sacramento.

Government leaders work in Sacramento to make important decisions for our state. The California State Legislature meets in the capitol building to write laws. Two houses make up the Legislature: the Senate and the Assembly. California citizens elect the members of the State Legislature to represent their interests.

The **governor** is the leader of the executive branch of a state's government. California's governor lives in the Governor's Mansion. Citizens elect the governor, who signs the laws that the State Legislature makes. The governor can appoint other officials to help carry out these laws.

The governor lives in a mansion, or large home, in Sacramento.

Another part of California's government makes sure that people understand and follow the laws. The governor chooses judges, and then other state officials confirm, or approve, them. The judges work in the state court system.

4. ☑ **Reading Check** On a separate sheet of paper, **identify** and write the name of your governor, as well as the state senator and assembly member that serve the area in which you live. Explain the work that they do and how they are chosen.

Chinese Americans in California celebrate Chinese New Year with colorful parades.

## Vocabulary

culture
explorer
immigrant
pop culture
celebrity

Each year, Mexican American communities celebrate their culture on *el Cinco de Mayo*, or the Fifth of May.

# California's Culture

California is a state rich in culture. **Culture** refers to the arts, beliefs, behaviors, and ideas of a group of people. It also includes the group's values, traditions, languages, religions, and so much more.

Our state's culture has changed over hundreds of years. California Indians were the first people living here. Explorers from Spain and other European countries came to learn about the land and discover riches. An **explorer** is someone who goes to an unfamiliar place to learn about it. Later, settlers moved here to build homes and raise their families. When gold was discovered in northern California, people from Australia, South America, Central America, Asia, and Europe came to work here.

Today, California's immigrant population has grown in size and is now larger than any other state. An **immigrant** is a person who moves from one country to settle in a different country. More than 10 million immigrants call California their home. They come from China, Mexico, the Philippines, and many other countries.

Our state is considered a land of many cultures. If you walk down a big city street or visit a small town, you can see traditions that people have brought here from around the world that make our state special.

5. ☑ **Reading Check** **Identify** and underline some of the countries that California's immigrants come from.

CA4

# California's Pop Culture

Pop culture is alive and well in California! **Pop culture** is activities and products that target a wide audience. Pop culture makes California a special place. Since the 1960s, California has produced many popular music artists and groups. For example, Katy Perry, the Beach Boys, and the Eagles all started in California.

Los Angeles is often called the "entertainment capital of the world." Many movies and television shows are made in Hollywood. Millions of people watch films created by Steven Spielberg and other well-known directors. People also enjoy TV shows made in and around Los Angeles. Most shows feature celebrities like Ellen DeGeneres. A **celebrity** is someone who is famous. When visiting Los Angeles, people often want to take a tour of a movie or TV studio. They hope to spot their favorite celebrity up close!

California has the most professional sports teams of any state. It has five professional baseball teams alone! Many teams moved to California from other cities. This happened to two baseball teams in 1958. The Brooklyn Dodgers and the New York Giants became the Los Angeles Dodgers and San Francisco Giants. The Philadelphia Warriors are now the Golden State Warriors. This popular sports team will move in 2019 from Oakland to a new arena in San Francisco. The latest team to move to California is a football team. The Los Angeles Rams used to be the St. Louis Rams.

6. ☑ **Reading Check** **Identify** your favorite California sports team. Turn to a partner and talk about the team. Tell your partner about your favorite player. **Describe** him or her.

Ellen DeGeneres is a celebrity who hosts a TV show in Burbank, near Los Angeles.

The Golden State Warriors play basketball at the Oracle Arena in Oakland.

# Geography Skills Handbook

## Using Maps

**Vocabulary**

political map
title
map legend
map key
symbol
scale
compass rose

The map titled "California" is a political map. A **political map** shows information such as state or national borders. Political maps often show the capital cities and major cities of states or countries.

Knowing how to read a map is an important skill. There are tools on the map to help you. Look at the political map of California and find each of these map tools.

**Title**: The title tells you what the map shows.

**Map legend** or **map key**: The legend or key explains the meaning of the symbols on the map.

**Symbol**: A symbol is a marking or color that stands for something else.

**Scale**: The scale on the map shows distance. It helps you see how far apart locations are.

**Compass rose**: A compass rose shows you the cardinal directions of north, south, east, and west.

1. ☑ Reading Check **Analyze** the map and answer these questions.

   **Locate** and circle the title on the map.

   Circle on the map the symbol that is used for the state capital.

   Find the scale on the map. About how far is Sacramento from the Pacific Ocean?

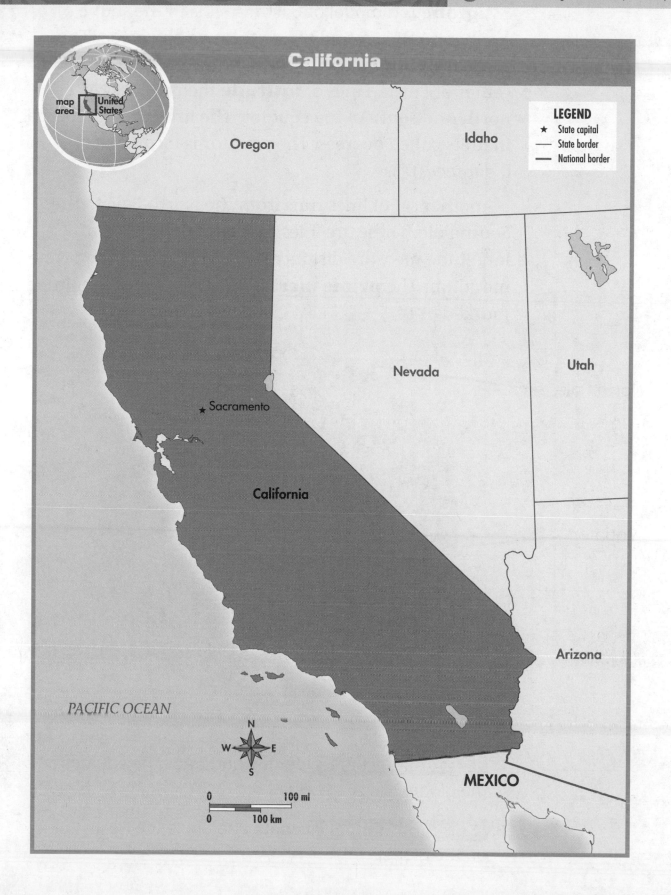

California

Oregon

Idaho

map area

United States

**LEGEND**
★ State capital
— State border
— National border

Nevada

Utah

★ Sacramento

California

Arizona

PACIFIC OCEAN

N
W E
S

MEXICO

0          100 mi
0          100 km

# Using Globes

A **globe** is a model of Earth, so it is in the shape of a sphere. You can find the equator on the globe. The **equator** is an imaginary line that extends around the center of Earth. Lines of **latitude** measure distances north and south of the equator. The lines are numbered in units called degrees. The equator is located at 0 degrees (0°).

Another set of lines runs from the North Pole to the South Pole. These are lines of **longitude**. Lines of longitude measure distances east and west of the prime meridian. The **prime meridian** is the line of longitude marked as 0°.

North Pole

Equator

South Pole

2. ☑ **Reading Check** **Identify** and trace the equator on the globe.

3. ☑ **Reading Check** **Locate** and circle the North Pole on the globe.

The equator and the prime meridian divide Earth into hemispheres, or parts. Each **hemisphere** is half of Earth. The equator divides Earth into the Northern Hemisphere and the Southern Hemisphere. The prime meridian and the line opposite it on the other side of Earth form the Western Hemisphere and the Eastern Hemisphere. The United States is in the Northern Hemisphere and the Western Hemisphere.

**Vocabulary**

globe
equator
latitude
longitude
prime meridian
hemisphere

### Western Hemisphere

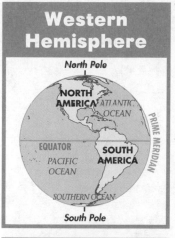

### Eastern Hemisphere

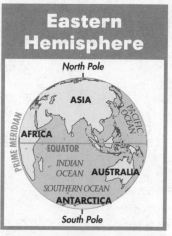

### Northern Hemisphere

### Southern Hemisphere

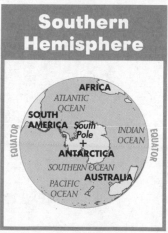

4. ☑ **Reading Check** **Identify** the hemisphere that all of South America is located in.

_____

5. ☑ **Reading Check** **Identify** the line that separates the Northern Hemisphere from the Southern Hemisphere.

_____

# Absolute Location

**Absolute location** tells the exact location of a place on Earth. A place's absolute location does not change. You can find the absolute location of a place on a map or globe by finding its latitude and longitude. For example, the absolute location of San Francisco is 38° N, 122° W.

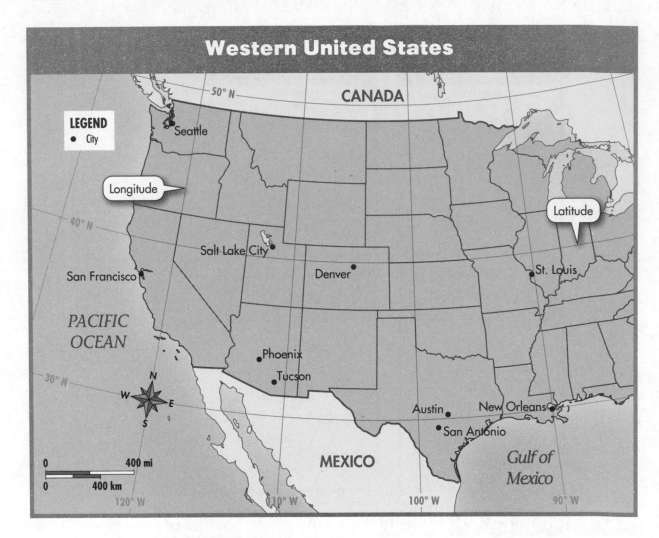

**Western United States**

6. ☑ **Reading Check** **Determine** the absolute location of New Orleans.

_____

# Relative Location

**Relative location** describes where a place is in relation to another place. You might say that your school is across the street from the park. You can also use the directions in the compass rose to explain the relative location of a place. Look at the map titled "Western United States." San Francisco is south of Seattle.

The importance of a place's relative location can change over time. For example, after gold was discovered in California, the land became much more valuable for a time. Harbors and port cities also became more valuable because people and goods needed places to come and go.

**Vocabulary**

absolute location

relative location

7. ☑ **Reading Check** Use the map titled "California" to **describe** the relative location of California.

_____

_____

_____

_____

_____

8. ☑ **Reading Check** In what ways do you think California's relative location has become an advantage or disadvantage over time?

_____

_____

_____

_____

# Physical Geography

The natural features of a place are its **physical geography**. Natural features include landforms, such as mountains, deserts, valleys, and plains. They also include bodies of water, such as rivers, lakes, and oceans. A **physical map** shows the landforms and bodies of water found in a place.

A physical map may also show elevation. **Elevation** is the height of land above sea level. For example, valleys have lower elevations than mountains. The legend helps you understand what the colors on the map mean. Different colors show lower and higher elevations.

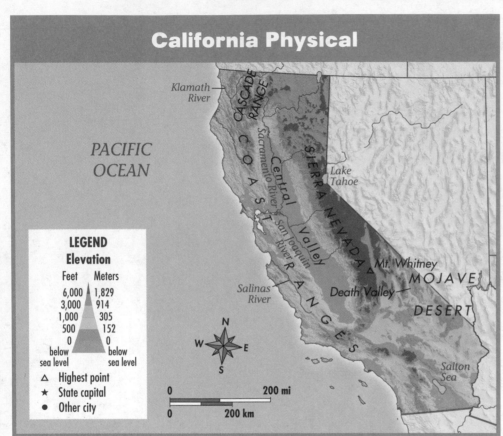

9. ☑ **Reading Check** Choose one physical feature shown on the map. **Describe** how people might use it.

_____

_____

_____

10. ☑ **Reading Check** Circle your community on the map. Write what the elevation range is there.

_____

This table also gives information about elevation, as well as other facts about California's features.

**Vocabulary**

physical geography
physical map
elevation

| California's Amazing Features | |
|---|---|
| Highest elevation | Mt. Whitney: 14,494 feet |
| Lowest elevation | Death Valley: 282 feet below sea level |
| Largest desert | Mojave Desert: more than 25,000 square miles |
| Longest river | Sacramento River: 382 miles long |
| Largest lake | Lake Tahoe: 193 square miles (also in part of Nevada); Clear Lake: 67 square miles (largest lake completely in California) |
| California coastline | about 1,100 miles long |

Source: *U.S. Geological Survey; Encyclopaedia Britannica*

11. ☑ **Reading Check** Circle the feature on the table that is located nearest to your community.

Graphs can also help you learn about physical geography. This graph shows how much land is covered by water in California and nearby states.

12. ☑ **Reading Check** About how many more square miles are covered by water in California than in Oregon?

_____

_____

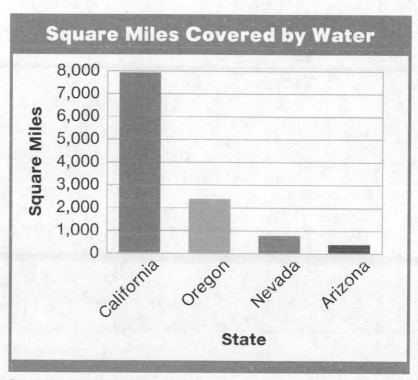
**Square Miles Covered by Water**

Source: *U.S. Census Bureau*

# Human Geography

**Human geography** explains how people affect the Earth's surface. For example, people may build a tunnel through a mountain or build a dam on a river. These actions change the land. When people build roads or towns, they also change the land. Often when people change the land, those changes can make a place unique. For example, the Golden Gate Bridge is a unique human characteristic of San Francisco.

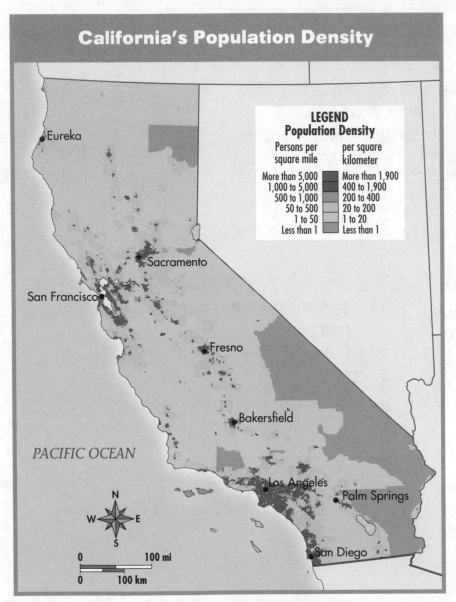

**California's Population Density**

LEGEND
**Population Density**

| Persons per square mile | per square kilometer |
| --- | --- |
| More than 5,000 | More than 1,900 |
| 1,000 to 5,000 | 400 to 1,900 |
| 500 to 1,000 | 200 to 400 |
| 50 to 500 | 20 to 200 |
| 1 to 50 | 1 to 20 |
| Less than 1 | Less than 1 |

Eureka

Sacramento

San Francisco

Fresno

Bakersfield

PACIFIC OCEAN

Los Angeles

Palm Springs

San Diego

N W E S

0    100 mi

0    100 km

Some maps show the human geography of a place. A **population map** shows where people live. Cities in California are centers of business and government. Many people live and work near them. Other parts of California have fewer cities and jobs. Fewer people live there.

**13.** ☑ **Reading Check**
Look at the population map. **Identify** how many people per square mile live in your community.

Charts can also show the human geography of a place. The chart on this page shows the ten cities in California where the most people live.

**Vocabulary**

human geography
population map

| California's 10 Largest Cities, 2010 | |
| --- | --- |
| Name | Population |
| Los Angeles | 3,792,621 |
| San Diego | 1,307,402 |
| San Jose | 945,942 |
| San Francisco | 805,235 |
| Fresno | 494,665 |
| Sacramento | 466,488 |
| Long Beach | 462,257 |
| Oakland | 390,724 |
| Bakersfield | 347,483 |
| Anaheim | 336,265 |

Source: *U.S. Census Bureau*

14. ☑ **Reading Check** Use the chart and population map to **determine** which area of California has the most populous cities. Why do you think this is so?

_____

_____

_____

_____

_____

# Writing Workshop

## Keys to Good Writing

Good writers follow five steps when they write.

| | |
|---|---|
| **Plan** | • Brainstorm to choose a topic.<br>• Find details about the topic.<br>• Take notes from sources.<br>• Write down your sources.<br>• Plan how to use the details. |
| **Draft** | • Write down all of your ideas.<br>• Think about which ideas go together.<br>• Put ideas that go together in groups.<br>• Write a sentence for the introduction and write a sentence for the conclusion. |
| **Revise** | • Review what you wrote.<br>• Check that your ideas and organization make sense.<br>• Add time-order words and transitions (words and phrases such as *because* or *for example*).<br>• List any more sources that you used. |
| **Edit** | • Check for correct grammar, spelling, and punctuation. If using a word processor, use spell-check.<br>• Make a final copy. |
| **Share** | • Use technology to print or publish your work.<br>• Make sure that you list all of your sources. |

1. ☑ **Reading Check** **Explain** Why is it important to edit?

_____

_____

_____

There are three main writing genres. They are opinion, informative, and narrative writing. They all have a different purpose.

## Opinion Writing

When you write an opinion piece, you share your point of view on a topic. Your goal should be to make your viewpoint clear. You also need to support your point of view with evidence. Read the steps and sample sentences below to see how to write effective opinion pieces.

Tools used to dig for gold

| | |
|---|---|
| **1** | **Introduce the topic.** *People came to California for different reasons, but many came to find gold during the Gold Rush.* |
| **2** | **State your opinion.** *The people who came to California in 1849 were smart because there was an opportunity to get rich.* |
| **3** | **Support your opinion with reasons and evidence.** *James Marshall discovered gold in California in 1848. People who came to California in 1849 after gold was found were called Forty-Niners.* |
| **4** | **Make sure that your ideas are clear and organized to support your purpose.** |
| **5** | **Support your opinion statement with a conclusion.** *I think that the people who came to California in 1849 were smart because many people at that time did find gold.* |

2. **☑ Reading Check Analyze** How might using technology make your writing more effective?

_____

_____

California Indians relied on the natural resources available to them.

# Informative Writing

Informative writing is also called explanatory writing. When writing an informative piece, your purpose is to inform, or tell. Credible, or reliable, sources are very important to use in this kind of writing. Make sure to avoid plagiarism. This means using someone else's words without giving that person credit. Take notes on your sources, including what they say and where you found them. Read the steps and sample sentences below.

**1**
**Introduce the topic.**
*Many different groups of California Indians lived off the land before settlers came.*

**2**
**Develop the topic with facts, definitions, and concrete details.**
*The California Indians used the natural resources in their environment to live. Natural resources are things in nature that people use, such as water, soil, plants, and trees. Some groups that lived on the coast used shells for jewelry and for money to trade. Another natural resource that they used for money was beads.*

**3**
**Use precise language and content words.**
*The Chumash made bead money from Olivella shells, which came from sea snails. Some shells were rare, so they were very valuable.*

**4**
**Write a conclusion that supports your introduction.**
*California Indians lived off the land by using the natural resources available to them.*

3. ☑ **Reading Check** **Infer** Discuss with a partner the following question: What could be added to the conclusion?

# Narrative Writing

Writing a narrative is telling a story. The story can be about a real or made-up event or experience. Use sensory words to show, rather than tell, the reader what happened. Sensory words describe what a person sees, hears, touches, tastes, or smells. The events in your narrative should be clear, in order, and connect to each other. Read the steps and sample sentences below.

**4.** ☑ **Reading Check** Based on the description in the story, **underline** the setting, or place where an event takes place.

| 1 | **Introduce the story and characters.** *Lin was getting ready for the Chinese New Year.* |
|---|---|
| 2 | **Use dialogue and sensory words.** *"Mrs. Chen, would you like some oranges? We just unloaded them from the farmer's truck. They're sweet and juicy." Mrs. Chen bit into an orange slice and it squirted Lin in the face. Lin wiped the sticky juice away from her cheek.* |
| 3 | **Use details to develop your writing.** *Lin dashed to the front of the store to help her mother at the cash register. A long line twisted around the shelves of fresh fruit she had stocked early that morning.* |
| 4 | **To connect the events in your writing, use words that express sequence.** *Finally, it was 1:00 and time to close the store to get ready for the parade.* |
| 5 | **Make sure that the order of events in your story is organized.** |
| 6 | **Write a strong conclusion to close the narrative.** *As Lin grabbed her sweater, someone in a colorful dragon costume passed by the shop. Lin called out to her parents, "Let's follow that dragon!"* |

## Researching on the Internet

Look at sites before you use information from them. Web sites with .org, .edu, or .gov are good choices. You cannot always rely on facts and details from sites that end in .com. If you do use them, check one or two other sources from a .org, .edu, or .gov site.

5. ☑ **Reading Check**

**Infer** Discuss the following question with a partner. How might you use your Library Media Center to find information on California Indians who lived where you live today?

## Using a Library Media Center to Write a Research Paper

When you are writing a research paper, it is helpful to use the resources available in your Library Media Center. To use them effectively, make sure that you:

- use both print and electronic sources and also make sure the sources are reliable to use.
- use more than one source and check the information in the sources to see if it matches.
- take short notes from your sources.
- ask a librarian for help if you are unsure which sources to use for your topic.

Follow these steps to write a research paper:

1. Write down two or three questions to help you with your research.
2. Use reliable sources to answer the questions you wrote. Change your questions if needed.
3. Based on the answers to your questions, organize your topic so that details for each part of your topic are together.
4. Write a sentence about your topic based on your research. This will become your introduction.
5. Use details, examples, and quotes to support your statement.
6. Use transitions and clauses to connect ideas and events.
7. Write a strong conclusion that goes back to what you stated in the introduction.
8. Make a list of your sources.

# Using Primary and Secondary Sources

**HSS** 3.2, 3.2.3, 3.3.1, 3.3.3
**Analysis** RE.1, RE.2

## Primary and Secondary Sources

A **primary source** is a source made or written by a person at an event. A primary source can be a historical document, such as the California Constitution. Other examples of primary sources are letters, diaries or journals, and photographs. Maps and artwork are also primary sources. Even **architecture**, which is how buildings are designed, can be a primary source. It helps us understand the people who designed the buildings.

A **secondary source** is material that was written or made by someone who did not witness an event. This textbook is a secondary source. Encyclopedias, online or in print, are also secondary sources. Secondary sources may include primary sources. For example, textbooks include photographs and often journal entries that are primary sources. Encyclopedias include information about people, places, and events from other sources.

Artifacts like this basket made by the Pomo Indians are considered to be primary sources. An **artifact** is an object that was made and used by people.

A **biography** is a story about a person's life that was written by someone else. Because the author did not see or live through the events he or she describes, a biography is a secondary source.

**Vocabulary**

primary source
architecture
secondary source
artifact
biography
oral
eyewitness

California Indian basket

1. ☑ **Reading Check** **Underline** in the text one example of a primary source and **circle** one of a secondary source. **Explain** your answers to a friend.

Miners panning
for gold

Primary sources can also be oral or spoken. Family stories that are told to children and grandchildren are **oral**, or spoken, histories. Oral histories can tell us how individual people contributed to the history of a place. Songs can also be oral histories. Read the words below from a song written by a miner who did not have the money to go home after he came to California to find gold. Note that *lousy* means "of poor quality." As you read, think about who wrote the song and why. Also think about what it tells you about the past.

## Primary Source

It's four long years since I reached this land,
In search of gold among the rocks and sand;
And yet I'm poor when the truth is told,
I'm a lousy miner,
I'm a lousy miner in search of shining gold. . . .
Oh, land of gold, you did me deceive [trick],
And I intend in thee my bones to leave;
So farewell, home, now my friends grow cold,
I'm a lousy miner,
I'm a lousy miner in search of shining gold.

–"The Lousy Miner," from *Put's Original California Songster*,
edited by John A. Stone, 1854

2. ☑ **Reading Check** **Draw Conclusions** What does the song tell you about why the writer came to California? How do you know that it is a primary source?

_____

_____

_____

# Distinguishing Between Primary and Secondary Sources

To distinguish between primary and secondary sources, think about who created the source and when. If a person at an event creates the source, it is a primary source.

An **eyewitness** is a person who sees or experiences an event. Eyewitness accounts are primary sources. A journal entry about witnessing the horse and buggy being replaced by the first car would be a primary source. If you wrote a report about the different kinds of transportation people have used over the past 100 years, the report is a secondary source. Your report is a secondhand account because you were not there 100 years ago.

A film can be a primary or secondary source. If you make a video of your family or friends at the beach, that video is a primary source. You are creating a film or video while you are experiencing the event. A film is a secondary source if it is made about a time in the past, such as a movie about people who immigrated to California in the 1800s. The film might include primary sources like historical documents or photographs, but the film itself is a secondary source. The people who made the film were not alive when the events in the film took place.

Making videos of the sunset

3. ✓ **Reading Check** **Analyze** and **describe** how a film can be either a primary source or a secondary source.

_____

_____

# How to Interpret a Primary Source

We can learn who, what, where, and when from primary sources. Read the journal entry written by Father Font. He met with American Indian groups when he traveled to California with Spanish settlers.

## Primary Source

In order that the horses and mules, which were in bad condition, might be refreshed with the good grass around this pond, it was determined that we should remain here. Many Indians of the Cajuenche nation, who live from here on farther down the river, came joyfully, and brought to the camp a great many watermelons, pumpkins, and other provisions [food supplies], which they traded for beads.

—With Anza to California, 1775-1776: The Journal of Pedro Font,
December 7, 1775

Asking questions about sources helps us identify what type of source we are using. Questions also help us understand what the source can teach us.

4. ☑ **Reading Check** Answer these questions based on the primary source.

**Who** wrote the journal entry? _____

**What** does the journal entry tell about the California Indians of the Cajuenche nation? _____

_____

**Where** did the journal entry take place? _____

**When** was the journal entry made? _____

# How to Interpret a Secondary Source

Your textbook has information about the California Indians, but the information was not written by someone who was there, like Father Font. The authors did not see or live through the events that are described. They got their information by reading other people's writing or looking at other primary sources, like photographs, diaries, and artifacts. We can ask the same questions to interpret secondary sources that we used to interpret primary sources. Read the passage below from your textbook that talks about the California Indians.

> By about 500 years ago, nearly 300,000 people probably lived in California. California Indians did not have a lot of conflict with other groups. In fact, many groups traded goods with each other.

The textbook is different from the journal because the writers of the textbook were not there 500 years ago. They did not meet the California Indians in person. Notice that the writers do not use *I* or *we*. They did not interact face to face with the California Indians.

5. ☑ **Reading Check** **Compare** the journal entry and the textbook excerpt. **Write** how they are different.

_____

_____

_____

_____

_____

_____

# California's Geography and Resources

GO ONLINE FOR
DIGITAL RESOURCES

- ▶ VIDEO
- 👆 INTERACTIVITY
- 🔊 AUDIO
- 🎮 GAMES
- ☑ ASSESSMENT
- 📖 ETEXT

**The BIG Question**

▶ VIDEO

## How do we interact with our environment?

## Jumpstart Activity

People interact with their environment in many different ways. Think about all the different things you like to do outside. Stand up and pretend you are doing your favorite outdoor activity.

HSS 3.1, 3.1.1, 3.1.2 **Analysis** RE.1, HI.2 **ELA** RI.3.1, RI.3.2, RI.3.4, RI.3.7, RI.3.9, RF.3.3.b, W.3.2, W.3.6, SL.3.1

 AUDIO

# California, Land of Many Traits

Preview the chapter **vocabulary** as you sing the rap:

On the West Coast of the United States
Sits California, a land of many traits

**Landforms** make up a good part of the Earth's
   surface
Each and every one has a specific purpose
Let's talk about a few that you'll find in this area
Mountains so high the **elevations** might scare ya'

Look down from a hill or a mountain and see
A huge, low, flat stretch of land they call a **valley**
The **desert** is another one of the features
Very dry with all kinds of creatures

The Pacific Ocean sits all the way to the West
The coastlines are considered to be some of
   the best
But that's not the only water, you know there's
   more
Many lakes and rivers you'll find near and far
   from the shore

1

# Quest
## Project-Based Learning

# Come to California!

California is a great place to live, or just to visit! People can go skiing on a mountain, play volleyball on a beach, or go for a hike in a valley—all in one day! Visitors are important to California's economy. One way to persuade people to come to California is to create a video advertisement.

## Quest Kick Off

Hello, Californians! We need more people to visit California. Your mission is to write and perform in a video ad to show and describe your community's best features. Convince people to come!

## 1 Ask Questions

What are your favorite places in your community? Which places in nature would you invite people to see?

.................................................................

.................................................................

.................................................................

.................................................................

## 2 Research

👆 **INTERACTIVITY**

Complete the activities
to get started on your
advertisement.

Watch several travel videos about California on the Internet. Use search words such as "California travel videos" to help you find examples. What features are advertised?

......................................................................

......................................................................

......................................................................

......................................................................

## 3 Look for *Quest* Connections

Turn to the next page to begin looking for Quest connections that will help you write and perform in your video ad.

## 4 *Quest* Findings
## Write and Perform Your Video Ad

Use the Quest Findings page at the end of the chapter to help you write and perform in your video ad.

**INTERACTIVITY**

Participate in a class discussion to preview the content of this lesson.

## Vocabulary

physical geography
landform
elevation
range
valley
desert
irrigate
ecosystem

## Academic Vocabulary

feature
area
interact
common

**Unlock The BIG Question**

I will know about the physical features found in California.

### JumpStart Activity

As a class, draw a simple map of your community on the board. Working one person at a time, draw a part of the map. Include your school, homes, roads, trees, parks, hills, and any bodies of water. What things are part of nature? What things are made by people?

What does the land look like where you live? Is it hilly, or flat? You might live near a body of water, like the ocean or a lake. Does the place where you live get hot during the summer? Perhaps it gets cold enough to snow in the winter.

Sierra Nevada mountains

The land, water, and other natural **features** of a place are its **physical geography**. The physical geography and features of California are what make it unique, or not like any other state. California's physical geography is made up of a variety of landforms and bodies of water. A **landform** is a natural part of Earth's surface. Mountains, deserts, and valleys are all types of landforms.

## Mountains and Hills

California is dotted with mountains and hills. A hill has a lower elevation than a mountain. **Elevation** is the height of land above sea level. The higher the elevation of a place, the cooler its temperature. A mountain's peak can rise to very high elevations.

Mountains are usually found in a **range**, or group, of other mountains. California has a number of major mountain ranges, such as the Sierra Nevada mountain range. Hills also come in groups, like the Montezuma Hills in Northern California. A hill found next to a mountain is called a *foothill*.

HSS 3.1, 3.1.1 Analysis HI.2
ELA RI.3.1, RI.3.2, RI.3.4, RI.3.7, RF.3.3.b

**Academic Vocabulary**

**feature** • *n.*, an important or interesting part of something

1. ☑ **Reading Check**
**Compare and Contrast** Study the landforms in the photos. **Identify** and circle two differences you see between the mountains and the hills.

Montezuma Hills

## Valleys and Deserts

A **valley** is an **area** of low land between
mountains and hills. Valleys can be flat in places.
They can be long and large, too. If the land in a
valley gets enough rain, it can be good for farming
crops. There is a large valley that runs through the
center of California called the Central Valley.

In places where little or no rain falls, a **desert**
can form. A desert is an area of very dry land
where few plants grow. Deserts can be very hot or
they can be very cold, depending on the time of
year or the location.

2. ☑ **Reading Check**
**Main Idea and Details**
Fill in the chart by
**identifying** physical
characteristics of valleys
and deserts.

| Valleys | Deserts |
|---|---|
|  |  |
|  |  |
|  |  |

## Bodies of Water

California's physical geography includes many
different bodies of water. The state's entire western
coast borders the Pacific Ocean. California also
has many beautiful lakes. Some, like Lake Tahoe in
Northern California, are very large and deep.

Californians enjoy going to Laguna Beach along the Pacific Ocean.

Californians use water from the state's lakes and rivers for drinking and for farming. Farmers **irrigate**, or supply water to, their land with water from lakes and rivers. However, low rainfall and using too much water have lowered the amount of water in the state.

California's bodies of water also provide fun things to do. Along the Pacific Ocean, people go to the beach or surf. People enjoy boating and canoeing in California's lakes and rivers.

3. ☑ **Reading Check** **Explain** how California's bodies of water help make it a unique place.

_____

_____

_____

_____

Which physical features are in your community?

 **INTERACTIVITY**

Explore the physical features in your community.

# Ecosystems

Landforms often have ecosystems. An **ecosystem** includes all the living and nonliving things that **interact** in a certain place.

California's mountainous areas are covered in forests of pine trees. Bears and cougars live there. Forests are also found along California's northern coast. Tall trees called *redwoods* grow there. Other coastal areas are home to palm trees and the Monterey cypress.

Woodlands, grasslands, and wetlands are **common** ecosystems found in the state's valleys. Everything from farm animals like cattle to deer and skunks live in California's valleys.

4. **☑ Reading Check** **Use Evidence from Text**
Underline in the text details about the ecosystems found in California's valleys.

**Academic Vocabulary**

interact • *v.*, to act together
common • *adj.*, not rare or unusual

**Word Wise**

A suffix is a letter or group of letters added to a base word to create a new word. Notice the word *mountainous*. It has the suffix *-ous* added to the base word *mountain*. A *mountain* is a noun. The suffix *-ous* is added to nouns to make them into adjectives. What do you think *mountainous* means?

The Monterey cypress is a tree found along California's coast.

Deserts are also located in valleys, and they are home to plants like cactus and brittlebush. Rattlesnakes and horned toads live in the desert.

Even bodies of water have ecosystems. Fish, shellfish, and plants like coral live in the Pacific Ocean. Fish and plants live in the state's lakes and rivers.

Western diamondback rattlesnakes live in California's desert.

INTERACTIVITY

Check your understanding of the key ideas of this lesson.

## ✓ Lesson 1 Check

 HSS 3.1.1 **Analysis** HI.2
ELA RI.3.1, RI.3.7, RI.3.9

5. **Compare and Contrast Identify** the differences between mountains and valleys. Consider their ecosystems as part of your answer.

_____

_____

_____

_____

6. **Describe** what kind of ecosystem is located in or near your community.

_____

_____

_____

7. **Quest** Connections Choose one of the physical features mentioned in this lesson. **Explain** how you have interacted with it.

_____

_____

# Compare and Contrast

When you compare two things, you find ways that they are alike. When you contrast them, you find how they are different. Comparing and contrasting is a great way to understand more about California's physical geography. Read the text below about California's deserts and bodies of water. Think about how you can compare and contrast them.

California's bodies of water are part of its physical geography. The Pacific Ocean forms California's western coast. People surf and sunbathe on its beaches. Beautiful rivers such as the American River provide visitors with a place to canoe and fish. California's rivers and lakes provide water for irrigation and personal use.

California's deserts are also part of its physical geography. People enjoy visiting deserts, but not very many people live there. The weather is often dry, and deserts lack resources to support life, such as water.

## Fun Fact

Bighorn sheep that live in the deserts of California often go without drinking water for a week or longer in the summer.

## Your Turn!

HSS 3.1.1 **Analysis** HI.2
**ELA** RI.3.1, RI.3.9

**1.** How are deserts and bodies of water similar and different? Fill in the Venn diagram below. On the left, write what is true only for deserts. On the right, write facts about bodies of water. In the middle, write what both have in common.

**INTERACTIVITY**

Review and practice what you learned about Compare and Contrast.

Deserts          Both          Bodies of Water

**2.** Write how deserts and bodies of water are similar and different. Then write whether you think these two features are very similar or very different from each other.

_____

_____

_____

_____

_____

# Regions of California

**INTERACTIVITY**

Participate in a class discussion to preview the content of this lesson.

Unlock
The **BIG**
Question

I will know the region of California that I live in.

## Vocabulary

region
bay
tourist

## Academic Vocabulary

primary
series

## Jumpstart Activity

Imagine that your classroom is the entire state of California. Follow your teacher's instructions and stand with a partner in one of four areas: coast, mountain, valley, and desert. You and your partner are going to film a movie in that area. Together, act out a scene from your movie. What kind of scene might take place in your particular area?

San Diego is California's second largest city.

HSS 3.1, 3.1.1 **Analysis** HI.2
**ELA** RI.3.1, RI.3.7

California is divided into four regions. A **region** is a large area of land with similar features that is different from other areas. California's four regions are coast, Central Valley, mountains, and desert. Each region is defined by its features and landforms.

## Coastal Region

Along the western side of California, the coast of the Pacific Ocean extends for more than 1,000 miles. The coastal region is home to California's largest cities.

Forests cover much of the land along the state's northern coast. Redwood National Park is famous for its very old, tall trees. It starts in the far north in Crescent City and stretches 40 miles down the coast.

About 300 miles south of Redwood National Park is the San Francisco Bay Area. A **bay** is a body of water that is part of an ocean and partly surrounded by land. This area is home to the big cities of San Francisco and Oakland.

California's central coast is marked by rocky cliffs. A 100-mile stretch of coast called Big Sur is known for its beautiful views of the Pacific Ocean. The central coast is also home to Santa Cruz, Monterey, and other smaller cities.

Farther south, the state's coast offers some of the finest beaches in the world. This area also has very mild weather. Beach cities like Santa Monica and Redondo Beach attract millions of tourists every year. A **tourist** is a person who travels for pleasure. The southern coast is also home to Los Angeles and San Diego, two of California's biggest cities.

1. ☑ **Reading Check**
**Draw Conclusions**
**Discuss with a partner** why you think many of California's largest cities are located in the coastal region.

# The Central Valley

2. ☑ **Reading Check**
**Identify** the region of California in which you live by circling it on the map.

The Central Valley runs through the center of the state. It is quite long but only about 40 miles wide. The cities of Bakersfield, Fresno, Stockton, and the state capital of Sacramento are all found in the Central Valley.

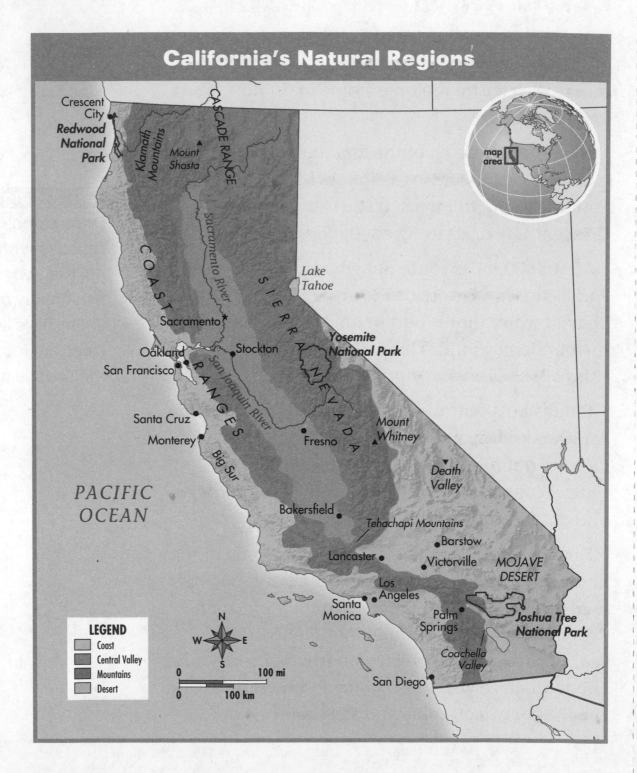

California's Natural Regions

Crescent City
Redwood National Park
Klamath Mountains
Mount Shasta
CASCADE RANGE
Sacramento River
COAST
Lake Tahoe
SIERRA NEVADA
Sacramento
Oakland
San Francisco
Stockton
Yosemite National Park
San Joaquin River
RANGES
Santa Cruz
Monterey
Fresno
Mount Whitney
Big Sur
Death Valley
PACIFIC OCEAN
Bakersfield
Tehachapi Mountains
Barstow
Lancaster
Victorville
MOJAVE DESERT
Los Angeles
Santa Monica
Palm Springs
Joshua Tree National Park
Coachella Valley
San Diego
map area

**LEGEND**
Coast
Central Valley
Mountains
Desert

N W E S

0        100 mi
0        100 km

The Central Valley is California's **primary** farming area. It is good for farming because it has a long growing season and rich soil. Farmers in the Central Valley grow fruits, vegetables, and grains. Ranchers raise cattle there.

Because the region has little rain, most farms need to irrigate the land. Two major rivers, the Sacramento River and the San Joaquin River, are used to bring water to farmland. The Central Valley's two parts are named for these rivers. The Sacramento Valley is in the north, and the San Joaquin Valley is in the south.

## California's Mountains

Surrounding the Central Valley on all sides is a **series** of mountain ranges. On the valley's northeastern side is the Cascade Range. Mount Shasta, with its two peaks, is located in the Cascade Range. The Klamath Mountains are to the Central Valley's northwest.

Along the Central Valley's western edge are the Coast Ranges. To the south are the Tehachapi Mountains. These mountains make a border between Central and Southern California.

Towering over the Central Valley's eastern side are the mighty Sierra Nevada. Mount Whitney, the state's highest mountain peak, is part of the Sierra Nevada. The Sierra Nevada attract many tourists each year. People come to hike, ski, and enjoy the scenery of places like Yosemite National Park and Lake Tahoe.

**Quest** Connections

Which region do you live in? What are its geographical features?

**INTERACTIVITY**

Take a closer look at California's regions.

# California's Deserts

Much of the southeastern part of California is covered in sandy and rocky deserts. The largest desert in the state is the Mojave Desert. This desert lies to the south of the Sierra Nevada and to the southeast of the Tehachapi Mountains. Despite its very hot summers and cold winters, people do live in the Mojave Desert in towns like Lancaster and Barstow. In the graph, you can see that the populations of desert cities are much lower than the populations of major California cities.

The Mojave Desert includes an area called Death Valley. It has the lowest land in North America. It lies 282 feet below sea level. Very few people live in Death Valley.

Other areas of interest lie near the Mojave Desert. Palm Springs is located in the Coachella Valley. It is a popular spot for vacationers and Hollywood movie stars. Joshua Tree National Park is famous for its beautiful desert landscape. The unique Joshua trees need little water to survive in the desert.

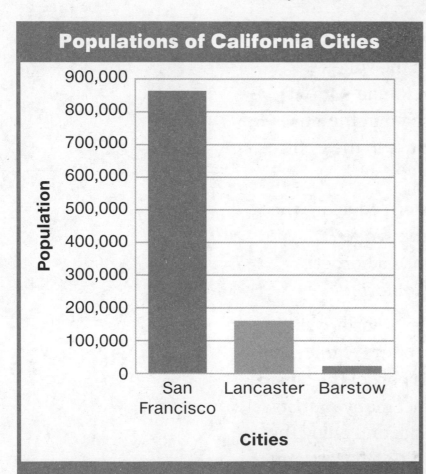

Populations of California Cities

| Features of California's Regions | | | |
|---|---|---|---|
| **Coast** | **Central Valley** | **Mountains** | **Desert** |
|  |  |  |  |

3. ☑ **Reading Check** Fill in the chart and **identify** one place or geographical feature for each region.

INTERACTIVITY
Check your understanding of the key ideas of this lesson.

☑ **Lesson 2 Check**   🌐 **HSS** 3.1.1 **ELA** RI.3.1, RI.3.7, RI.3.9

4. **Compare and Contrast Identify** the differences between the physical features of California's desert and coastal region.

_____

_____

5. **Describe** the region that you live in.

_____

_____

6. **Quest Connections** Which geographical feature in your region might be the most attractive to visitors? Explain.

_____

_____

_____

# Analyze Images

You can learn more about social studies topics by analyzing images. Images include modern photographs and pictures from history. They can show people, places, and events. Paintings, magazine covers, and Web site pictures are other kinds of images.

When you see an image in your book, look closely at its details. Think about what you have already learned about the topic. This can help you understand any new information the image offers.

You can look at clues in pictures to help you identify the region of a place. Look at the images on these two pages. Notice the physical features in each image. As you look for details, think about what you have already learned about California's four regions.

## Your Turn!

1. Look at each photograph on these two pages. Which region is shown in each of the photographs? Label each image with the name of the region.

2. What details helped you know what region each photograph shows? Write at least one detail in each image that helped you identify it.

_____

_____

_____

_____

_____

# Ecosystems and Resources

 **INTERACTIVITY**

Participate in a class discussion to preview the content of this lesson.

**Unlock The BIG Question**

I will know how we use and protect California's resources.

## Vocabulary

natural resource

environment

agricultural region

adapt

mineral

renewable resource

nonrenewable resource

conserve

## Academic Vocabulary

modify

process

refine

### JumpStart Activity

Stand in one of the four areas of your classroom that represent California's regions. Pick a partner in another group and invite the person to your area. Tell your partner what is special about your region and why your partner should visit. Then, go to your partner's area. Listen to your partner tell you what is special about that region.

California's geography affects how people live and what people do for fun and for work. People use the state's natural resources in different ways. A **natural resource** is anything found in nature that people use. Water, trees, and soil are all examples of natural resources. People in California and across the United States use California's resources.

People use natural resources to make things that people buy and sell. Examples include clothing, food, and shelter. People are also hired to work at jobs in which they make things or complete tasks for others. Jobs are one way California's natural resources support communities.

# Forest Resources

**HSS** 3.1, 3.1.2 **Analysis** HI.2
**ELA** RI.3.1, RI.3.2, RI.3.7

Each of California's ecosystems has natural resources. In the state's forests, trees are cut down and sawed into lumber. Lumber is wood that is used for building things like houses. Wood is also used to make paper. People such as loggers work in California's forests. Park rangers work in places like Muir Woods National Monument, where tourists visit to admire the beauty of nature.

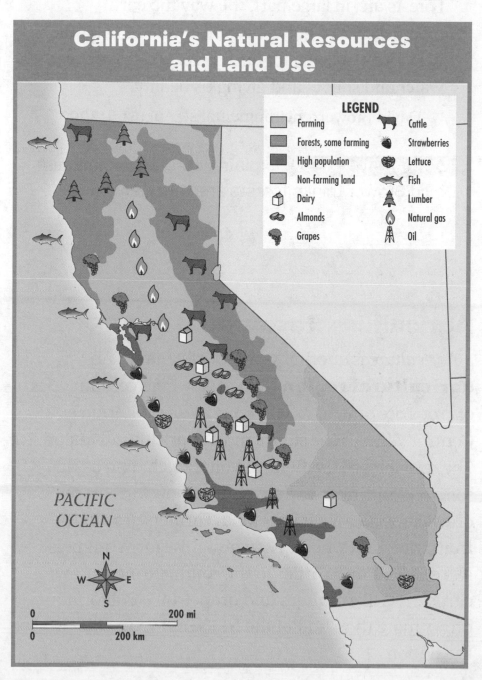

**California's Natural Resources and Land Use**

**LEGEND**

- Farming
- Forests, some farming
- High population
- Non-farming land
- Dairy
- Almonds
- Grapes
- Cattle
- Strawberries
- Lettuce
- Fish
- Lumber
- Natural gas
- Oil

PACIFIC OCEAN

0    200 mi
0    200 km

**1.** ☑ **Reading Check**

Use the map to **identify** which natural resources are found in California's forests. Circle the resources on the legend.

People **modify** their environment to meet their needs. The **environment** is the natural world in which people, plants, and animals live. Making changes to a place can have bad effects, too. For example, when people cut down trees, certain birds and animals lose resources. Also, thinner forests can catch fire more easily.

### Primary Source

Forests are, in large part, the way the earth breathes. We've got to become aware of what the wild forest is doing for us: It is . . . taking care of water and soil . . . and giving us beauty.

—David Brower, environmentalist, August 5, 2000

2. ☑ **Reading Check** **Explain** why environmentalist David Brower thinks forests are important.

_____

_____

### Word Wise

A homophone is a word that sounds the same as another word but has a different spelling or meaning. *Rays* are beams of light from the sun. Look for a word in the text that sounds the same. Explain the different meanings.

## Agriculture Resources

*Agriculture* is another word for "farming." An **agricultural region** is an area where certain types of crops are grown. As you have read, California's Central Valley is the state's major agricultural region. The resources of the Central Valley, including its rich soil, flat land, and warm climate, allow farmers to grow crops nearly all year long. Farmers grow nuts, fruits, rice, and wheat. They also raise farm animals, like chickens and cattle. To the south, farmers grow citrus fruits like oranges and grapefruits. California grows more than half of the fruits and vegetables in the nation.

Smaller communities in the Central Valley are supported by the buying and selling of agricultural goods. For example, in Yuba City, people work at a company that **processes** dried fruits.

Farming is a good example of people adapting to their environment. To **adapt** means to change in order to live in a new environment. Over time, people learned to farm crops that grow best where they lived. They also learned the best time to plant certain crops and how to protect the soil. Today, farmers rotate, or move around, their crops to keep the soil healthy and insect-free.

Most of the state's oranges are grown in Fresno, Kern, and Tulare Counties.

**Academic Vocabulary**

**process** • *v.*, to change something into another form

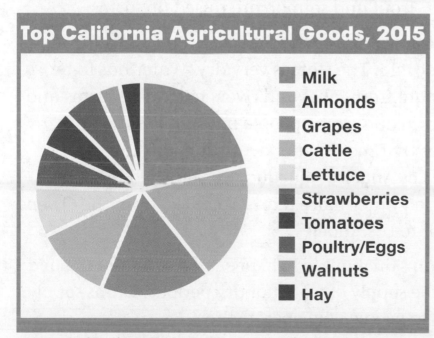

**Top California Agricultural Goods, 2015**

- Milk
- Almonds
- Grapes
- Cattle
- Lettuce
- Strawberries
- Tomatoes
- Poultry/Eggs
- Walnuts
- Hay

*Source:* **California Department of Food and Agriculture**

3. ☑ **Reading Check** This graph shows the ten agricultural goods in California that brought the most money into the state in 2015. **Circle** the three goods that brought the most money into California.

In Northern California is the Shasta Dam, which was built across the Sacramento River.

## Water Resources

Many natural resources can also be found in California's bodies of water. The Pacific Ocean offers fish, such as tuna and sardines, and also squid and crab. Trout and salmon are raised on farms.

Fresh water is a very important resource for California. The state is very dry. Water has to be brought from lakes and rivers to irrigate farms and for drinking. Some people have built aqueducts, or pipes that move water across long distances. The first Los Angeles Aqueduct was finished in 1913. It carried water more than 200 miles, from the Owens River to Los Angeles.

Dams are built to help prevent floods and to build up the supply of water for dry periods. Dams supply jobs to people who operate them.

**4.** ☑ **Reading Check** **Main Idea and Details** Write why people modify their environment by building dams.

_____

_____

## Underground Resources

California is also rich in minerals. A **mineral** is a resource that comes from under the ground. In the city of Long Beach, oil is drilled, **refined**, and turned into gasoline and other products. Many areas of the Sacramento Valley produce natural gas. Underground sand and gravel mines have been built in places like Stanislaus and Shasta.

California's minerals are used to make things. Oil is used to make plastic bottles. Most cars are fueled by gasoline, but some run on natural gas. People use natural gas in homes for heating, cooking, and drying clothes. Sand and gravel are turned into concrete, which is used to build highways and buildings. Many Californians work at places that produce and process these resources.

**Academic Vocabulary**

**refine** • _v._, to take away the unwanted parts in something

Oil is refined into gasoline in Long Beach.

The Tehachapi Wind Farms are located north of Los Angeles.

## Conserving Resources

Not all natural resources will last forever. **Renewable resources**, like trees, can be replaced. **Nonrenewable resources**, like oil and natural gas, cannot be replaced. Therefore, people must work to **conserve**, or protect, resources. By conserving resources, people make fewer changes to the environment. It also ensures that there will be resources for people in the future.

There are many ways to conserve resources. People can try to use less energy. Another way is to use new sources of energy. For example, in Tehachapi, wind farms turn wind into electricity. In the Mojave Desert, solar energy, which comes from sunlight, is produced. Wind and solar energy are renewable resources. People can also recycle, which means to use something again. Plastic bottles, metal cans, and paper can all be recycled.

| Renewable Resources | Nonrenewable Resources |
|---|---|
|  |  |
|  |  |
|  |  |

5. ☑ **Reading Check**
Fill in the chart by **identifying** examples of renewable and nonrenewable resources.

**INTERACTIVITY**

Check your understanding of the key ideas of this lesson.

☑ **Lesson 3 Check**   🔊 **HSS** 3.1.2 **ELA** RI.3.1, RI.3.7, RI.3.9

6. **Compare and Contrast  Compare** the ways underground resources and water resources are similar and different.

_____

_____

_____

_____

7. **Describe** which resources are located near you. How are they used?

_____

_____

_____

8. **Explain** why conserving resources is important.

_____

_____

# I Love You, California

A primary source is a source created at an event or during a certain time period. Secondary sources are created after an event or time period. A state song is a primary source. California's state song is called "I Love You, California." A state song is a way that people celebrate their state.

**Vocabulary Support**

over ......................................

**fertile**, *adj.*, producing many crops

**rugged**, *adj.*, rough and uneven

**chorus**, *n.*, a part of a song that is repeated and sung between verses

I love you, California, you're the greatest state of all.

I love you in the winter, summer, spring and in the fall.

I love your fertile valleys; your dear mountains I adore.

I love your grand old ocean and I love her rugged shore.

Chorus

When the snow crowned Golden Sierras

Keep their watch o'er the valleys bloom,

It is there I would be in our land by the sea,

Every breeze bearing rich perfume.

It is here nature gives of her rarest. It is Home Sweet Home to me,

And I know when I die I shall breathe my last sigh

For my sunny California.

—F. B. Silverwood, "I Love You, California," 1913

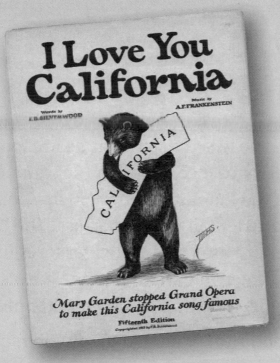

Mary Garden stopped Grand Opera
to make this California song famous

Fifteenth Edition

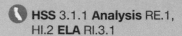

This drawing decorated
the sheet music for
the song when it was
written in 1913.

## Close Reading

**1.** Look at the words of the chorus. In what area of California
would the person in the song like to be?

_____

_____

**2. Circle** the physical features that are mentioned in the state
song on the previous page.

### Wrap It Up

Why do you think "I Love You, California" mentions so many of the
state's landforms, features, and regions?

_____

_____

_____

_____

# Hallie M. Daggett
## First Female Fire Lookout

Hallie M. Daggett was a woman who took on a big responsibility. She was the first female fire lookout hired by the Forest Service. Beginning in the summer of 1913, she worked in the Klamath National Forest atop a high mountain peak. Her job was important. She had to look out over the entire area and watch for forest fires. She had to deal with terrible weather, too. She also had to be careful of grizzly bears and other wild animals.

Perhaps most difficult of all, Daggett's job required her to spend many hours all alone atop Klamath Peak. It was 9 miles away from her home. The other lookouts—all men—never thought she would continue working. They were wrong. She loved her job and worked hard at it for 14 years.

## Find Out More

1. In what way did Hallie M. Daggett have a lot of responsibility?

_____

_____

_____

2. There are a lot of people in your community who have jobs with a lot of responsibility, such as police officers, doctors, and firefighters. Ask an adult who works in one of those jobs to talk about his or her responsibilities. Report back to the class what you learn. Would you like to have a job with a lot of responsibility?

Use these graphics to review some of the key terms and ideas from this chapter.

## The Regions of California

**Mountains**
**Geographical Features:** mountains grouped in ranges, higher elevation than hills
**Places:** Cascade Range; Klamath Mountains; Tehachapi Mountains; Sierra Nevada; Yosemite National Park

**Central Valley**
**Geographical Features:** farmland, low land between mountains, long and flat
**Places:** capital city of Sacramento; Sacramento Valley, San Joaquin Valley

**Desert**
**Geographical Features:** dry area with little or no rain, can be very hot or cold, Joshua trees
**Places:** Mojave Desert; Death Valley; Palm Springs

**Coast**
**Geographical Features:** Pacific Ocean, forests, rocky cliffs, beaches
**Places:** big cities like Santa Monica and Los Angeles; Redwood National Park

Map labels: KLAMATH MTS.; Mt. Shasta; Redwood National Park; CASCADE RANGE; Cape Mendocino; COAST RANGES; Sacramento Valley; PACIFIC OCEAN; SACRAMENTO; SIERRA NEVADA; Yosemite National Park; San Francisco; SIERRA NEVADA; Monterey Bay; Monterey; Fresno; San Joaquin Valley; Death Valley; Desert; TEHACHAPI MTS.; Mojave Desert; Santa Monica; Joshua Tree National Park; Palm Springs; Los Angeles; Channel Islands; Sonoran Desert; San Diego

# ☑Assessment

🎮 **GAMES**

Play the vocabulary game.

## Vocabulary and Key Ideas   🕐 **HSS** 3.1.1 **ELA** RI.3.7

1.  Write the letter of the correct term next to its definition.

    a. ecosystem  _____  a natural part of the Earth's surface

    b. region  _____  to protect resources

    c. conserve  _____  all the living and nonliving things that interact in a certain place

    d. landform  _____  a large area of land with similar features

2.  **Compare and Contrast** What is the difference between a renewable resource and a nonrenewable resource?

    _____

    _____

3.  **Identify** Study the image. Which region is it most likely showing?

    _____

4.  **Define** Fill in the circle next to the best answer.
    In which of the following are mountains usually grouped together?

    Ⓐ a valley

    Ⓑ a landform

    Ⓒ a range

    Ⓓ an area

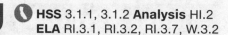
5. **Identify** Which region in California is home to most of the state's major cities? Give examples.

_____

_____

_____

6. **Describe** California's mountains. What are their primary characteristics? Where in California are they found?

_____

_____

_____

7. **Main Idea and Details** In what ways are California's desert regions unique?

_____

_____

_____

_____

8. **Revisit the Big Question** What is one way that we interact with California's bodies of water?

_____

_____

_____

9. **Writer's Workshop: Write Informative Text** On a separate piece of paper, identify the region of California in which you live. Describe its physical geography, including its natural features, landforms, and ecosystems. What are some ways that you interact with the landforms in your community?

Any fool can destroy trees . . . God has cared for these trees . . . but he cannot save them from tools—only Uncle Sam can do that.

–John Muir, "The American Forests," 1897

10. John Muir was an environmentalist, or a person who works to protect the environment. What does he think the United States government should do to care for the environment? (Hint: "Uncle Sam" means the same thing as the United States government.)

_____

_____

_____

## Compare and Contrast ● ELA RI.3.9

11. Fill in the Venn diagram to compare California's Coastal Region to the Central Valley.

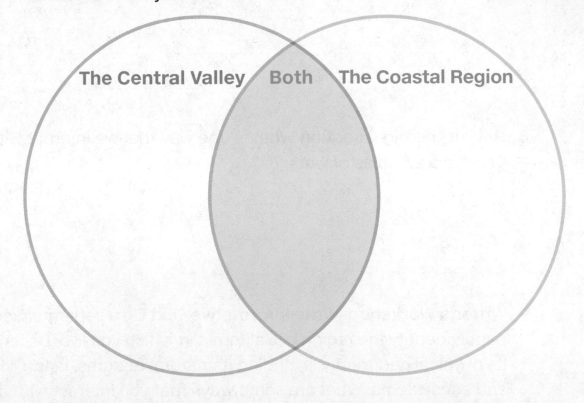

The Central Valley    Both    The Coastal Region

# Quest Findings

## Create Your Advertisement

You've read the lessons in this chapter, and now you are ready to write and perform in your video advertisement. Remember that you are trying to persuade someone to visit California.

**INTERACTIVITY**

Use this activity to help you prepare your advertisement.

### 1 Prepare to Write

Decide on three physical features in your community that you think people would love to visit. Write them down on a piece of paper and make a few notes about each.

### 2 Write Your Script

Use your notes and write a short script in which you tell visitors about each of the features. Include:

- which region you live in;
- the name of your community;
- why each physical feature is special to you; and
- how you interact with each feature.

### 3 Perform and Film Your Ad

With an adult's help, use a camera (or a camera on a smartphone) and film your video ad. Hold your script a little bit below your face. Look right into the camera as you read your script. Try to look up from your script as much as possible—and smile!

### 4 Review

After you've performed your ad, watch it with a classmate. Do you notice any mistakes or spots where you could improve? If you do, you may wish to film it again.

Chapter 2
# American Indians of California

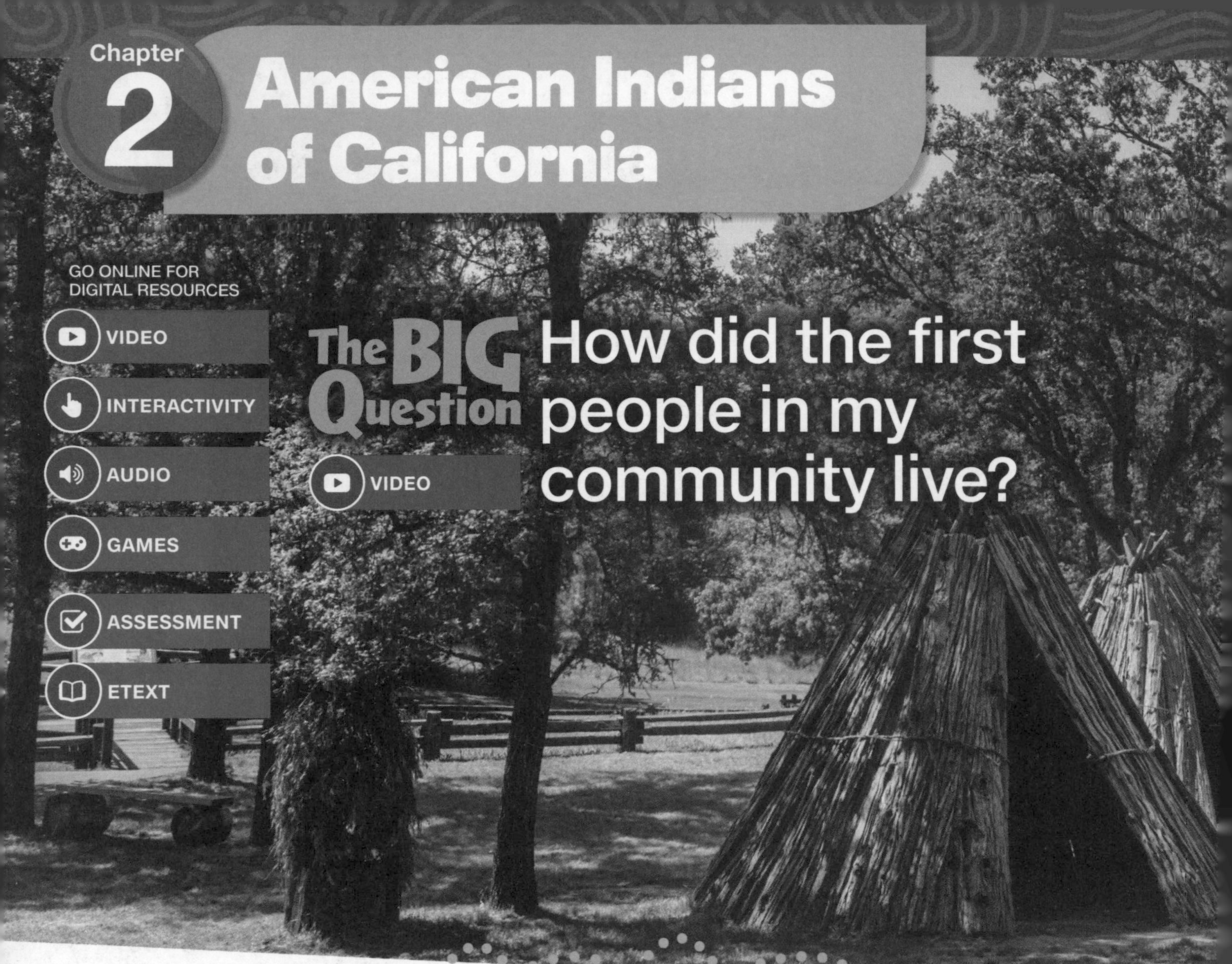

GO ONLINE FOR DIGITAL RESOURCES

- VIDEO
- INTERACTIVITY
- AUDIO
- GAMES
- ASSESSMENT
- ETEXT

## The BIG Question

How did the first people in my community live?

VIDEO

Lesson 1
California Indians

Lesson 2
Daily Life

Lesson 3
Customs, Art, and Folklore

## Jumpstart Activity

INTERACTIVITY

Throughout history, geography has played a big role in how people lived. Geography still has an impact today. Work with a partner to create a list of activities that people do in your community that depend on geography. Remember the main features from Chapter 1: deserts, mountains, valleys, hills, coastal areas, oceans, and lakes.

______________________________

______________________________

______________________________

______________________________

**HSS** 3.1.2, 3.2, 3.2.1, 3.2.2, 3.2.3 **Analysis** RE.1, HI.2 **ELA** RI.3.1, RI.3.2, RI.3.7, RI.3.9, RF.3.4.c, RL.3.1, RL.3.2, W.3.2, SL.3.2

# Rap About It!

◀)) AUDIO

# Settling Down

Preview the chapter **vocabulary** as you sing the rap:

Ten thousand years ago people came to this
place
Following their food or animals they'd chase
They came to California, as it's known today
They **settled** and called it home and were here
to stay

The variety of land throughout the region
Allowed groups to thrive from season to season
**Hunting and gathering** is how they met their
needs
So many foods: animals, berries, nuts, and
seeds

They modified the land in order to thrive here
Like building dams to trap the salmon, called
a **weir**

Many Indian **customs** are still in effect
**Traditions** kept alive today in full respect

# Life Today and Long Ago

Was daily life in California long ago very different than it is today? Comparing your daily life with the life that California Indians lived long ago is a great way to learn more about them.

## *Quest* Kick Off

Can you help me tell people how life today is alike and different from how American Indians lived in the past? You can write about it so others can learn.

## 1 Ask Questions

What is your daily life like? What foods do you eat? What clothes do you wear? What do you do for fun?

......................................................................................

......................................................................................

......................................................................................

......................................................................................

## 2 Plan

What do you need to know about how California Indians lived? What kinds of pictures or other sources might help? Write down some ideas.

.....................................................................
.....................................................................
.....................................................................
.....................................................................

INTERACTIVITY

Complete the activities to get started on your informative/explanatory text.

## 3 Look for Quest Connections

Turn to the next page to begin looking for Quest Connections that will help you write your informative/explanatory text.

## 4 Quest Findings

## Write Your Informative/ Explanatory Text

Use the Quest Findings page at the end of the chapter to help you write your informative/explanatory text.

# Lesson 1

# California Indians

**INTERACTIVITY**

Participate in a class discussion to preview the content of this lesson.

**Unlock The BIG Question**

I will know the names, characteristics, and history of California Indians.

## Vocabulary

settle
hunter-gatherer

## Academic Vocabulary

conflict
develop

### JumpStart Activity

What might California have looked like more than 10,000 years ago? Would the plants and animals have looked different? How about the land? Stand with a partner and share what you think might look the same and what might look different.

Many scientists believe people first came to North America from Asia. They became hunter-gatherers in places like California.

HSS 3.1.2, 3.2, 3.2.1, 3.2.2 **Analysis** HI.2 **ELA** RI.3.1, RI.3.2, RI.3.7, RF.3.4.c

More than 10,000 years ago, the first people to live in California arrived. Many scientists believe they came from Asia, following groups of animals that they could hunt and eat. Over time, these people stayed in California. There, they began to **settle**, or organize and live on, the land.

## The First Californians

The first people who settled in California lived among many landforms and bodies of water. These included forests in the north, deserts in the southeast, what were then marshes in the Central Valley, and California's coast along the Pacific Ocean. To survive, early Californians learned to adapt to and modify their environment. California's physical geography also had many natural resources that helped them to adapt.

The different landforms of each region affected how each group of California Indians lived. They used their region's resources in many ways. For example, early Californians lived as **hunter-gatherers**. They hunted animals and gathered nuts and plants for food. They used the resources around them to build homes on mountains, in valleys, along the coast, and in deserts.

By about 500 years ago, nearly 300,000 people probably lived in California. California Indians did not have a lot of **conflict** with other groups. In fact, many groups traded goods with each other.

1. ☑ **Reading Check** Main Idea and Details
   Underline the ways early Californians used their region's resources.

**Academic Vocabulary**

**conflict** • *n.*, disagreement

# California Indian Groups

Hundreds of American Indian groups lived in their own communities across what is today the state of California. They **developed** their own ways of life and spoke their own languages.

**Academic Vocabulary**

develop • *v.*, to create

## Shasta, Yurok, and Hupa

In the northwest, Indian groups including the Shasta, Yurok, and Hupa settled around the deep redwood forests. People in these groups modified the environment to meet their needs. They cut down the giant trees and carved canoes out of them. Then they traveled on rivers in the canoes to search for food. They also used the wood to make houses. For food, people fished for salmon along forest streams.

## Modoc

A group called the Modoc lived in the northeast among marshes, rivers, and lakes. The Modoc used many plants as a food source and as medicine. They also used plants for clothing and baskets. They hunted antelope, deer, sheep, and birds.

## Washoe

The Washoe lived in the Sierra Nevada mountains. They hunted animals such as rabbit, antelope, and deer. The Washoe and other groups that lived in the mountains depended on plants that grew there. The Washoe are known for their beautiful baskets.

2. ☑ **Reading Check** Circle the California Indian group on the map that lives nearest to your community.

# California Indian Regions

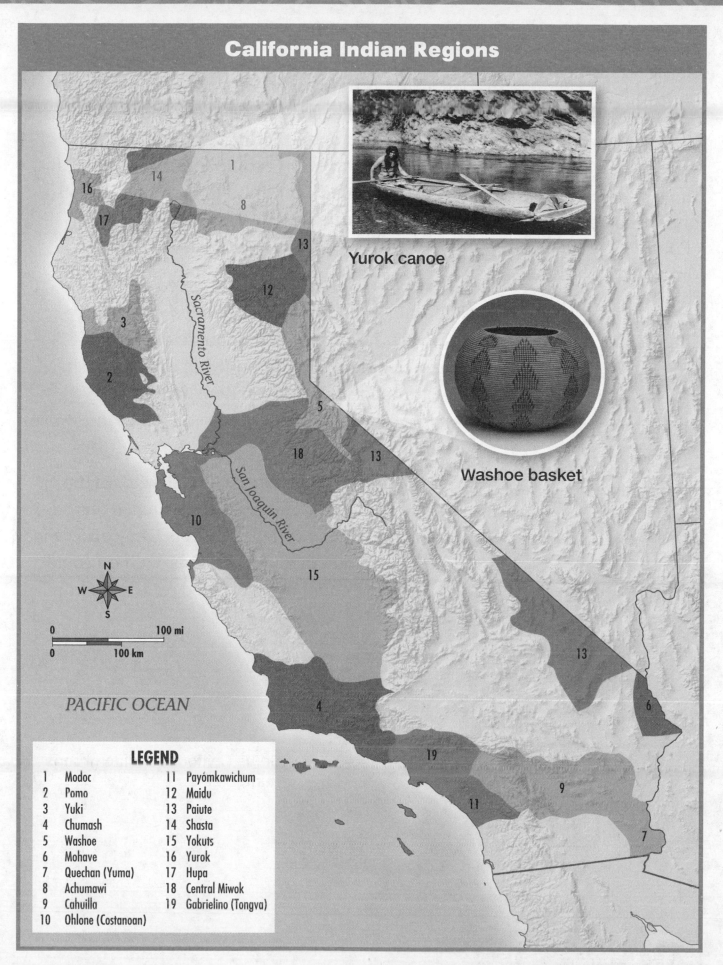

Yurok canoe

Washoe basket

*Sacramento River*

*San Joaquin River*

PACIFIC OCEAN

N W E S

0       100 mi
0       100 km

## LEGEND

| | | | |
|---|---|---|---|
| 1 | Modoc | 11 | Payómkawichum |
| 2 | Pomo | 12 | Maidu |
| 3 | Yuki | 13 | Paiute |
| 4 | Chumash | 14 | Shasta |
| 5 | Washoe | 15 | Yokuts |
| 6 | Mohave | 16 | Yurok |
| 7 | Quechan (Yuma) | 17 | Hupa |
| 8 | Achumawi | 18 | Central Miwok |
| 9 | Cahuilla | 19 | Gabrielino (Tongva) |
| 10 | Ohlone (Costanoan) | | |

## Miwok and Yokuts

Today, California's Central Valley is an area of rich farmland. However, long ago, much of this land was watery marsh. California Indians in this area depended on gathering resources rather than farming to survive. For example, the Miwok and the Yokuts hunted deer, rabbit, and elk. They also picked acorns and fished for salmon in rivers.

## Pomo

California Indian groups that lived along California's Pacific Coast depended on the ocean to survive. The ocean was a source of food for all coastal people. People caught fish and shellfish. They trapped seals and sea lions, too. These animals provided fur that could be made into warm clothing.

Some Pomo villages were located inland, in the Russian River valley. These groups searched for animals and plants in nearby forests. They also fished for salmon in inland streams. Salmon could be eaten fresh, or dried and eaten later.

Some California Indian groups hunted elk.

The Gabrielino used the resources along the coast for food and clothing. This modern photo shows a traditional Gabrielino celebration.

## Gabrielino

The Gabrielino (Tongva) lived along the southern coast where Los Angeles and Orange County are today. This group settled there because of the many resources available to them. They hunted, fished in lakes and streams, and picked acorns and other plants. They used tule, a long grass, to make their homes.

## Mohave and Yuma

Among the California Indian groups that settled in the southeastern desert were the Mohave and the Yuma. Long ago, the area that is now the Mojave Desert was much greener. The Colorado River would flood every year. This allowed the Mohave to farm crops like corn. The Yuma farmed pumpkins, melons, and beans.

3. ☑ **Reading Check** **Main Idea and Details** Fill in the chart and **identify** details about California Indian groups and the environments or regions in which they lived.

| California Indian Group | Environment/Region |
|---|---|
|  | forest |
| Washoe |  |
|  | Central Valley |
| Pomo, Gabrielino |  |
|  | desert |

A Mohave woman carries water in a pot on her head.

**INTERACTIVITY**

Check your understanding of the key ideas of this lesson.

✓ **Lesson 1 Check**

🔊 **HSS** 3.1.2, 3.2, 3.2.2 **Analysis** HI.2
**ELA** RI.3.1, RI.3.2, RI.3.7

4. **Main Idea and Details** Give two examples of how California Indians modified their natural environment.

_____

_____

_____

5. How did California Indian groups living near the ocean use that resource?

_____

_____

6. Why do you think the Mohave and the Yuma did not leave the hot, dry deserts of the southeast and settle somewhere else?

_____

_____

_____

# Main Idea and Details

A paragraph usually has a main idea and supporting details. Finding these parts can help you understand important ideas about a subject. The main idea tells what the paragraph is about. Often the first sentence of a paragraph is the main idea. The details support, or tell more about, the main idea.

The Payómkawichum (also called Luiseño), a California Indian group, lived near what is today Los Angeles. They depended on the area's many resources. Those living inland in valleys gathered acorns, seeds, and fruits. They also hunted using bows and arrows. Those living along the Pacific Ocean fished for shellfish like crabs and mussels.

Use the organizer on the next page to list the main idea and supporting details of the paragraph you just read. As a first step, find a partner and take turns reading the paragraph to each other.

A Payómkawichum woman stands next to an olla, a jar used to hold water.

**HSS** 3.1.2, 3.2, 3.2.2
**ELA** RI.3.2, SL.3.2

**1.** After reading and listening to the paragraph, fill in its main idea in the organizer below. Then fill in three supporting details.

**Main Idea**

_____

_____

_____

_____

_____

**Supporting Detail**

_____

_____

_____

**Supporting Detail**

_____

_____

_____

**Supporting Detail**

_____

_____

_____

**2.** Read the paragraph in Lesson 1 under the heading "Shasta, Yurok, and Hupa." Write the main idea and one supporting detail on the lines below.

_____

_____

_____

_____

# Lesson 2 · Daily Life

 **INTERACTIVITY**

Participate in a class discussion to preview the content of this lesson.

## Vocabulary

weir
obsidian
climate

## Academic Vocabulary

obtain
structure

This Pomo woman gathers seeds with a tool called a seed beater.

 **Unlock The BIG Question**

I will learn about the daily life of California Indians.

### JumpStart Activity

California Indians often traded goods. Write five things you use every day but cannot make yourself. Swap lists with a classmate. Then pretend to trade to get the things on the list that you wrote.

You have seen how California Indian groups were alike in that they all used natural resources to survive. They were alike in other ways, too. When faced with a problem in their daily lives, they adapted. For example, areas covered in bushes were burned to make traveling and hunting easier. Tools were crafted from stones and animal bones. With those tools, people gathered food. The Paiute, for example, dug up wild hyacinth flowers, which had roots that could be eaten. How else were Indian groups alike and different?

## Obtaining Food

As you have read, most California Indian groups were alike in that they were not farmers. Instead, they **obtained** food by fishing and hunting animals. They also gathered their food from plants.

Some groups adapted to what they ate. For example, some roasted pine cones and ate the seeds that were inside. The Cahuilla ate the pods covering the seeds of mesquite trees. They also made the seeds into soup or bread. Many California Indians also used acorns to make bread and soup. A group that settled around Mono Lake ate a food called *kutsavi*. It was made from larvae, or newly hatched flies. An explorer named William H. Brewer described *kutsavi* in his journal:

**Academic Vocabulary**

obtain • *v.*, to acquire, or get

### Primary Source

The [larvae] are dried in the sun, the shell rubbed off, when a yellowish kernel remains, like a small yellow grain of rice. This . . . forms a very important article of food. The Indians gave me some; it does not taste bad . . .

—*Up and Down California in 1860–1864,*
William H. Brewer, 1930

1. ☑ **Reading Check**
**Discuss** with a partner some ways that California Indians adapted to get food.

The Hupa, like the Yurok, used weirs to catch salmon.

## Traps and Tools

Finding food to eat was not always easy. California Indian groups had to come up with ways to hunt, trap, trade, or travel for food.

Groups that hunted animals came up with creative ways of capturing them. For example, the Achumawi set traps for deer. They would dig holes in the ground and cover them. Then they would use fire to scare the deer, who would run into the traps.

The Yurok had a unique way of catching salmon in the Klamath River. They built dams called **weirs** across the river. Holes in the weirs were covered with nets that trapped the salmon.

California Indian groups created tools from animal bones and antlers, or horns. The Hupa shaped the antlers of elk into spoons and other tools. Some groups used a black glass-like material called **obsidian** to make tools. People used obsidian to make knives and arrowheads used for hunting animals.

These are Miwok arrow and spear points made of obsidian.

# Trading Resources

Some regions of California lacked certain resources. California Indians traded with people in other areas to get what they needed.

Groups traded items that were unique to their people and made from resources where they lived. For example, the Achumawi traded obsidian tools. The Yuki traded animal furs for seafood. The Pomo traded dried meat and shells, and the Paiute traded bows and arrows. Chumash beads made from sea snail shells were highly desired. The Yurok even traded entire canoes for acorns from the Hupa. Canoes allowed people to travel on rivers and trade their goods with other groups.

2. ☑ **Reading Check**
Why do you think the Chumash needed to trade for obsidian tools? **Explain** your answer.

_____

_____

_____

_____

_____

The picture shows one example of items that were traded between different California Indian groups. The Chumash traded bead necklaces for obsidian tools from people who lived inland.

Yurok houses were made from wood.

Cahuilla houses were made from willow and palm trees.

## California Indian Homes

California Indians built homes to suit their local climate. **Climate** is the weather that a place has over a long period. If a group lived in an area that had harsh winters, their homes had to be sturdy and warm. However, desert groups needed homes that shaded them from the hot sun. Indian groups built their homes from resources in their environment.

Groups like the Shasta, Yurok, and Hupa lived in the cool forests of the north. They made homes out of wood from trees. People built these **structures** to be strong and protect them from the rain. Homes also had fire pits used for cooking and heating. The Maidu lived in the mountains. Part of Maidu homes were built into the ground where it was warm during the winter.

**Academic Vocabulary**

**structure** • *n.*, a building

The Yokuts of the Central Valley built rows of homes out of tule. The homes were open, allowing fresh air to come inside. They had roofs made from bark to keep out the rain. The Miwok, who lived in the same region, also lived in these cone-shaped homes made out of tule and bark.

In the desert, the Cahuilla built homes that would stay cool and shady. They were made from branches of desert willow trees and leaves of fan palm trees. These trees grew in the hot, dry climate of the desert.

3. ☑ **Reading Check** **Compare and Contrast** Fill in the Venn diagram and **identify** details about Yurok and Cahuilla houses.

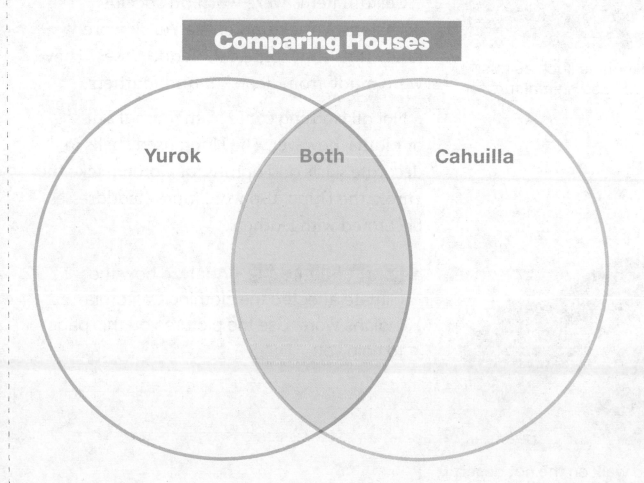

## Comparing Houses

Yurok          Both          Cahuilla

California Indians such as this Yokuts man used animal furs for warmth.

## Types of Clothing

Most California Indian clothing came from animal skins or plants. Like their homes, the clothing California Indians wore also depended on the climate they lived in.

Groups in the north and in the mountains needed the warmest clothes. Furs from many different animals, including deer and elk, were used to make warm coverings. The Paiute made blankets from soft rabbit fur. To adapt to snowy winters, the Maidu made snowshoes out of willow branches and deerskin.

Certain items were worn on special occasions. For example, the Yurok wore fancy hats that some call headdresses. They were made from deerskin and feathers.

Not all clothing came from animal skins or plants, however. The Hupa used shells to decorate skirts and aprons for women. Like the Yurok, the Hupa also wore fancy headdresses decorated with feathers.

4. ☑ **Reading Check** **Analyze** how the climate affected the clothing California Indians wore. Use the pictures on this page to help you.

_____

_____

_____

_____

In order to walk on the hot desert ground, the Cahuilla wore shoes like these.

The Yokuts used animal skins for clothing, but they also used plants. You have already learned that this group made their homes out of tule. They made some of their clothing out of it, too! Tule was woven into a cloth and then made into clothes.

Groups that lived in the desert had to adapt to the hot, rough ground. These groups made sandals from deerskin and the fibers of yucca plants.

 **Quest** Connections

How are the clothes you wear different than the clothes shown and described here?

 **INTERACTIVITY**

Take a closer look at American Indian clothing.

**INTERACTIVITY**

Check your understanding of the key ideas of this lesson.

## ✓ Lesson 2 Check

🚫 **HSS** 3.2, 3.2.2 **Analysis** HI.2
**ELA** RI.3.1, RI.3.2, RI.3.7

5. **Main Idea and Details Explain** how the desert climate affected the daily life of the Cahuilla.

_____

_____

_____

_____

6. **Identify** one way that the Hupa adapted to their natural environment.

_____

_____

7. **Quest** Connections What parts of California Indian daily life do the images in the lesson show?

_____

_____

# Compare Points of View

When you express your point of view on an issue, you are giving your opinion. People can have different points of view about the same issue. They may agree on some points but disagree about others. You can compare more than one point of view to discover where they agree and disagree.

So far in this chapter, you have read about how the California Indians modified and adapted to the land around them. Land use is still an issue today. Read the two points of view below.

## Point of View 1

People should be eating more vegetables, but only those that are not grown using chemicals. Farming without chemicals is a more natural way to grow vegetables. It does not use any chemicals to control pests and disease. This causes less pollution and saves water and soil. Vegetables grown this way are also healthier for you.

## Point of View 2

All farming methods that produce more plants and vegetables should be encouraged. For example, there are special chemicals that can help control pests. This helps farmers not lose their crops. Also, certain chemicals can increase the number of crops grown in a single season. More vegetables mean healthier communities.

## Your Turn!

ELA RI.3.1, RI.3.9

**1.** Fill in the Venn diagram with the ways in which the points of view are similar and different.

**INTERACTIVITY**

Review and practice what you learned about comparing points of view.

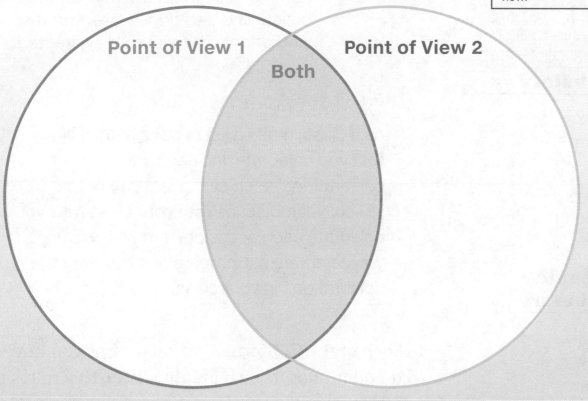

Point of View 1          Both          Point of View 2

**2.** What is your point of view on the topic of growing vegetables with chemicals? Tell which point of view you agree with, and why.

_____

_____

_____

# Lesson 3 Customs, Art, and Folklore

**INTERACTIVITY**

Participate in a class discussion to preview the content of this lesson.

## Vocabulary

identity
custom
elder
tradition
ceremony
folklore

## Academic Vocabulary

arrange
display
support

**Unlock The BIG Question**

I will know how California Indian communities functioned, what their beliefs and traditions were, and the kind of art and folklore they created.

## JumpStart Activity

As a class, make a list of special occasions that you celebrate. Include simple celebrations, such as the last day of the school year. Discuss with your class how you celebrate each occasion, and with whom you celebrate it. Compare and contrast the celebrations in your class.

Each of the California Indian groups you have read about has its own identity. **Identity** refers to all the things that make people who they are. Each group's identity is made up of its **customs**, or ways of doing things. That includes everything from the food they ate to the beliefs they had. Today, members of Indian groups continue to share and celebrate their customs and common identity.

## Organized Societies

Long ago, California Indians organized their societies, or communities, in different ways. For example, some lived in one large village. Others lived in smaller villages and traveled to large villages for important events.

HSS 3.2, 3.2.1, 3.2.3
Analysis HI.2
ELA RI.3.1, RI.3.2, RI.3.7

Within each village, people worked together. Many California Indian communities had a single leader. The leaders were usually men. However, the Pomo allowed women to be village leaders, too. Leaders had many duties, including organizing how food was obtained. They also made all major decisions, settled conflicts, and took charge in times of trouble. Often villages had a group of **elders**, or older leaders, who helped make decisions.

Family was also a key part of each group's identity. The village leader usually came from an important family. Families **arranged** marriages between men and women. Parents provided food to their children, but other family members such as grandparents helped raise the children.

## Academic Vocabulary

**arrange** • *v.,* to plan or decide

1. ☑ **Reading Check** **Main Idea and Details** Underline the duties of village leaders.

A modern family dresses in traditional clothing at a gathering in Mariposa, California.

61

# Traditions and Ceremonies

Each California Indian group had its own traditions that helped to form its identity. A **tradition** is a way of life that is handed down over many years. California Indian traditions affected what people wore, ate, and believed.

California Indians held special ceremonies. A **ceremony** is a special activity held for an important reason. Ceremonies were often based on people's religion. Healers who believed in spirits often led ceremonies. Healers could be men or women. Some villages had more than one.

Religious ceremonies had traditional symbolic clothing and adornments, music, and dancing. For example, every summer and fall, the Hupa conducted two traditional dances. Each dance lasted for ten days. The Hupa believed these dances helped protect their people and improved their hunting and fishing. Participants wore headdresses made of woodpecker and duck feathers while they danced and sang prayers. They **displayed** shell necklaces, obsidian knives, and deerskins on long, wooden poles.

**Academic Vocabulary**

**display** • *v.*, to show off

This Hupa man is wearing symbolic clothing and adornments for the White Deerskin Dance, a Hupa ceremony.

Other groups held ceremonies that had different customs. For example, the Miwok played handmade musical instruments during their ceremonies. In winter, men would make whistles out of small bones. Flutes were made from reeds, or long grasses. The Miwok also played wooden clapper sticks.

**Quest Connections**

What traditions do you have? How do you celebrate special occasions?

▶ **INTERACTIVITY**

Explore family celebrations.

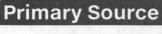

A Payómkawichum gourd rattle is decorated with sea turtles.

2. ☑ **Reading Check** Main Idea and Details **Explain** one way California Indians used musical instruments.

_____

_____

_____

_____

# Folklore

One of the most important traditions of California Indians was storytelling. People told or sang stories to pass on their beliefs, history, traditions, and customs to younger members of their groups. The traditional beliefs, customs, and stories of a group that are passed down by word of mouth are called **folklore**. People continue to learn their identity through folklore today.

Some stories explained things in nature. For example, the Pomo told a story that explained the sun and the moon. In many California Indian stories, animals act like people. For instance, in some stories, Turtle creates the Earth. In other stories, Coyote makes trouble by creating floods. People also told stories about daily life, recent events, and tales that taught important lessons.

California Indians told stories in which animals like turtles and coyote acted like people.

A Pomo woman makes a traditional basket.

## Pottery and Baskets

Many California Indians practiced traditions such as making clay pottery and woven baskets. They used materials from their natural environment to make these objects. Groups who lived in the desert, like the Cahuilla, made pots from clay. People dug mud from riverbeds to use as clay. Clay pots were very useful. They could store water, corn, and beans. They could also be used for cooking.

Most California Indians wove baskets. Groups made their baskets in different ways and from different materials depending on where they lived. Pomo baskets were made from parts of willow trees and a plant called sedge. After these plants were woven together, the Pomo would decorate their baskets with the feathers of different birds, like quail, woodpeckers, or ducks.

3. ☑ **Reading Check**
**Discuss with a partner** why storytelling is an important tradition to California Indians.

Yokuts made their baskets from tule and sedge. They decorated the baskets with shells. The Paiute used willow branches, and the Cahuilla made their baskets from palm tree leaves and grasses. Over time, California Indian baskets and pottery have come to be viewed as pieces of art. Today, California Indian artists continue to create this beautiful artwork.

## California Indians Today

American Indians still live in California. In fact, many California Indian groups continue to live in their local region. They still celebrate and share their customs and traditions.

Some groups are successful in business. For example, today the Cahuilla have nine smaller groups. One is called the Agua Caliente. The Agua Caliente run a large hotel in Rancho Mirage. They also **support** the Los Angeles Clippers basketball team.

**Academic Vocabulary**

**support** • *v.*, to help by giving money to

California has the largest population of American Indians in the United States. However, the current population of each California Indian group is small compared to what it was long ago.

The Agua Caliente Cultural Museum is in Palm Springs.

**4.** ☑ **Reading Check** **Summarize** how California Indians keep their traditions alive today.

_____

_____

_____

☑ **Lesson 3 Check**     🖐 **HSS** 3.2, 3.2.1, 3.2.3 **Analysis** HI.2
**ELA** RI.3.1, RI.3.2, RI.3.7

👆 **INTERACTIVITY**
Check your understanding of the key ideas of this lesson.

**5. Main Idea and Details Analyze** how Indian groups used natural resources to create art and music. Give two examples.

_____

_____

**6. Describe** some examples of how California Indians live today. Include culture and business in your answer.

_____

_____

_____

_____

**7. Quest Connections** What stories have adult members of your family told you about their past?

_____

_____

_____

# Great Tellings

California Indians passed down their beliefs orally as part of their folklore. These stories often describe traditions, explain nature, or retell events from a group's history. They also may offer a moral, or lesson. To find the moral of a story, look for moments when a character is being taught something. California Indian stories are considered primary sources because they were created over time within an American Indian group.

Read the story below that comes from the Mohave. The Mohave call these stories Great Tellings.

**Vocabulary Support**

a period of time long ago

the creator god of the Mohave people

Only people lived during the First Times. There were no animals or crops to eat. So the spirit Mastamho stuck a willow stick in the ground. When he pulled out the stick, water flowed onto the land. This water became the Colorado River. It was filled with ducks and fish. Then Mastamho taught the Mohave how to plant seeds to grow crops. He also showed them how to make fire. Later, he taught them how to make pots to use for cooking.

–Great Tellings

# Close Reading

1. **Identify** and circle three things that Mastamho taught the Mohave.

2. **Analyze** the story's central message. Does this story offer a moral or describe something in nature? **Explain** your answer.

_____

_____

_____

_____

The Colorado River runs through the Mojave Desert.

## Wrap It Up

Why do you think the Mohave have passed down this story to younger members of their cultural group? Think about what you have learned in the chapter about traditions, folklore, customs, and identity.

_____

_____

_____

_____

_____

**Quality:**
Problem Solving

# Archie Thompson
## Saving the Yurok Language

As one of the last living speakers of the Yurok language, Archie Thompson faced a problem. There was a risk that, in time, no one would know how to speak the Yurok language anymore. Thompson knew he needed to keep the important language alive.

Thompson had grown up with his grandmother, who spoke only Yurok. He understood the importance of the traditions of the Yurok people. Thompson helped to save the Yurok language. He taught the language at schools in the area. He helped workers at the Yurok Language Project create Yurok dictionaries. Thompson also made recordings of himself speaking the language. The efforts of Thompson and other elders paid off. Today, the Yurok language is taught in high schools in Del Norte and Humboldt counties. In 2013, the year Thompson died, more than 300 people were able to speak Yurok.

### Find Out More

1. In what way did Archie Thompson help solve the Yurok language problem?

_____

_____

_____

_____

2. Choose a partner and exchange stories of when you solved a problem. What was the most difficult part of solving it?

# Visual Review

Use these graphics to review some of the key terms, people, and ideas from this chapter.

## Details About Some California Indian Groups

| Name | Region or Environment | Examples of Food | Examples of Clothing | Houses | Examples of Culture |
|------|----------------------|------------------|---------------------|--------|---------------------|
| Shasta, Yurok, and Hupa | forest (NW) | salmon, elk, acorns | headdresses of feathers; skirts and aprons with shells | wood from redwood trees | traditional spiritual dances |
| Washoe, Paiute, and Maidu | Sierra Nevada; eastern mountains | rabbit, deer, pine cone seeds, acorns | rabbit fur; snowshoes of willow branches and deerskin | parts were built into the ground (Maidu) | woven baskets |
| Miwok and Yokuts | Central Valley | rabbit, deer, elk, acorns, salmon | made from tule | tule and bark | wooden clapper sticks; whistles of bones; woven baskets |
| Pomo, Gabrielino, Chumash, and Payómkawichum | Pacific coast | fish, shellfish, inland animals and plants, acorns, fruits | made from seal and sea lion fur | tule | sun and moon story; woven baskets; beads made from shells |
| Mohave, Yuma, and Cahuilla | desert | grew corn, melons, and beans; mesquite tree seeds | sandals of deerskin and yucca plant fibers | fan palm trees and willow branches | woven baskets, clay pots |

# ☑ Assessment

 **GAMES**

Play the vocabulary game.

## Key Terms and Ideas  ⓘ **HSS** 3.1.2, 3.2, 3.2.1 **ELA** RI.3.1, RI.3.7

1. Fill in the blank with the correct word from the word bank.

   **weir**          **climate**          **custom**          **folklore**

   a. dam built across a river to catch fish _____

   b. the identity and ways of doing something _____

   c. all the traditions, customs, and beliefs of a group
      of people _____

   d. the weather that a place has over a long period _____

2. **Define** Fill in the circle next to the best answer.
   Which of the following terms best describes most of the earliest
   Californians?

   Ⓐ hunter-farmers

   Ⓑ hunter-gatherers

   Ⓒ fisher-gatherers

   Ⓓ fisher-farmers

3. **Identify** Study the image. What
   Indian group built this house? How
   do you know?

   _____

   _____

   _____

   _____

4. **Summarize** How did the Yokuts use tule?

_____

5. **Summarize** Identify and draw one example of the art or folklore of a California Indian group.

6. **Revisit the Big Question** Identify one California Indian group that lived (and may still live) in your local region and describe them. Think about their food, clothing, houses, and cultural identity.

_____

_____

7. **Writer's Workshop: Write Informative Text** Study the map of Indian groups in Lesson 1. Then review the California regions map in Chapter 1. Using both maps, choose one California Indian group and identify the region they lived in. Then, on a separate sheet of paper, describe the ways in which the physical geography of that region affected how the group adapted to their environment.

Two young brother bears fell asleep on a rock. As they slept, the rock grew and became a mountain. Mother Bear worried because she could not find her bear cubs. Finally, the animals saw the brothers at the top of the mountain. Many big and strong animals tried to leap or climb to the top of the mountain. But none could help. Finally, a tiny inchworm crawled all the way to the top. He took a very long time. But the inchworm showed the brother bears how to get down safely.

—A Very Small Hero

**8.** What is the moral, or lesson, of this traditional Miwok story?

_____

_____

**9.** Read the two points of view. Then describe how they are similar and different.

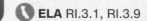

| Point of View 1 | Point of View 2 |
| --- | --- |
| When we recycle, we are saving our resources. Recycling means to destroy something and turn it into something new. An old computer can become a new computer. So recycling means less trash, too! | Reusing resources is better than recycling. When we reuse something, we don't have to destroy it. And the process of recycling can be expensive and cause pollution. So donate that old computer. |

_____

_____

_____

# Quest Findings

## Write About California Indians

You have read the lessons in this chapter, and now you are ready to write your informative/explanatory text. Remember that you are going to compare your daily life today with the life of California Indian groups long ago.

### 1 Prepare to Write

Choose three areas of daily life that you are going to compare. Write them down on a piece of paper and make a few notes about each.

### 2 Write a Draft

Use your notes and your answers to the chapter's Quest Connections to write an informative/explanatory text in which you compare each area of daily life. Make sure you are clear about what is similar and different.

### 3 Share with a Partner

Exchange your draft with a partner. Tell your partner what you like about the draft. Ask for some ideas on how you could improve your draft. Listen closely as your partner speaks.

### 4 Revise

After you have thought about your partner's suggestions, make changes to your draft. Also check for spelling and grammar errors.

GO ONLINE FOR
DIGITAL RESOURCES

- ▶ VIDEO
- 👆 INTERACTIVITY
- 🔊 AUDIO
- 🎮 GAMES
- ☑ ASSESSMENT
- 📖 ETEXT

The **BIG** **How does life change**
**Question** **throughout history?**

▶ VIDEO

## JUMPstart Activity

👆 INTERACTIVITY

Find and circle items in the photo that are different from today. Your teacher will give you one minute to find differences.

HSS 3.1.2, 3.2, 3.2.4, 3.3, 3.3.1, 3.3.2, 3.3.3 **Analysis** CST.1, CST.2, CST.3, CST.4, RE.1, RE.2, HI.2, HI.3 **ELA** R1.3.3, RI.3.4, W.3.1

# Rap About It!  AUDIO

# The Times Are Changing

Preview the chapter **vocabulary** as you sing the rap:

In the 1500s great changes came about
As European **explorers** searched for
 trade routes
North America was new land to them
But Indians lived there first, had since way
 back when

What is now California is where some explored
The Spanish and English were two who
 went ashore
Soon the Spanish built **missions** up and down
 the coast
Nearby formed **presidios, pueblos,** and **ranchos**

People still came, the place kept right
 on growing
The Gold Rush and railroad kept them coming
 and going
In the **present** culture makes our state great
Growing and changing as the **future** awaits

# Quest

**Project-Based Learning**

# Then and Now

Have you ever wished you could travel back in time? If you could look at your community long ago, how would it be different? What would look the same? You can look at pictures of your community from the past. You can also use what you learn in this chapter and your imagination to think about what your community looked like long ago.

## Quest Kick Off

For this Quest you will create a picture that has two parts. One part will show what your community looked like long ago. The other part will show what it looks like now.

## 1 Ask Questions

What has changed? What has stayed the same? Write two more questions.

.................................................................................

.................................................................................

.................................................................................

# 2 Research

Talk with your teacher and others about where you can find pictures of your community long ago. Look for what has changed and what has not. Write some things you can put in your pictures.

_____

_____

_____

# 3 Look for Quest Connections

Turn to the next page to look for Quest Connections that will help you plan your pictures.

# 4 Quest Findings Create Your Pictures

Use the Quest Findings page at the end of the chapter to help you make two drawings.

👆 **INTERACTIVITY**

Participate in a class discussion to preview the content of this lesson.

## Vocabulary

century
wealth
explorer
voyage

## Academic Vocabulary

job
claim

Unlock
The **BIG**
Question

I will know the explorers who came to California and why they explored.

### JumpStart Activity

You are going to explore in your classroom. Walk around the room and list everything you find that would be helpful for studying about United States history.

Juan Cabrillo is greeted when he arrives in early California.

Why do people explore? Perhaps they are looking for resources. They might hope to find riches. Maybe they want to learn about new places. Why would you want to visit a new place?

## Europeans Explore North America

In the 1500s and the 1600s, people from Europe explored the world. The 1500s and 1600s are centuries. A **century** is 100 years. Some European countries wanted to gain more power and **wealth**. They explored to control new lands and find riches. They also explored to find faster routes for shipping and trading. England and Spain were among many European countries that explored North America. They wanted to use its many natural resources. They also wanted to expand their power as world leaders.

An **explorer** is a person who goes to an unknown place to learn about it. Explorers are adventurers. They left Europe in ships not knowing what they would find. Their **job** was to find wealth. Spain also wanted to spread the Catholic religion to other lands. However, exploration led to Europeans taking over the lands of American Indians who lived there.

**Academic Vocabulary**

job • *n.*, what a person is supposed to do; duty

1. ☑ **Reading Check** Reread to **identify** text that **explains** why explorers traveled to North America. Then write three reasons below.

_____

_____

_____

A statue of Juan Rodríguez Cabrillo stands near San Diego Bay.

## Cabrillo and California

Juan Rodríguez Cabrillo was a Portuguese explorer and soldier. He served the Spanish. In 1542, the leader of New Spain ordered Cabrillo to explore up the Pacific coast. He explored north to present-day California. The Spanish called the area "Alta California."

Cabrillo set out on the **voyage**, or sailing trip, with three ships. Cabrillo and his crew may have been the first Europeans to see the California coast. In 1542, they sailed into what is now San Diego Bay. Even though there were American Indians living in the area, Cabrillo **claimed** the land for Spain.

Cabrillo and his crew then sailed north along California's coast. They saw many California Indians. Some experts think that at least 135,000 American Indians lived in that area.

### Academic Vocabulary

**claim** • *v.*, to say that the land belongs to a certain country

### Primary Source

Always there were canoes because the whole coast is very populated.

–from *An Account of the Voyage of Juan Rodríguez Cabrillo*, translation of record of Cabrillo's voyage, 1999

Some of the California Indians were helpful and showed the explorers where to get fresh water. The California Indians even gave the explorers sardines to eat.

Not all of the meetings were peaceful, however. At one stop, Cabrillo got in a fight. He was injured. He later died of his injuries, but his crew continued on.

2. ☑ **Reading Check** **Describe** where Cabrillo's voyage went.

_____

_____

_____

# More Explorers Come to California

Francis Drake, an Englishman, sailed around the world. Along the way, he raided ports and ships. He took their gold, silver, and other treasure. By the time Drake's ship got to California in 1579, it was loaded with treasures. It also needed repair. Drake and his crew spent more than a month near Point Reyes, close to what is now San Francisco. Some historians believe they visited the Miwok village. Before Drake left the area, he claimed California for England.

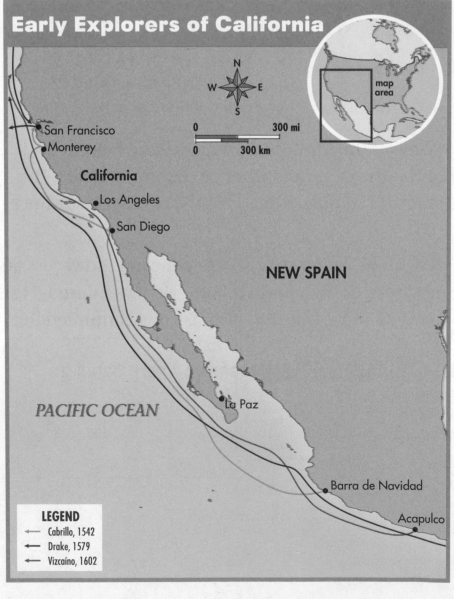

**Early Explorers of California**

map area

0 300 mi
0 300 km

San Francisco
Monterey

**California**

Los Angeles

San Diego

**NEW SPAIN**

*PACIFIC OCEAN*

La Paz

Barra de Navidad

Acapulco

LEGEND
← Cabrillo, 1542
← Drake, 1579
← Vizcaíno, 1602

Meanwhile, Spain was interested in finding new harbors in California to support sea voyages. Sebastián Vizcaíno was a Spanish explorer. Spain chose him to find a place to build a port in California for Spain. Spain also wanted him to map the coastline. Vizcaíno set off with three ships. One of the ships was named the *San Diego*. In 1602, Vizcaíno arrived in the area Cabrillo had explored. Vizcaíno named the area *San Diego*. As he and his ships sailed north up the coast, Vizcaíno wrote reports about what he found. He also named Monterey, Santa Catalina Island, and Santa Barbara. Vizcaíno returned with a report about what he saw.

**Word Wise**

**Word endings** The word *explore* means "to travel through a new area or look closely to learn about something." Knowing this word helps you understand some other words, such as *exploration*, *explorer*, and *explorative*.

3. ☑ **Reading Check** **Sequence** the voyages of Drake, Vizcaíno, and Cabrillo. Fill in the chart with names and the dates they arrived in California. Put the names and dates in order from oldest to newest.

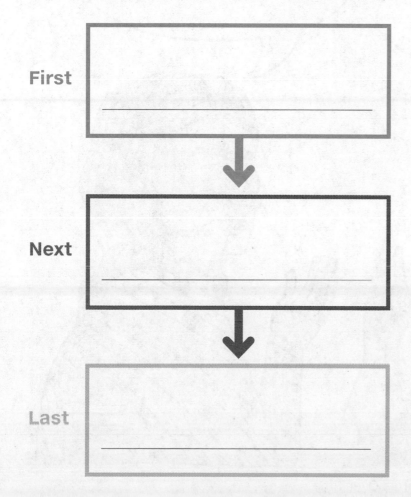

First

Next

Last

# Indian and European Views

Both Spain and England claimed California, but the land was not empty. Groups of California Indians already lived on the land. How did these groups feel about European explorers?

We know that some California Indians helped the explorers. Other groups were hostile, or angry, toward the strangers. The explorers and Indian groups looked different from each other. They had different clothing, weapons, languages, and tools. They also had different viewpoints about land.

**4.** ☑ **Reading Check**
**Summarize** what you learned. Fill in the speech bubbles. Show how explorers and California Indians viewed exploration differently.

Europeans believed in borders and land ownership. They also did not believe the Indians could own the land. American Indians did not have these same beliefs. They had no use for borders, and the land was where they lived.

The explorers and the people who already lived in the area had different ideas about claiming land. The actions of Europeans brought big changes to the California Indians.

**INTERACTIVITY**

Check your understanding of the key ideas of this lesson.

☑ **Lesson 1 Check** 🕐 **HSS** 3.3.1

**5. Explain** what the explorers wanted to find.

_____

_____

**6.** Draw lines to **match** the names of the explorers to the details.

Francis Drake

Juan Rodríguez Cabrillo

Sebastián Vizcaíno

In 1542, explored present-day San Diego

In 1602, explored and named San Diego and Monterey

In 1579, landed near Point Reyes while his ship was repaired

**7. Explain** why claiming land for a country might be good for some people and not for others.

_____

_____

_____

_____

# Lesson 2 Early Settlement

👆 **INTERACTIVITY**

Participate in a class discussion to preview the content of this lesson.

**Unlock The BIG Question**

I will know why settlers came to California and what life was like for them.

## Vocabulary

settlement
mission
presidio
pueblo
rancho
decade
entrepreneur

## Academic Vocabulary

convert
property

### JumPstart Activity

You are a settler. You want to choose a place to live. Which would be most important: living near water, being near other people, having good soil for growing crops, or having many animals for hunting or fishing? You will vote by standing in a place in the classroom.

It took more than 160 years after Vizcaíno's explorations before Europeans built communities in California. Why did Europeans wait so long? Spain did not know whether building there would make enough money to be worth it. England was more interested in exploring eastern North America.

## New Spain

In the mid-1700s, things changed. Russia began to explore the California coast. New leaders in Spain also began to think that parts of North America would earn them money. Spain decided it needed to build settlements in California. California was part of an area the Spaniards called New Spain. A **settlement** is a place where people live.

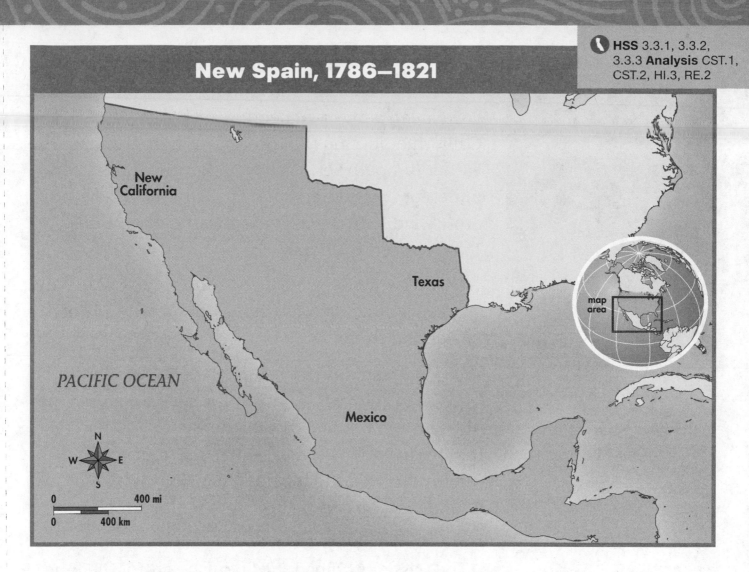

## New Spain, 1786–1821

HSS 3.3.1, 3.3.2, 3.3.3 Analysis CST.1, CST.2, HI.3, RE.2

New California

Texas

map area

PACIFIC OCEAN

Mexico

N
W E
S

0        400 mi
0      400 km

Starting in the mid-1700s, Catholic priests from Spain built settlements in the northern part of New Spain. The priests wanted to teach California Indians there about the Catholic religion. To help, priests built religious communities called **missions**.

1. ☑ **Reading Check** **Relative Location** Describe the location of what is now California within New Spain.

_____

_____

_____

Father Junípero Serra statue in front of the Spanish mission San Antonio de Padua, in Monterey County, California

## Academic Vocabulary

**convert** • *v.*, to change; to take on a different religion, opinion, or political idea

# California Missions

In 1769, a Spanish official named Gaspar de Portolá led a group of people north into what is now California. Joining that group was a priest named Father Junípero Serra. They took cattle, horses, and mules for new settlements. The trip was hard. The group had to travel over deserts and mountains. The weather was harsh.

The first mission was called San Diego de Alcalá. Workers built it out of wood, with a roof made of leaves and straw.

The Spanish built 21 missions along a 650-mile trail. The trail went from San Diego to Sonoma. The missions were built close to where many American Indians lived. Missionaries then used American Indians to build the missions. Missions were also built along the coast. They were built near good land for farming and sources of water.

The missions helped the Spanish control the land in California. Sometimes missions had **presidios**, which were forts that protected the missions. Spanish priests **converted** some California Indians to the Catholic religion. Over time, settlements called **pueblos** grew up around the missions. Pueblos were mostly used for farming.

2. ☑ **Reading Check** Why did Spain set up missions in California?

_____

_____

_____

_____

# Ranchos in California

Some people who lived in the part of New Spain that is now Mexico were unhappy with Spanish rule. In 1821, they fought to be free from Spain. They won. When Mexico became a new country, California became part of Mexico. It was no longer New Spain.

From the 1830s to the 1840s, mission lands were divided up into large ranches. These ranches were called **ranchos**. Rather than belonging to the church or a country, the land became private **property**. People owned the land. People drew maps of their land. These maps were called *diseños*. The *diseños* included landmarks, such as rivers, hills, and forests.

## Academic Vocabulary

**property** • *n.*, something that belongs to, or is owned by, someone

This hand-drawn *diseño* from the 1840s shows the land that made up Rancho La Cienega o Paso de la Tijera.

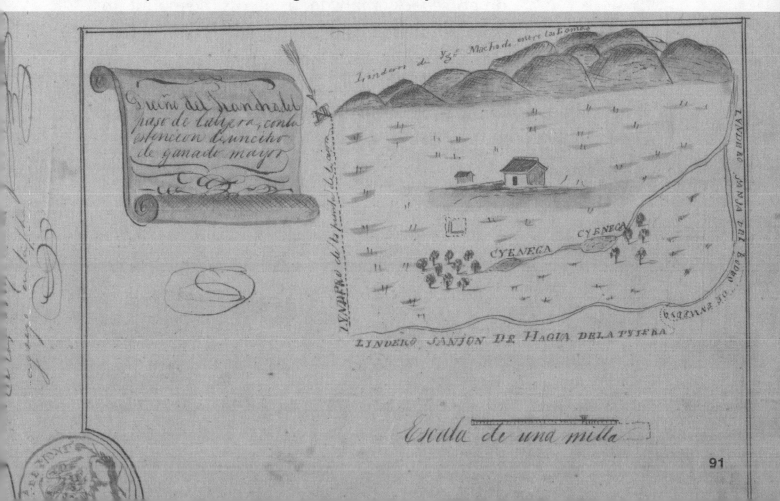

91

# A Rush to California

During the first half of the 1800s, settlements grew in California. The Spanish pueblos brought in people to farm the land. In time, pueblos became larger towns and even cities.

However, in the mid-1800s, the discovery of gold brought people to California by the thousands. In 1848, news got out that gold had been found close to a sawmill near the American River. James Marshall, who found the gold, said, "My eye was caught by . . . something shining in the bottom of the ditch." The owner of the sawmill was John Sutter. Soon miners from all over set up camps on Sutter's land. The California Gold Rush had begun.

The gold miners who came to California were called "forty-niners," because many arrived in 1849. Some came by ship to San Francisco. Others came on horseback or in wagons across the mountains from the eastern and central United States. They all came with dreams of striking it rich in California. The 1850s was a **decade**, or period of ten years, that saw large increases in the number of people in California.

Gold miners with shovels and picks on a hillside in El Dorado, California, in the mid-1800s.

Life for a gold miner was hard. Miners used metal pans to collect gold pieces from water. They also dug gold from pits. "Panning" and digging for gold was not easy. Mining camps were crowded. Supplies were few. While many people hoped for riches, few got wealthy from gold mining.

## Primary Source

Thou shalt not steal a pick, or a shovel, or a pan from thy fellow-miner.

—James M. Hutchings, "Miners' Ten Commandments," *Placerville Herald*, 1853

Miners used tools like these to pan for gold in streams and to break apart large rocks.

Many who became rich in the decade of the Gold Rush were entrepreneurs. An **entrepreneur** is someone who sets up a business. Entrepreneurs ran hotels, restaurants, and stores. One entrepreneur, Levi Strauss, learned that miners needed sturdy pants. He started a business making pants for miners. Even though Strauss did not mine for gold, he made money from the Gold Rush.

3. ☑ **Reading Check** Identify and list some effects of finding gold near a small town.

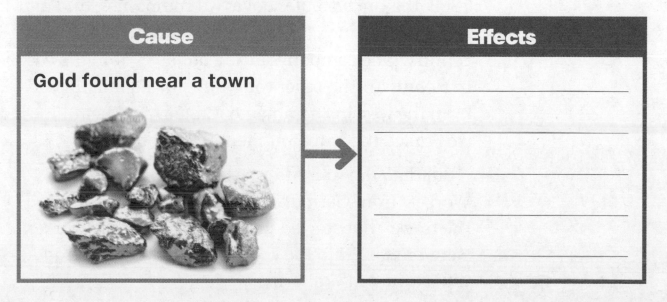

| Cause | Effects |
|---|---|
| **Gold found near a town** | _____ _____ _____ _____ _____ |

This photo shows a Chinese camp and construction train during the building of the Transcontinental Railroad. Chinese workers blasted tunnels through mountains, like the one shown. They also laid track on steep slopes.

## The Transcontinental Railroad

In the years after Mexico's independence from Spain, the United States and Mexico had disputes over land. Soon the two nations were at war. The United States won the Mexican-American War by 1848. The victory gave the U.S. large stretches of Mexican land, including California. In 1850, California joined the United States as the 31st state.

Many people wanted to move to California, but they had to take either a long sea trip or a hard wagon trip to get there. The U.S. government also wanted an easier way for people to travel west. In 1862, the United States gave two companies land and loans in exchange for building a railroad across the country. One company started building from the east in Nebraska. The other company started building from the west in Sacramento, California. The railroad was called the Transcontinental Railroad.

Building the railroad was hard and dangerous. Workers from Germany and Ireland helped build the tracks that started in Nebraska. Chinese workers were brought into the country to build the railroad that started in California.

On May 10, 1869, the tracks from east and west finally met. The final spike that connected the two tracks was made of gold. People across the country celebrated the joining of the tracks and the connecting of the nation. More railroads were built. Getting people and goods from one side of the country to the other became much easier. Now California was set to grow even more.

This is the golden spike that completed the Transcontinental Railroad.

4. ☑ **Reading Check** **Summarize** How did railroads change California?

_____

_____

_____

_____

☑ **Lesson 2 Check** 🖐 **HSS** 3.3.1, 3.3.2 **ELA** RI.3.3

**INTERACTIVITY**

Check your understanding of the key ideas of this lesson.

5. Cabrillo claimed the land that would become California for the nation of

_____

6. Why did Spain build missions in California?

_____

_____

7. What geographic features made settling California difficult?

_____

# Interpret Timelines

A timeline shows the order of events. You read most timelines from left to right just like you read a sentence. When studying a timeline, it is important to know how much time is shown. Look for dates to help you.

On the timeline below, each mark stands for 100 years. Notice that some events happen close together in time.

Circle the event on the timeline that happened first.

Put checkmarks by two events that happened close together.

## Exploration and Growth in California

1542
Cabrillo explores San Diego Bay.

1602
Vizcaíno explores the California coast.

1500     1600     1700

1579
Drake lands near San Francisco.

**1.** What do the numbers on the timeline show?

_____

_____

**INTERACTIVITY**

Review and practice what you learned about interpreting timelines.

**2.** Why are the spaces between events different?

_____

_____

_____

_____

**3.** List three events that have happened in your community. Circle the one you would place first on a timeline.

_____

_____

_____

**1821**
Mexico wins independence from Spain.

**1850**
California becomes the 31st state of the United States.

**1800**

**1900**

**1769**
First California mission is founded.

**1848**
Gold is found at Sutter's Mill.

**1869**
The Transcontinental Railroad is finished.

## Lesson 3

# Influence of Settlers on American Indians

 **INTERACTIVITY**

Participate in a class discussion to preview the content of this lesson.

 **Unlock The BIG Question**

I will know how California Indians and the new settlers interacted.

## Vocabulary

treaty
reservation

## Academic Vocabulary

discover

### JumpStart Activity

Choose one of these words: *shy, afraid, happy, sad*, or *curious*. Write the word on paper, but do not tell anyone the word. When your teacher tells you to start, walk around the room and talk to your classmates. Act like the word you chose. How did people act toward you? Did classmates guess your word?

California mission with priests, Spanish soldiers, and California Indians. What questions do you have about this scene?

When settlers first arrived in North America, American Indian groups already were living there. Over time, as the United States became a country and grew, American Indian groups were pushed off the land. Would things be different in California?

## California Indians and Early Visitors

How did explorers and California Indians interact? Some California Indians and explorers traded gifts, but trade was rare. Sometimes the explorers and the California Indians fought. Also, explorers and settlers brought deadly diseases to many California Indians. Some historians say that by the time of the Gold Rush, two out of three California Indians had died from diseases that visitors had brought.

1. ☑ **Reading Check**
**Analyze** and **underline** what happened when Europeans and California Indians interacted.

99

# California Indians and Missions

When the Spanish built missions, they used California Indians as workers. Some Indians decided to convert to the Catholic religion by being baptized. Baptism is a ceremony that, according to Catholic beliefs, makes a person a Catholic. After doing so, Indians were forced to work and could not leave. Some who did not convert still worked for the missions but could leave whenever they wanted. Indians built churches and housing, planted crops, and cared for animals.

Life of mission workers was not easy. Indians were given clothing and food, but they had to work hard jobs. Those who had converted lost their freedom and some of their beliefs.

2. ☑ **Reading Check** **Identify** and add details to the graphic organizer to support the main idea.

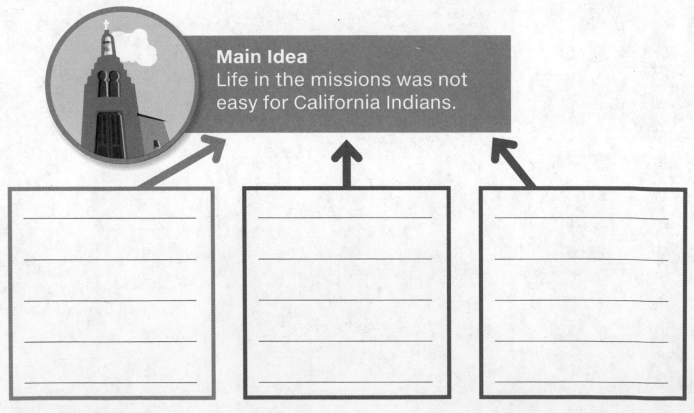

**Main Idea**
Life in the missions was not easy for California Indians.

A miner pans for gold in an 1849 California Gold Rush camp. What questions do you have about this scene?

## California Indians and the Gold Rush

California Indians had used the land for centuries as they hunted and gathered. Many California Indians had a close bond with nature, especially in their religious practices.

When gold was **discovered** in 1848, people came to California to try to get rich. They brought a different idea about land. Land ownership and private property were part of the settlers' culture. American Indians continued to suffer from diseases that the newcomers brought. There were even outbreaks of violence between the newcomers and Indians.

**Academic Vocabulary**

**discover** • *v.*, to find

This photo shows a California Indian family in front of an adobe building. Behind it is another building made of branches. Indians on this reservation farmed the land. But because of droughts, insect pests, and crop diseases, many crops were lost. Cattle and sheep of nearby settlers also ate the crops. The reservation was closed in 1864. What questions do you have about this photo?

## Conflicts and Treaties

In the 1800s, some groups of California Indians signed treaties with the United States. A **treaty** is a written agreement. But the Senate refused to approve many of them. Even though some treaties were signed, the United States government often did not honor them.

Beginning in the 1850s, California Indians were forced to live on reservations. A **reservation** is an area of land controlled by an American Indian group. Often reservations were located on the land on which California Indians had always lived. But Indians were forced to give up much of their land. California's government recognized few, if any, rights of California Indians. By 1930, there were 36 reservations for California Indians.

**Word Wise**

**Root Words** The word *reserve* means to save or put aside. How does this help you remember the meaning of *reservation*?

3. ☑ **Reading Check** **Describe** what happened to California Indian lands when Indians were forced to live on reservations.

_____

_____

_____

☑ **Lesson 3 Check** 🕐 HSS 3.2.4

4. **Identify** and circle two details that support the main idea that newcomers affected the lives of California Indians.

California Indians were forced onto reservations.

California Indians had a close bond with nature.

Some California Indians converted to the Catholic religion.

5. Discuss with a partner. **Explain** how the Gold Rush affected American Indians.

_____

_____

_____

6. Do you think settlers and the California government treated California Indians fairly? **Explain**.

_____

_____

_____

# Lesson 4
# Transforming the Land

**INTERACTIVITY**

Participate in a class discussion to preview the content of this lesson.

**Unlock The BIG Question**

I will know how people have changed the environment and used natural resources.

## Vocabulary

electricity
breakwater
mudslide
earthquake
boundary

## Academic Vocabulary

produce
energy

### JumpStart Activity

On a blank sheet of paper, make one change that can be undone. The paper can go back to the way it was before. Make another change that cannot be undone. The paper cannot go back to the way it was before. Compare your changes with those of a partner.

**Cathedral Beach, Yosemite National Park, California**

California has mountains, rivers, lakes, deserts, forests, and coasts. It is full of natural resources. Water, gold, trees, soil for growing crops, and wild animals are all natural resources. People used these resources to meet their needs. The ways people use resources over time can change the land.

## Communities Develop Near Resources

Think about the resources settlers needed. They needed clean water to drink, trees to build houses, open land to graze cattle, and good soil for growing crops. Settlers wanted to make their homes on land that would help them live. They chose to build near resources they needed. For example, it was wise to build homes near rivers. This way they could get water and fish easily.

**HSS** 3.1.2, 3.3, 3.3.3
**Analysis** CST.3, HI.2
**ELA** RI.3.4

**Quest Connection**

List natural resources that were available to the first people in your community. Then list resources that are still found there today.

**INTERACTIVITY**

Take a closer look at land and water changes.

1. ☑ **Reading Check** **Identify** and complete the web to show resources in California.

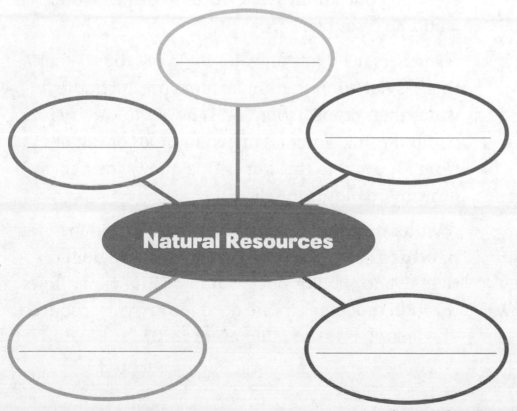

Natural Resources

Irrigation sprinklers water fields in Southern California.

## Using California's Water

Think of ways you use water each day. You need water for washing clothes, bathing, and brushing your teeth. You may like to ride in a boat or swim. You and your family need water to drink. Water is a valuable resource.

Farmers need lots of water to grow crops. When there is not enough rain, farmers must irrigate to water their crops. Irrigation is a way to water crops without rain. Water is carried in pipes or ditches from far away to the crops. This allows farmers to grow more plants to sell.

Water has many uses. Water can be used to **produce** electric power. Large dams are built on rivers. A dam holds back water. As the water flows through machines in the dam, **energy** is produced. The energy is turned into **electricity**.

### Academic Vocabulary

**produce** • v., to make or create

**energy** • n., usable power

Where does California get all this water? California gets water from melting snow, rivers, and from underground. California transports water all over the state. This water helps California meet the needs of its people. Since California does not always get as much rain as it needs, everyone must use water carefully. You can help by not wasting water at home or at school.

Although water is valuable, sometimes it causes damage. In some places, people build **breakwaters**. Breakwaters are walls that prevent waves from washing away the land. Breakwaters can be made out of concrete, sand, wood, metal, or other materials.

The next time you turn on a faucet, think about water as a valuable resource for farming, drinking, bathing, and more. The next time you see the ocean, a river, or even rain, think about how important water is for all of us.

2. ☑ **Reading Check**
**Use Evidence from Text** Underline details that support the main idea that water is an important resource.

Large waves splash over a breakwater on the California coast.

The first picture is a pen-and-pencil drawing of San Francisco, California, as it looked in the 1870s. The second one is a modern photo of downtown San Francisco today. Tell a partner about the changes that people have made.

## Word Wise

**Compound words**
A compound word is made of two smaller words. What smaller words make up *earthquake* and *mudslide*?

## Using the Land

Suppose you could fly over California when the first settlers came. Would you see the same forests, lakes, deserts, or mountains of today? Suppose you fly over your community today. Would you see the same things as in the past? Or would you see how a **mudslide**, a crack from an **earthquake** long ago, or humans changed the land?

People changed the land in many ways. Settlers, Indians, and Europeans cut down trees to build houses or make open fields for farms or ranches. Today, we build highways, parks, schools, bridges, and more. We change the land. When you plant a tree or grow a garden, you change the land.

Some changes are easy to see, like building a store or a dock. Other changes are easier to see on a map. A country or state might change a border or **boundary**. The name of a street or town might change. For example, San Francisco used to be called *Yerba Buena*. These types of changes have happened everywhere.

Think about how one community might change the land. Perhaps there was a forest before people arrived. People cut down some trees, built a few houses, and ran a small farm. A small town grew nearby. They gave the town a name. Later, a railroad was built nearby. More people came. They built more houses and stores. Much later, a highway was built, along with a shopping center and a hospital. The town became a city.

People change the land over time. What changes do you think will come next to your community?

3. ☑ **Reading Check**
**Analyze** what you have learned. Discuss with a partner how people have changed the land.

INTERACTIVITY

☑ **Lesson 4 Check**    ● HSS 3.1.2

Check your understanding of the key ideas of this lesson.

4. **Analyze** and **describe** why people built homes close to rivers or forests.

_____

_____

_____

5. **Describe** how people use water and land in California.

_____

_____

_____

6. **Understand the** *Quest* **Connections** How will the land, water, and other features look in your Then picture and your Now picture?

_____

_____

_____

# Cause and Effect

To understand what you read, look for causes and effects. A *cause* is the reason why something happens. An effect is the result. Suppose people need wood to build houses. Because of this need, loggers cut down trees for wood. Needing wood is the cause. Cutting down trees is the effect. You can use the word *because* in a sentence to help you figure out a cause. *Because* people need wood, loggers cut down trees.

An effect can have more than one cause. A cause may lead to more than one effect. As you read about events in California history, look for how events are connected and how one event might cause another.

Read the following paragraph and answer the questions on the next page.

People in California have built dams on some rivers. The dams produce electricity. When a dam is built, it changes the land and water. The water in the river backs up behind the dam and forms a lake. The lake floods some of the land. Controls on the dam let water from the lake flow through the dam, turning a turbine. The turbine produces electricity from the moving water.

**INTERACTIVITY**

Review and practice what you learned about cause and effect.

**1.** What is one effect from the cause below?

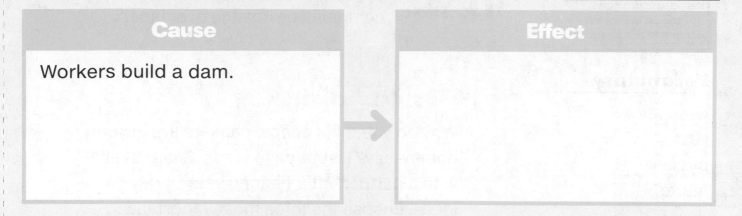

| Cause | Effect |
|-------|--------|
| Workers build a dam. | |

**2.** What is one cause of the effect below?

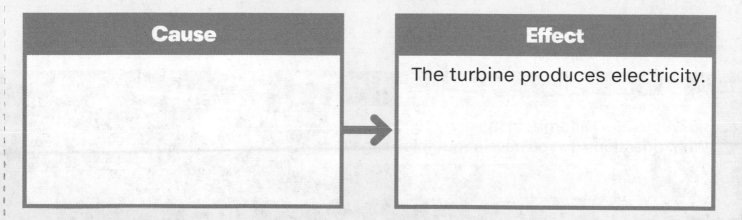

| Cause | Effect |
|-------|--------|
| | The turbine produces electricity. |

**3.** Use the photo and the text about the dam to create your own cause-and-effect chart.

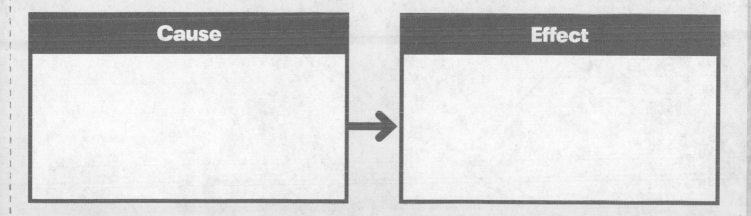

| Cause | Effect |
|-------|--------|
| | |

# 5 Changes Over Time

**Unlock The BIG Question**

I will know why locations are chosen for settlements and how communities change over time.

## Vocabulary

generation
past
present
future

## Academic Vocabulary

community
founded

### Jumpstart Activity

Why do you think people came to live in your community? List three reasons. Share them with a partner. After hearing your partner's ideas, choose the three most important reasons. Take a class vote on the most important reasons.

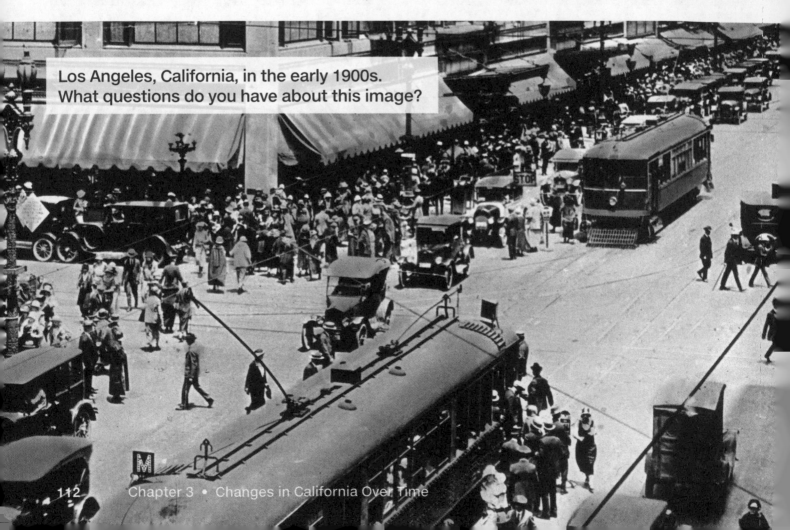

Los Angeles, California, in the early 1900s. What questions do you have about this image?

Do you know why your family came to this **community**? Many communities were **founded** because of nearby resources. Communities grew where there were enough resources such as clean water, good soil, or wooded forests. Today, people move from one town or city to another to be closer to family members or jobs and schools. Each time people move, they make a city or town grow larger or smaller.

HSS 3.3.3
Analysis CST.2, CST.3, RE.2

**Academic Vocabulary**

**community** • *n.*, a place where people live
**founded** • *v.*, started

## What Changes?

The story of William Wolfskill is an example of how businesses change. In the 1840s, Wolfskill started the citrus industry by selling a shipload of lemons to gold miners. The next year, he shipped oranges. Business grew. Wolfskill grew Valencia oranges. They became the most popular juice orange in the United States. Valencia, California, is named after the Valencia orange.

The way land is used also changes. A forest might become a factory. Still later, the factory might be torn down and the land used for a park. A **generation** is a period of time between the birth of parents and the birth of their children. Over generations, some things change. New neighborhoods and stores might be built. Some things also stay the same. You might use a library or ride on a street that has been around for generations.

1. ☑ Reading Check **Compare and Contrast** What are two things that might change and two things that might stay the same for generations?

_____

_____

_____

## Changes in Transportation

In the **past**, people traveled mostly to get what they needed to live. Today, in the **present**, we travel to visit family, to be entertained, or to go to work or school.

How we get from place to place has changed greatly. The California Indians walked or used canoes. The Spanish brought horses and mules to California. Horses and oxen pulled wagons for settlers. Ships and trains brought more settlers to California. Today, your family is likely to travel by car, bus, or airplane. How might you travel many years from now in the **future**?

Many years ago, there were animal footpaths. They became trails that Indians and settlers used. Then trails may have become streets or highways. Being close to transportation helps a community grow. Being near a railroad, highway, harbor, or airport can help businesses ship goods more easily. It can give people jobs.

In the past, people transported goods, like the cabbages in the top photo, using horses and wagons. Today, people use tractors and much larger containers, as shown in the carrot field in the bottom photo.

A ghost town in Bodie, California, preserves a general store as it might have looked long ago.

## Buildings Change

Buildings help tell the story of a community. What do you think was the first building in your community? It might have been a mission, a farmhouse, a store, or a train station. What is the oldest building you know about in your community? How does it help tell about your community?

Just as land uses change over time, building uses also change. A store that used to sell farm tools might now sell computers. An old factory might now be an apartment. What used to be a barn might now be a house. Are there empty buildings in your community? What might they become?

2. ✓ **Reading Check** **Identify** things that might cause a building to change from being used as a factory to being an apartment.

_____

_____

_____

_____

_____

**Quest Connection**

Underline some types of transportation and buildings you will include in your Then and Now pictures.

👆 **INTERACTIVITY**

Take a closer look at how buildings and transportation change over time.

## Making Decisions for Tomorrow

Every community faces problems. Some problems come from the need for change. Just like people, communities age. Buildings must be fixed or transformed into something new. Maybe the community needs to make a change to try to get more people to live there. Some communities might decide on a new way of doing something. Such decisions to change are not easy. Community leaders and the people who live there often come together to make those decisions.

Decisions made today affect communities in the future. If many families with children move to your city or town, will more schools be needed? Where will new schools be built? Will more cars mean that more roads will be needed?

Community and state leaders think about how to meet people's needs for years to come. Governments have to balance resources and money with people's needs. If the wrong decisions are made, problems could remain. However, there may not be resources to fix the problems. Each day, decisions are made that will affect the future.

Residents of Solana Beach, California, cross a wooden walkway in a park that has been fixed up.

### Word Wise

**Prefix** The prefix *trans* means "across" or "change." To *transform* means "to change form."

**3.** ☑ **Reading Check** **Identify** and **describe** an issue that you think California needs to work on now for a better future when you are an adult.

_____

_____

_____

● **INTERACTIVITY**

Participate in a class discussion to preview the content of this lesson.

☑ **Lesson 5 Check**    🜲 **HSS** 3.3.3

**4.** Choose a category, such as **transportation**, **buildings**, or **communities**. Write examples from the past and present. Then write what the future might have.

| Category | | |
|---|---|---|
| Past | Present | Future |
| _____ | _____ | _____ |
| _____ | _____ | _____ |
| _____ | _____ | _____ |

**5. Identify** and **describe** two events that might cause a community to grow.

_____

_____

**6. Understand the** *Quest* **Connections** What changes to transportation will you show in your Then and Now pictures?

_____

_____

# Adobe Days: A Book of California Memories

When someone writes about an event that they see, that writing is a primary source. We can learn about the past by reading a primary source, such as a letter or book, about life long ago. Sarah Bixby-Smith was born in 1871. She lived on a ranch. Her father raised sheep. She and her family moved to Los Angeles when she was seven.

Sarah wrote books that tell about California and her life there long ago. In her book *Adobe Days*, Sarah wrote about growing up. The following is from that book. As you read, look for words that describe changes.

**pastoral**, *adj.*, country life
**agricultural**, *adj.*, related to farming or growing crops
**kelp**, *n.*, a type of seaweed

"Now the sheep are all gone . . . pastoral life gave way to the agricultural, and that in turn to the town and city. There is Long Beach. Once it was a cattle range, then sheep pasture, then, when I first knew it, a barley field with one shed. . . . And the beach was our own private, wonderful beach. . . . Nobody knows what a wide, smooth, long beach it was. It was covered with shells and piles of kelp and a broad band of tiny clams; there were gulls and many little shore birds, and never a footprint except the few we made, only to be washed away by the next tide."

– Sarah Bixby-Smith, *Adobe Days: A Book of California Memories*, 1925

# Close Reading

1. **Identify** and underline ways people have used the land near Long Beach.

2. **Draw** a picture of the beach Sarah Bixby-Smith wrote about. Use exact words from the text to **describe** and label your drawing.

### Wrap It Up

How is this photograph of Long Beach today different from what Sarah Bixby-Smith described?

_____

_____

## Lesson 6 — Culture and Religion

**INTERACTIVITY**

Participate in a class discussion to preview the content of this lesson.

**Unlock The BIG Question**

I will know how different cultures and traditions influence California.

### Vocabulary

culture
ethnicity
legacy
preserve
heritage

### Academic Vocabulary

element
influence

**JumpStart Activity**

List celebrations you know about. Circle one of them. Tell a partner what you know about the celebration. How is the celebration the same or different from the celebration your partner chose?

There are certain events we celebrate as families. We share other celebrations as citizens or residents of the United States and of California. Our celebrations are part of what bring us together. What brings us together or makes us special?

## What Is Culture?

**Culture** refers to arts, beliefs, behaviors, and ideas of a group of people. Our religions, languages, music, art, stories, tools, ethnicities, dances, holidays, and more make up culture. People of one **ethnicity** share a common background or culture. Often they share a language or religion. We pass down some parts of our culture from one generation to another. In California, culture has **elements** from the groups that came before us and the groups of today. Our cultural traditions build a sense of community. They help us better understand one another.

### Academic Vocabulary

**element** • *n.*, a part or small bit

1. ☑ **Reading Check** **Analyze** and use your own words to **describe** culture.

_____

_____

_____

_____

Marchers perform a dragon dance on Market Street during San Francisco's annual Chinese New Year parade, which celebrates the Asian Lunar New Year.

A California Indian camp along the Merced River in California's Yosemite Valley, around 1700.

## California's Cultural Legacy

California has a strong legacy of culture in its history. A **legacy** is something handed down from the past.

California Indians have rich cultures with religion, music, and art. California Indians today are working hard to **preserve** and bring back the traditions and skills of their ancestors. For example, California Indians make baskets and other art using past traditions.

The **influence** of Spanish and Mexican culture on California is seen today. Spreading religion was a goal of some early Spanish settlers. They established missions and brought the Catholic religion to California. You can visit missions today that were built more than 200 years ago. Today, you can see mission-inspired buildings all around California.

Over time, people brought other religions to California. Today your community may have churches, mosques, synagogues, and other religious buildings.

## Academic Vocabulary

**influence** • *n.*, when one thing affects another

# Hispanic and Latino Influences

Hispanic culture is a large part of California's cultural legacy. Four of California's biggest cities have Spanish names: Los Angeles, San Diego, San Jose, and San Francisco. The capitol, Sacramento, is also a Spanish name. Does your community have places with Spanish names? Many California towns have central plazas. These plazas may have been influenced by Spanish and Mexican cities.

Many California buildings use Spanish and Mexican building styles, or architecture. Many communities also have colorful murals or mosaics. These can be traced to traditions in Spain, Mexico, or countries in Central and South America.

Olvera Street is in one of the oldest parts of Los Angeles. As you stroll through the Mexican Marketplace there, you can buy traditional pottery and leather goods. You can hear Spanish speakers. You can listen to mariachi music. Traditional dancers also perform there.

In California, you can learn about cultures from Central and South America. For example, you can attend the Taste of Ecuador Food Festival and Parade. There you can taste *patacones*, or fried plantains. There are many ways to learn about Hispanic and Latino cultures in California.

Shops and booths on Olvera Street in Los Angeles sell many kinds of Mexican goods.

2. ☑ **Reading Check** **Cite Evidence from Text**
Underline influences of Hispanic and Latino culture on cities in California.

# California's Cultural Heritage

American Indians who lived on the land before newcomers arrived had the first culture of California. As new people came to California, they brought their culture with them. During and after the Gold Rush and the building of the Transcontinental Railroad, many workers and settlers came from Africa, Europe, and Asia.

Communities may show off their cultural **heritage** with festivals. *Heritage* refers to traditions that are passed down from parent to child. Sacramento hosts an African Cultural Festival. It has art, food, and a fashion show. California Native American Day features dance, music, and food. In Torrance, you can visit Alpine Village and learn about German culture at Oktoberfest. Asian celebrations are popular in California. Have you seen the Dragon Boat Festival in Long Beach? Or the Asian Pacific Lunar New Year Festival in Riverside? What cultural festivals are held near you?

Chumash girl dances at a festival in Live Oak, Santa Ynez Valley, California. Joining the Chumash at the festival were American Indian groups from around the nation.

The United Sikh Mission celebrated Sikh culture with a float during the 2016 Tournament of Roses Parade in Pasadena.

Oral histories and letters can teach us about culture in the past. Letters are primary sources. Old letters were written long ago. They tell us about the past. Family stories that are told to children and grandchildren are oral histories. By listening to or reading stories about the past from people we know, we can learn about how culture and our communities changed over time.

3. ☑ **Reading Check** **Ask** a family member to share a letter or story from the past. Ask questions. Discuss with a partner what you learned from that letter or story.

**Quest** Connections

List cultural traditions that you can include in your Then and Now picture. Think about food, clothing, shops, or celebrations.

👆 **INTERACTIVITY**

Take a closer look at what makes up cultures.

👆 **INTERACTIVITY**

Check your understanding of the key ideas of this lesson.

## ☑ Lesson 6 Check   🔊 HSS 3.3.1

4. **Identify** and list an effect of a new cultural group moving into a community.

_____

_____

5. **Describe** why traditions are important.

_____

_____

_____

6. **Understand the Quest** **Connections** How will you show cultures in your Then and Now pictures?

_____

_____

## ★ Citizenship

**Quality:**
Honesty

# Delilah Beasley
## Reporting African American Life

Delilah Beasley was born in Cincinnati, Ohio. She loved to write. In 1910, she moved to Oakland, California. There she wrote for Oakland newspapers about events in the African American community. Beasley also stood up for African American rights in her newspaper writings.

Delilah wrote a book about African Americans in California. She researched the book for more than eight years. She studied primary sources such as diaries, letters, and government documents. She interviewed settlers and people who remembered family stories about the past. In 1919, the book was published. It was titled *The Negro Trail Blazers of California*. It is about black men and women who were early explorers or settlers in California.

### Find Out More

1. Reporters like Delilah Beasley need to be honest about what they write. Why is it important for a reporter or historian to be honest?

_____

_____

_____

2. About what issue or person in your school or community could a good newspaper story be written? Why?

_____

_____

# Visual Review

Use these graphics to review some of the key terms, people, and ideas from this chapter.

## California Events

**1769**
First mission is founded in California.

**1848**
Gold found at Sutter's Mill.

**1862**
Companies agree to build the Transcontinental Railroad.

| 1760 | 1780 | 1800 | 1820 | 1840 | 1860 | 1880 |
|------|------|------|------|------|------|------|

**1784**
First rancho land grant awarded.

**1850**
California becomes a state.

**1869**
Transcontinental Railroad is finished.

Music and dance

**Hello!** Language, stories, poems

Ethnicity

**Some Elements of Culture**

Food

Religion

Art and architecture

Celebrations

# Chapter 3 Assessment

**GAMES**

Play the vocabulary game.

## Vocabulary and Key Ideas

**HSS** 3.3.1 **Analysis** CST.1

**Circle** the best word to complete each sentence about explorers in California.

1. Explorers traveled in ships. An explorer's trip was called a ________. voyage, claim, tradition

2. Spain wanted to ________ California as part of Spain. voyage, claim, mission

3. A time period of 100 years is called a ________. decade, century, generation

4. **Interpret Timelines** Write on the lines above and below the timeline. Tell what happened in the years 1542, 1579, and 1602. **Draw** a line to show where each year goes on the timeline.

### Explorers in California

1542

1602

1500
1550
1600
1650

1579

**HSS** 3.2.4, 3.3, 3.3.1
**ELA** W.3.1

**5. Describe** some effects of newcomers on California Indians.

_____

_____

_____

**6.** Fill in the circle next to the event that happened first.

Ⓐ Ranchos were created in California.

Ⓑ Gold was discovered near Sutter's Mill.

Ⓒ Spanish missions were built.

Ⓓ Entrepreneurs sold goods to Gold Rush miners.

**7. Draw** land features that might cause people to settle in a place.

**8. Revisit the Big Question** How do communities change over time?

_____

_____

_____

**9. Writer's Workshop: Write Opinion Text** On a sheet of paper, write a paragraph to express your opinion. Who learns more, the people who share a culture or the people who learn about a culture? Use details to support your ideas.

## Analyze Primary Sources 🕭 HSS 3.3.3

Automobiles have changed over time. This car has a hand crank, used to start the engine.

**10.** What details tell you this is not a modern car?

_____

_____

_____

_____

## Cause and Effect 🕭 HSS 3.3.2 Analysis HI.3

**11.** How did businesses change because of the Gold Rush and the Transcontinental Railroad?

_____

_____

_____

_____

# Quest Findings

## Draw Your Pictures

You have read about how California changed. Now you are ready to draw pictures to show your community long ago and your community today. Think about changes to the land, buildings, roads, ways to travel, and people. Use labels to help everyone understand the changes.

### 1 Prepare to Create

List items you want to include in your Then picture and items you want to include in your Now picture. Check that you have included information about the land, buildings, ways to travel, and people.

### 2 Make a Sketch

A sketch is a simple drawing that shows where you will place each item. Remember to leave space for labels.

### 3 Share with a Partner

Trade sketches with a partner. Check that your partner has included all the items needed. Share ideas to make each drawing better.

### 4 Draw and Label

Complete your Then drawing and your Now drawing. Add labels telling what the drawings show.

# 4 Government, Landmarks, and Symbols

GO ONLINE FOR
DIGITAL RESOURCES

▶ VIDEO

👆 INTERACTIVITY

🔊 AUDIO

🎮 GAMES

☑ ASSESSMENT

📖 ETEXT

**The BIG Question** Why do we have government?

▶ VIDEO

## JumpStart Activity

INTERACTIVITY

Work in a small group. Suppose there were no rules or laws at all. Talk about some things that might happen.

_____

_____

_____

_____

_____

# Rap About It!

 AUDIO

# Our Constitution: The Government Plan

Preview the chapter **vocabulary** as you sing the rap:

Before creating a government, we made the
   **Constitution**,
An important document that we consider a
   solution,
A plan that explains how our country works
To serve the people and keep our safety first.

**Legislative** is the branch that makes the laws,
Two houses of **Congress**—each with its own
   cause.
The **executive** branch is headed up by the
   president,
The commander in chief for all our country's
   residents.
The **judicial** branch has a vital contribution:
Making sure laws are fair and sticking to the
   Constitution.

# *Quest*

# Government at Work

Our government is very big. Many people work for the government. Local government is the government of your community. You have seen local government workers, such as police officers, firefighters, librarians, and others who work for your town or city. You can research to find out more about what they do.

## *Quest* Kick Off

Hello, my first-grade students are having a career day! They will learn about local government jobs. Can you help? Choose a local government job, research it, and tell my students about it at career day.

## 1 Ask Questions

What local government job did you select? Write two questions you have about that job.

........................................................................

........................................................................

........................................................................

## 2 Research

Use online or text sources to find out more about the local government job. On the lines below, write some sources you can think of.

..............................................................................................

..............................................................................................

..............................................................................................

..............................................................................................

..............................................................................................

..............................................................................................

**INTERACTIVITY**

Complete the interactivity to learn more about local government jobs.

## 3 Look for Quest Connections

Turn to the next page to begin looking for Quest Connections that will help you learn about government jobs.

## 4 Quest Findings
## Present a Local Government Job

Use the Quest Findings page at the end of the chapter to help you tell about a local job.

# The American Government

 **INTERACTIVITY**

Participate in a class discussion to preview the content of this lesson.

**Unlock The BIG Question**

I will know how the federal government is organized.

## Vocabulary

constitution
federal
legislative
Congress
executive
judicial

## Academic Vocabulary

consequence
violate

### JumpStart Activity

Name three things you and a partner know about the United States government. Then walk around the room with your partner and talk with other pairs. Describe four things you and others know about the nation's government.

On April 30, 1789, George Washington (holding the sword) was sworn in as the first president of the United States. The ceremony took place in New York City.

In the 1700s, Americans wanted to break away from British rule. This led to the American Revolution. The Americans won this struggle. After the revolution, the United States needed a plan for government.

## Forming Our Government

During the revolution, American leaders wrote the Declaration of Independence. One idea from it is that government gets its power from "the consent of the governed." This means that the people take part in government. But how? A plan was needed.

In 1787, leaders wrote the United States Constitution. A **constitution** is a plan for how a country will work. The U.S. Constitution lists goals of the government. It also tells how the government is set up. The states approved the Constitution and must approve any new changes to it today. Also, state laws cannot go against national laws. All Americans depend on the Constitution. It helps to make our country's government work for the people.

1. ☑ **Reading Check** **Summarize** List key information about the United States Constitution.

| What Is a Constitution? | Why Is the U.S. Constitution Important? |
|---|---|
| | |
| | |
| | |

Donald Trump was elected president of the United States in 2016. He took office in 2017.

## Three Branches of the Federal Government

The U.S. Constitution splits the **federal**, or national, government into three parts, or branches. Each branch has some power. No branch has all the power. All three branches meet in the same city. They work in our nation's capital, Washington, D.C.

The **legislative** branch makes the laws. **Congress** is the legislative group. Congress is made up of the Senate and the House of Representatives. People in the states elect legislators—the people who represent them in Congress. Legislators must listen to the people who elect them. They also must do what they believe is best for all the people in the country.

The president of the United States leads the **executive** branch. This branch carries out the laws that the legislative branch makes. The president can sign into law what Congress passes or send it back for changes. The executive branch is also in charge of the departments that make the government work. Some of the departments print money, take care of our national parks, keep our food safe, and protect us.

The **judicial** branch makes certain the laws follow what is in the U.S. Constitution. The judicial branch is made up of federal courts, with the Supreme Court above all other courts. It is important for people to obey the rules and laws. There are **consequences** if people **violate**, or do not follow, laws. It is also important that laws are used in ways that are fair for all.

It takes all three branches to make our national government work. It also takes everyone in the country doing their part by telling legislators what is important, voting, and following the rules and laws.

**Academic Vocabulary**

**consequence** • *n.*, the result or effect of an action

**violate** • *v.*, to break or fail to follow a rule

2. ☑ **Reading Check** **Discuss** and **list** some duties of each branch of government.

## What Does Each Branch of Government Do?

| Legislative (Congress) | Judicial (Supreme Court) | Executive (President) |
|---|---|---|
| Makes the laws | Make sure the laws follow the U.S constiution. | Carries out the laws |

**Root words** The word *legislate* means "to make laws." Knowing this word helps you understand other words. *Legislators* are people who make laws.

## National Leaders

Congress, the legislative branch, is made up of senators and representatives from each state. They are elected by the people of each state. Every state elects two senators. The number of representatives differs by state. States with more people elect more representatives. California has the greatest population of any state. It has 53 representatives in the House of Representatives. It has more representatives than any other state!

California was the first state to have two female U.S. senators serving at the same time (Dianne Feinstein, left, and Barbara Boxer, right).

The president and the vice president of the United States lead the executive branch. They are elected by the whole country, rather than just by one state. They need to represent all of the people. What happens when people do not agree on what the country needs to do? This often happens. It is a hard job to be the president and try to do what is best for the whole country.

The Supreme Court is the highest court of the judicial branch. Members of the Supreme Court are judges, or justices. They are not elected. The president suggests a justice to be on the Supreme Court. The members of the Senate then vote on the president's choice. The head of the Supreme Court is called the chief justice.

Ronald Reagan was the governor of California. Later he was elected president of the United States.

3. ☑ **Reading Check** The three branches of government have different leaders. **Identify** and **list** the leaders of each branch.

| Who Leads Each Branch? | |
|---|---|
| Legislative | |
| Executive | |
| Judicial | |

People vote to elect their leaders in government.

## States and the Nation

The federal government makes laws that people in all states must follow. For example, a federal law tells how old you must be to vote anywhere in the country. There are many national laws. Some tell what you can carry on an airplane, what wild animals are protected, how food is kept safe, or that everyone can apply for jobs.

How do people make a difference in the federal government? You know that people vote for the leaders in Congress and vote for president and vice president. People across the country also pay taxes to the national government. These taxes help pay for the military that protects us, highways we travel on, and many other things. Some people may choose to become part of the federal government by becoming a ranger in a national park, joining the military, or even running for Congress. A person can even run for president!

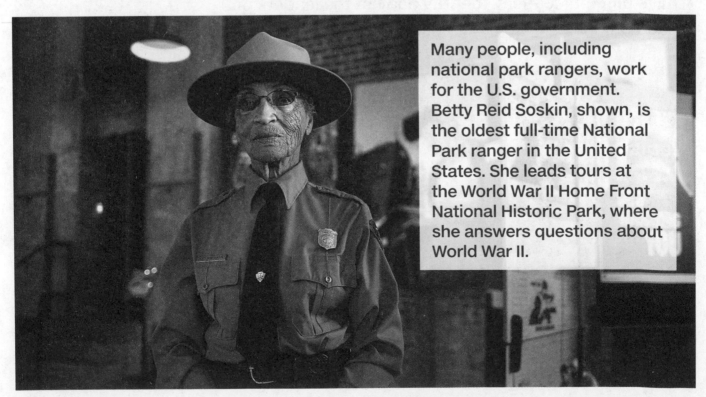

Many people, including national park rangers, work for the U.S. government. Betty Reid Soskin, shown, is the oldest full-time National Park ranger in the United States. She leads tours at the World War II Home Front National Historic Park, where she answers questions about World War II.

People also make a difference by following the rules and laws. One of the most important ways that all of us can participate is to let our leaders know what we think. Leaders need to know what issues people think are important and what problems need to be solved. People of all ages have a responsibility to speak up and make suggestions. You can make a difference.

4. ☑ **Reading Check** **Underline** details that show how people take part in the federal government.

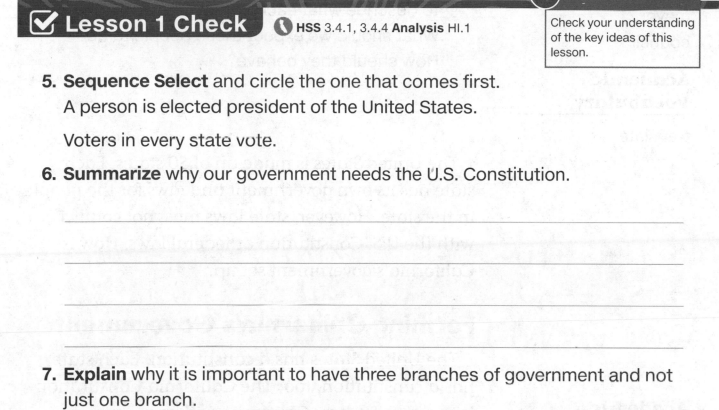

**INTERACTIVITY**

Check your understanding of the key ideas of this lesson.

☑ **Lesson 1 Check** ⓘ **HSS** 3.4.1, 3.4.4 **Analysis** HI.1

5. **Sequence Select** and circle the one that comes first.

A person is elected president of the United States.

Voters in every state vote.

6. **Summarize** why our government needs the U.S. Constitution.

_____

_____

_____

_____

7. **Explain** why it is important to have three branches of government and not just one branch.

_____

_____

_____

_____

# The California Government

INTERACTIVITY

Participate in a class discussion to preview the content of this lesson.

**Unlock The BIG Question**

I will know how our state and local governments are organized.

## Vocabulary

legislature
governor
charter
mayor
council

## Academic Vocabulary

translate

### JumpStart Activity

Move around the room to the charts your teacher has put up. Write words on each chart to describe what each person should be like. What should we expect these people to do? How should they behave?

The United States is made up of 50 states. Each state has its own government and laws for the people in the state. However, state laws must not conflict with the U.S. Constitution or federal laws. How is California's government set up?

## Forming California's Government

The United States has a constitution. Each state has a constitution, too. The California Constitution is the plan for how California will be governed. The first version of the state constitution was **translated** into Spanish. It was adopted in 1849, before California became a state. Today's constitution was adopted in 1879.

## Academic Vocabulary

**translate** • *v.*, to put words into a different language

The California constitution begins like this:

HSS 3.4.2, 3.4.4, 3.4.5 **Analysis** HI.1
**ELA** RI.3.3

## Primary Source

We, the People of the State of California, grateful to
Almighty God for our freedom, in order to secure and
perpetuate its blessings, do establish this Constitution.

—Preamble to the California State Constitution, 1849

The state government must do many things. It collects
state taxes, manages the state budget, and determines
what is taught in state schools. California spends much
of its budget on educating its students. The state also
takes care of state parks and state roads.

1. **✓ Reading Check** **Sequence** **Discuss with a partner**
which was first—the United States or the California
Constitution. Explain how you know.

## Word Wise

**Multiple-Meaning Words** California is a state. The word *state* can also mean "to say something." You could state that you love living in the state of California!

California spends money on its schools for teachers, books, school buildings, and other things needed for learning.

The California capitol building looks much like the U.S. capitol.

Jerry Brown was governor of California longer than any other person. He was elected four times.

## Three Branches of California's Government

The U.S. government has three branches. California's government also has three branches. In some ways the national and state branches are alike, and in some ways they are different.

In California, the legislative branch writes laws and sets state taxes. The California State **Legislature** is made of up the California State Senate and the California State Assembly. There are 40 state senators and 80 members of the State Assembly. Each of the legislators represents a part of the state of California.

The leader of California's executive branch is the **governor**. The lieutenant governor also helps run the executive branch. The people of California elect both the governor and the lieutenant governor. The governor signs or rejects laws that the legislature writes.

California's judicial branch decides if laws are used correctly and helps everyone understand the laws. The California Supreme Court heads the judicial branch. There is a chief justice of the California Supreme Court, just as the U.S. Supreme Court has a chief justice. There are also other state courts in California.

California's state government has tried many new ideas. Sometimes these ideas have been adopted by other states. Sometimes the ideas are even used for the whole nation. For example, California led the way in many environmental and educational issues.

2. ☑ **Reading Check** **Compare and Contrast**
**Complete** the diagram to show how California's government and the national government are alike and different.

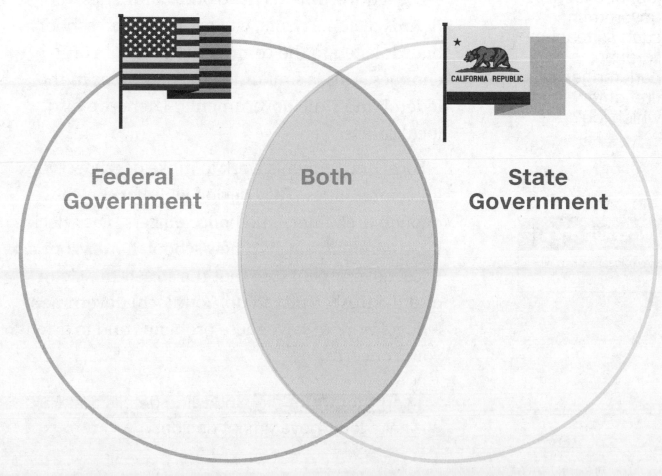

Federal Government

Both

State Government

# Our Local Government

The federal and state governments work on issues that affect many people. Sometimes local people are better at handling local issues. We need local governments that are close to our own communities. Local governments may be made up of our neighbors and people we see every day.

California has 58 counties. Within those counties there may be cities, towns, and special districts for water or fire protection. A local government may have a **charter**, which is similar to a constitution. It tells the plan for how the organization will work. A **mayor** or city manager is usually the leader of local government. Some mayors are elected by the people. Some mayors are appointed by the city **council**. A council is made up of a group of local leaders.

Local governments have other branches, too. Boards of supervisors, city councils, and school boards listen to the community and vote on changes. This is similar to what happens in the federal and state governments. There are also local courts.

Local governments work to make good decisions for communities. They decide whether they have enough firefighters and police officers. They decide if a community needs a new school, library, or park. Local governments see that the streets are clean and the trash is picked up. Your local government leaders work to solve these problems and to listen to your concerns.

3. ☑ **Reading Check** Underline details that tell what a local government decides.

**Quest Connection**

Think about your worker. Does the worker do a job for a local government, such as teacher, librarian, park ranger, or firefighter? If so, which job?

👆 **INTERACTIVITY**

Take a closer look at types of jobs people have.

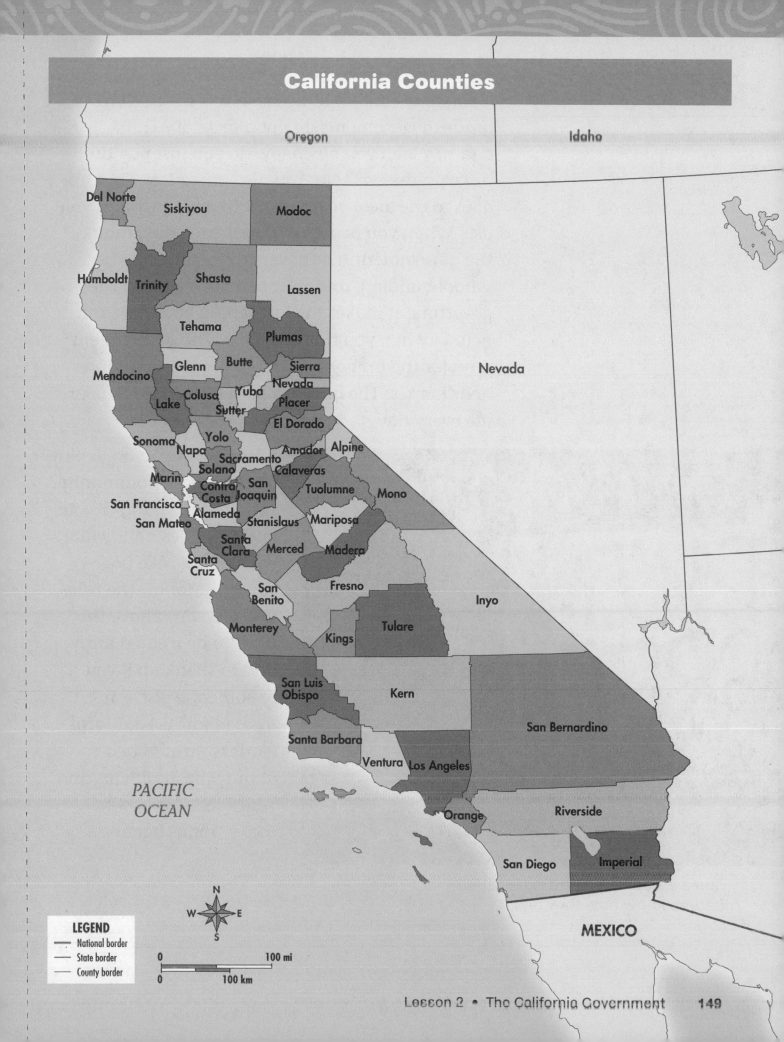

# California Counties

## Government and You

You may think that because you are in third grade, governments do not affect you. Think again. When you buy a toy, do you just pay the price on the box? No. You also pay a tax. That tax goes to the local government to pay for things you use. When you arrive at school each day, thank the government. The government pays for the school building, and your teacher's salary. The government makes the law telling you to wear a helmet when you ride a bicycle. The government pays for the firefighters who put out the wildfires near homes. The government plays a role in your life every day.

What can you do to play a role in your community? You are too young to vote, but that does not mean you cannot take part. You must follow the rules and laws. You have the right to be treated fairly and to speak up if you or someone else is not treated fairly. Your local leaders want to hear about your problems and your ideas for how to make things better.

These students are letting local leaders know how they feel.

You can join in on community projects that help others. You might collect books for children who need them. You can clean up trash outside your school or in a park. Perhaps your class can write letters to suggest a stop sign near your school. Maybe you and your friends can send thank-you letters to members of the military far from home. You can think of many ways to help and be involved.

4. ☑ **Reading Check**
**Connect** the reading to your life. **Underline** examples that show how you can make a difference in your community.

INTERACTIVITY

Check your understanding of the key ideas of this lesson.

## ☑ Lesson 2 Check   🌐 HSS 3.4.4, 3.4.5

5. **Cause and Effect** What effect does the United States Constitution have on state constitutions?

_____

_____

_____

6. **List** some titles of leaders in state and local government.

_____

_____

_____

_____

7. **Understand the** *Quest* **Connections** Think about the local government worker you will present in your Quest. Which tasks would not get done if a community did not have that worker?

_____

_____

_____

# The Preamble to the United States Constitution

The United States Constitution might be the most important document in our country. The Preamble is the introduction to the Constitution. It tells the goals of the nation and why the Constitution was written. The first words, "We the People of the United States" are perhaps the most meaningful. The power in our government is with the citizens, not a king, queen, president, or any other person.

**Vocabulary Support**

peace

protection from other nations

encourage the well-being of everyone

our children and their children

make into law

**union,** *n.*, country
**justice,** *n.*, fairness
**liberty,** *n.*, freedom

We the People of the United States, in Order to form a more perfect Union, establish Justice, insure domestic Tranquility, provide for the common defence, promote the general Welfare, and secure the Blessings of Liberty to ourselves and our Posterity, do ordain and establish this Constitution for the United States of America.

—Preamble to the United States Constitution

## Fun Fact

The Declaration of Independence and the United States Constitution were both signed in the same building in Philadelphia, Pennsylvania. That building is now called Independence Hall.

# Close Reading

1. Who does this primary source say is creating the United States Constitution?

_____

_____

2. Using simpler language than the Preamble, write the six reasons the United States Constitution was written. Number each reason.

_____

_____

_____

_____

_____

_____

## Wrap It Up

In what ways do state governments, local governments, and American Indian governments have the same goals as the United States Constitution?

_____

_____

_____

_____

_____

# American Indians and Government

 **INTERACTIVITY**

Participate in a class discussion to preview the content of this lesson.

**Unlock The BIG Question**

I will know how American Indian governments work.

## Vocabulary

tribal government
sovereign

## Academic Vocabulary

participate
contribute

Members of the Acjachemen Indian group in San Juan Capistrano, California

### JumpStart Activity

Work in a team of three. You will each take a role. One will be a student from a classroom. This classroom has a rule of no running on the playground. Another will be a student from a different classroom. This classroom allows running on the playground. The third will be the problem solver. When both classes are on the playground, there are problems. Act out what happens. Discuss how the problem solver can fix the problems.

Before there were any federal or state governments in California, American Indians were living here in smaller family groups or larger bands. They had set up forms of government to protect and take care of the group. This government was centered around family life. When the settlers came, they had different governments. They had different rules. What would the two groups do?

## Sovereign Governments

Many American Indian groups helped create and build the United States. Some groups helped settlers find food and grow crops. Many settlers might have starved without the help of the native people who had been living in the area for centuries. American Indians have continued to help our nation. They serve as guides on journeys. They serve in the military. And they help protect the environment.

Today an American Indian is a citizen of the United States and a citizen of a state. American Indians pay taxes, vote, and obey the laws just as all citizens do. They may also **participate** as citizens under a **tribal government**. Many Indian groups are **sovereign**. This means they have the power to govern themselves. The United States government recognizes more than 560 sovereign American Indian groups in 35 states.

**Academic Vocabulary**

**participate** • *v.*, to take part, to be involved

1. ☑ **Reading Check** **Identify** and **underline** words that tell how American Indians are part of several governments.

# Tribal Governments

There are over 100 federally recognized American Indian groups in California. Many others are seeking to be recognized. Look at the map to see which groups live near you.

Each American Indian government must follow federal laws, but they may make other laws too. Each group creates a plan or constitution to make it clear how its government will work. Citizens under a tribal government vote for their leaders. Those leaders make important decisions for their group. A leader may be called a chairperson, chief, elder, president, or governor.

Indian governments can be organized in different ways. Many have a council to help make decisions. The leaders might help determine how land and water will be used. Groups may form a court system to settle disputes. Some American Indian governments have their own police and fire departments.

**Word Wise**

**Antonyms** A *dispute* is an argument or disagreement. What word means the opposite of dispute?

2. ☑ **Reading Check** **Compare** and list ways American Indian governments are similar to national and state governments.

_____

_____

_____

_____

# Lands of Some California Indian Groups

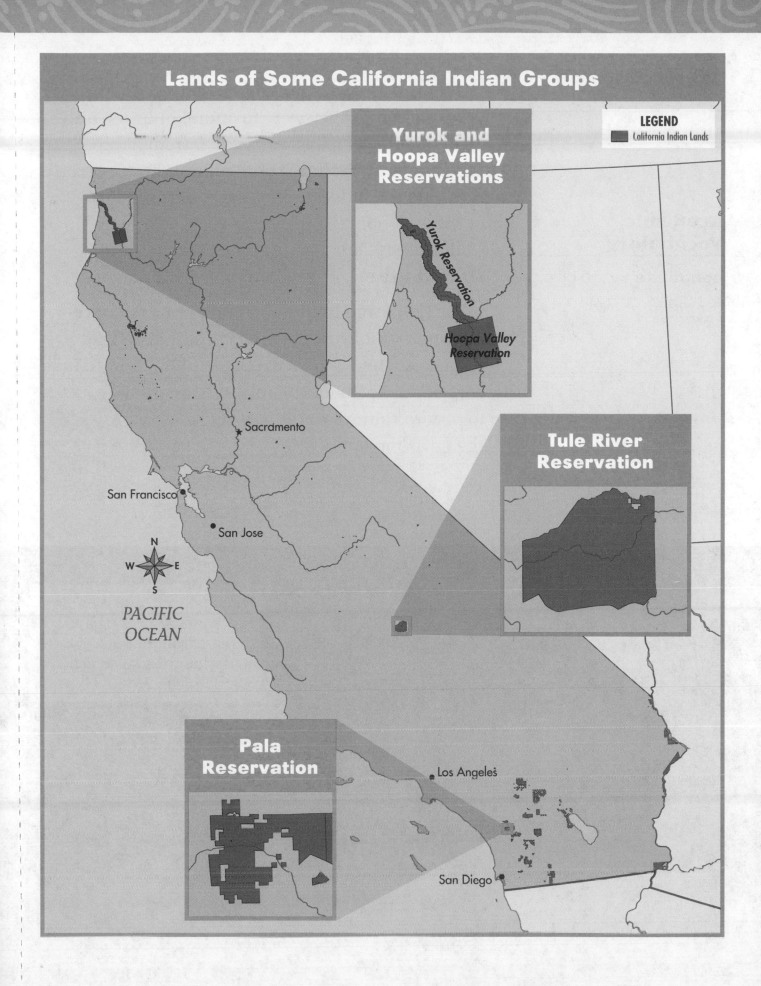

**Yurok and Hoopa Valley Reservations**

Yurok Reservation

Hoopa Valley Reservation

**Tule River Reservation**

**Pala Reservation**

LEGEND
California Indian Lands

Sacramento

San Francisco

San Jose

PACIFIC OCEAN

N
W · E
S

Los Angeles

San Diego

# Working Together

California Indians have lived on this land for a very long time. They were farming, hunting, and fishing here when explorers came from Europe. The land, water, plants, and animals have special meaning to California Indians. The careful use of these resources is important. The efforts of California Indian groups to conserve resources **contribute** to the well-being of us all.

The California Indian Environmental Alliance is a group that works to protect California's resources. They also train people about how to take care of our Earth for the future. This group works to restore cultural traditions. It also works to keep the environment healthy.

The Sycuan Golden Eagles Hotshots are a Sycuan Indian firefighting crew. They fought a large fire in California in 2016.

American Indians have also helped our nation by serving in the military. There is a long tradition of military service among native people. General George Washington valued their efforts in the American Revolution. And they have been fighting for our country in every war since then. In 2012, there were more than 22,000 American Indians serving in the United States military. More than 27 American Indians have received the nation's highest military award, the Medal of Honor.

3. ☑ **Reading Check** **Summarize** How do American Indians contribute to California and the nation?

_____

_____

**INTERACTIVITY**

Check your understanding of the key ideas of this lesson.

## ☑ Lesson 3 Check   🕐 HSS 3.2.3, 3.4.5

4. **Sequence** Circle the event that came first.

   The United States Constitution was signed.

   American Indian groups settled in California.

5. **Explain** how an American Indian can be a citizen of more than one group.

_____

_____

_____

6. **Opinion** Do you think an American Indian group should have land use rules that are different from state rules? Explain your thinking.

_____

_____

_____

## Sequence

When you learn about past events, it is important to understand when they happened. The order in which events took place is their sequence. Sometimes you can look for words that signal a sequence, such as *first, then, shortly after, next, before,* and *years later*. As you read about these events in California history, look for dates and key words that help you understand the sequence.

California joined the United States in 1850. It was the 31st state. Before Mexican and U.S. settlers came, California was home to American Indians who did not have borders to their lands. Settlers built missions and towns when they arrived. In 1821, Mexico gained independence from Spain. Then Mexico claimed the area of California. Later, more settlers from the United States came to California. The United States acquired California in 1848. To become a state, a state constitution had to be written. The California State Constitution was adopted in 1849. Another constitution was adopted in 1879.

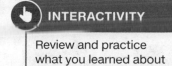
1. You read about some events in California's history. Put the events in sequence. Begin with what happened longest ago and write the events in order. If a year is given in the text, include it on the lines.

**INTERACTIVITY**

Review and practice what you learned about sequence.

## Events in California

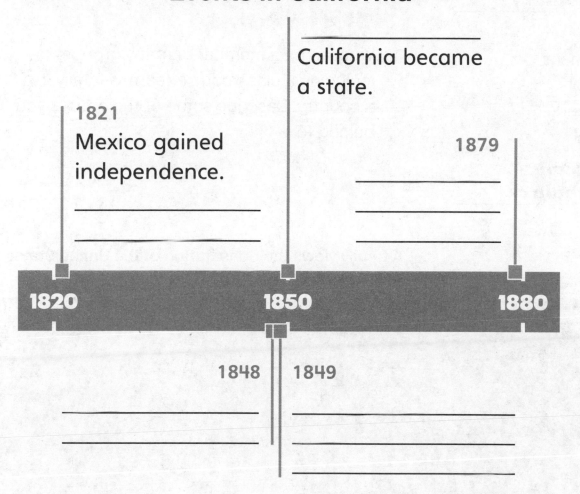

California became a state.

1821
Mexico gained independence.

_____

_____

1879

_____

_____

_____

**1820**          **1850**          **1880**

1848          1849

_____          _____

_____          _____

_____

2. What words in the text helped you understand the sequence?

_____

_____

# Landmarks, Symbols, and Documents

**INTERACTIVITY**

Participate in a class discussion to preview the content of this lesson.

**Unlock The BIG Question**

I will know some of the documents, symbols, and landmarks that bring us together.

## Vocabulary

ideals
document
symbol
landmark
official

## Academic Vocabulary

value
original

**JumpStart Activity**

You can be a member of many groups, including a classroom, a team, a family, or a country. Describe some of the groups you belong to.

A family views the Constitution of the United States at the National Archives in Washington, D.C.

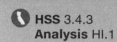
We belong to many groups. We have things in common with people in those groups. Perhaps we all like the same sport or the same music. What do all Americans have in common? There are many beliefs that Americans share and that make us feel like we belong.

## Important Documents

Our American **ideals**, or ideas that we hope will come true, were first stated in 1776 in the Declaration of Independence. It said that the ideal nation would treat people equally. It said that people should have the right to "Life, Liberty, and the pursuit of Happiness." The Declaration of Independence is a **document**, or written record, that makes it clear what Americans **value**. It reminds us that we all believe in the freedom to be the best we can be.

As you know, the U.S. Constitution is another document that we share. Changes have been made to it after it was approved. The Bill of Rights is what we call the first ten changes, or amendments, to the Constitution. Many people value the Bill of Rights for the many rights it protects.

### Academic Vocabulary

**value** • *v.*, to think something is important

1. ☑ Reading Check **Summarize Write** one thing you have learned about the ideals Americans share.

_____

_____

_____

_____

In 1793, George Washington placed the first stone of the United States capitol building.

CAPITOL CORNERSTONE CEREMONY · 1793

**Academic Vocabulary**

original • *adj.*, first

The Statue of Liberty was a gift from France.

## National Symbols We Honor

If someone from another country visits, what American symbols would you show the person? A **symbol** is something that stands for something else and has meaning for people. The American flag is a symbol for our country. The 50 stars are symbols of the 50 states. The 13 stripes stand for the **original** 13 colonies.

What are some other symbols for our country? The eagle is a symbol of our country's strength. You see the eagle on money and some government buildings. The Statue of Liberty is a landmark that stands for freedom. A **landmark** is an important building, monument, or place that has great meaning to people. When people see the Statue of Liberty in New York harbor, they may be reminded that the United States has welcomed millions of immigrants to this country. The United States capitol building in Washington, D.C., is a landmark. It is where Congress meets. It is also a national symbol.

The U.S. capitol reminds us that we all have a voice and are represented in our country.

We also honor the United States when we stand and say the Pledge of Allegiance. We put our hand over our heart to show that we mean what we are saying with our whole heart:

### Primary Source

I pledge allegiance to the flag of the United States of America, and to the Republic for which it stands, one nation under God, indivisible, with liberty and justice for all.

—Pledge of Allegiance to the Flag of the United States, Adopted by U.S. Congress, 1942

Have you heard people singing the national anthem? When we sing "The Star-Spangled Banner," we are letting people know that we are proud of our country. Singing brings us all together. Americans joining together may be the best symbol of all.

The bald eagle became our national bird in 1782.

2. ☑ **Reading Check** **Ask Questions List** questions about two national symbols.

| National Symbol | A Question I Have | Where I Can Find the Answer |
|---|---|---|
|  |  |  |
|  |  |  |
|  |  |  |
|  |  |  |

## Symbols in California

States have symbols too. What symbols represent California? The California bear flag is a symbol of the state. The flag shows a grizzly bear, which is a symbol of strength. The bear flag became the **official** state flag of California in 1911. Where have you seen the state flag?

The California Constitution is a document that is a symbol of California. The original 1849 state constitution is stored at the California State Archives in Sacramento. It was written on parchment made of animal skins. Great care is taken to keep it safe.

California has some landmarks that are known across the country. The Golden Gate Bridge makes all Californians proud, not just those who live near San Francisco Bay. Some people say the Hollywood sign is their favorite California landmark. Perhaps the Mojave Desert or a beach on the Pacific Ocean is your favorite California landmark. What are some symbols or landmarks in your community?

**Quest Connection**

Think about how a local government worker can represent the community and its people.

**INTERACTIVITY**

Take a closer look at what symbols stand for.

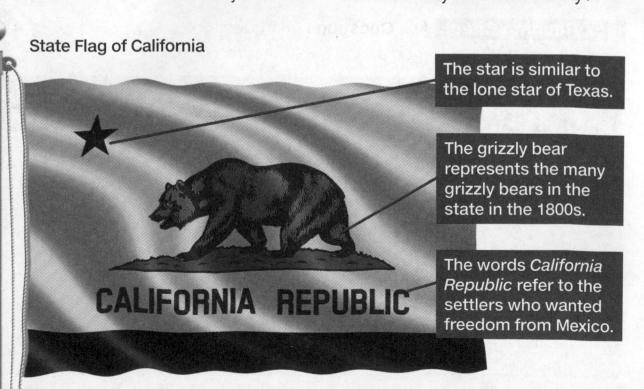

**State Flag of California**

The star is similar to the lone star of Texas.

The grizzly bear represents the many grizzly bears in the state in the 1800s.

The words *California Republic* refer to the settlers who wanted freedom from Mexico.

**CALIFORNIA REPUBLIC**

California has many symbols. Look at this chart to learn about more of them.

## California Symbols

| | | |
|---|---|---|
| State Flower | California poppy |  |
| State Tree | California redwood |  |
| State Bird | California quail |  |
| State Animal | Grizzly bear |  |
| State Seal | Great Seal of the State of California |  |
| State Mineral | Gold |  |
| State Motto | Eureka! (I have found it.) | EUREKA! |
| State Prehistoric Artifact | Chipped stone bear | 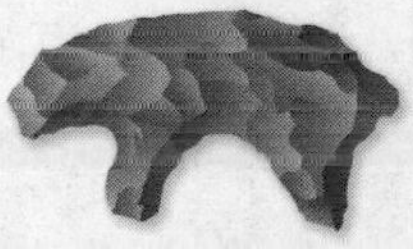 |

3. ☑ **Reading Check** **Write** four words to **describe** one California symbol. Have a partner guess your symbol.

_____

_____

Celebrating Independence Day is a proud American tradition.

Many people remember the men and women who served our country in the military.

## Patriotic Celebrations and Traditions

We all love celebrations. We might celebrate weddings or birthdays with our families. We celebrate as communities and a country as well. Our country celebrates a "birthday" on Independence Day. Each July 4 we remember when our country declared its independence. The U.S. Constitution was signed on September 17, 1787. We celebrate Constitution Day in September to remind ourselves of our country's ideals. The American flag gets remembered on a special day, too. We celebrate the flag and what it stands for on Flag Day on June 14.

Our country honors people who have made and keep our country great. Veterans Day (November 11) and Memorial Day (the last Monday each May) remind us to thank and honor those who have served in our nation's military. Each year on Presidents Day (the third Monday each February) we remember our founders and those who have come after them to serve as leaders for our country.

**4.** ☑ **Reading Check** **Summarize** Why do we have patriotic celebrations?

_____

_____

_____

☑ **Lesson 4 Check**   ⬤ **HSS** 3.4.3

**INTERACTIVITY**

Check your understanding of the key ideas of the lesson.

**5. Compare and Contrast** How is a landmark different from a celebration?

_____

_____

**6. Explain** how symbols and celebrations bring people together.

_____

_____

_____

**7. Understand the** _Quest_ **Connections** How can local government workers make us proud of our state?

_____

_____

_____

# Interpret Graphs

A graph shows information in a visual way. A graph makes it easier to understand relationships between numbers. Some graphs help us see how things change over time.

When studying a graph, it is important to look at the title. Look also at the labels on the side and bottom of the graph. Notice the source of the data. Then look at how the graph changes.

The federal government employs people to work in our country and the world. These jobs include working for the military, caring for the environment, enforcing laws, or checking that foods and medicines are safe. This graph shows the number of federal government workers in different years. Not every year is shown.

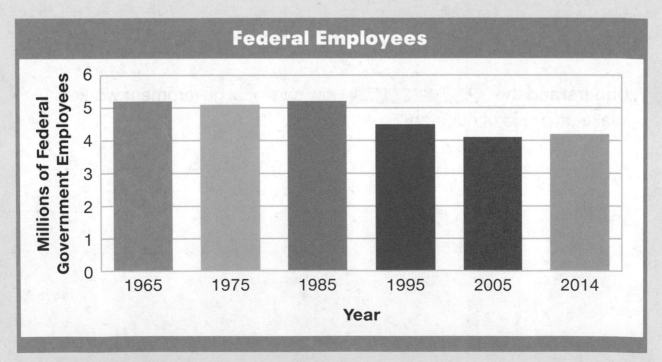

**Federal Employees**

*Source*: Office of Personnel Management

# Your Turn!

1. What do the numbers on the side of the graph show?

_____

**INTERACTIVITY**

Review and practice what you learned about interpreting graphs.

2. What do the numbers at the bottom of the graph show?

_____

3. What generalizations can you make based on the graph? Tell how you know.

_____

_____

_____

_____

_____

★ **Citizenship**

**Quality:**
Leadership

# Earl Warren
## A Life of Law and Leadership

Earl Warren was born in Los Angeles, but he lived much of his childhood in Bakersfield, California. Even as a young boy he knew he wanted to be a lawyer. When older, he went to law school and became a lawyer. He enjoyed helping his community. He ran for governor of California in 1942 and was elected. He served three terms. He was even nominated to be the vice president of the United States. He did not win that election.

Mr. Warren became the Chief Justice of the United States Supreme Court in 1953. One of the most important rulings while he led the Supreme Court was the ruling that made schools open to children of all races.

### Primary Source

We conclude that in the field of public education the doctrine of "separate but equal" has no place. Separate educational facilities are inherently unequal.

—Chief Justice Earl Warren, ruling
on *Brown* v. *Board of Education*, 1954

### Find Out More

1. There was something very unusual about the election for California's governor in 1946. Research and find out what that was.

2. When Chief Justice Warren was on the Supreme Court, the court ruled that a child's race should not determine what school the child attends. Talk with a partner about why this is important.

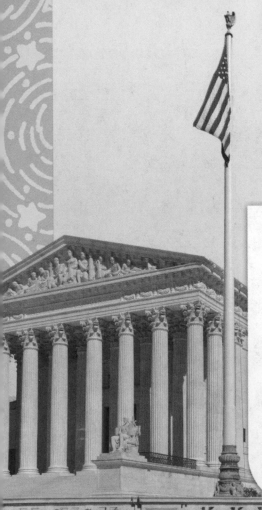

# Visual Review

Use these charts to review some key terms, people, and ideas from the chapter.

## Governments in the United States

| | Federal Government | State Governments | Local Governments | American Indian Governments |
|---|---|---|---|---|
| **Who Is Governed?** | The United States | One state, such as California | A city or community | An American Indian group |
| **Some of the Leaders** | • President<br>• Vice president<br>• Senator<br>• Representative<br>• Supreme Court justice | • Governor<br>• Lieutenant governor<br>• State senator<br>• Member of the State Assembly<br>• State Supreme Court justice | • Mayor<br>• City manager<br>• Supervisor<br>• School Board member | Each Indian nation may have a different title for the leader, such as chairperson, chief, elder, president, or governor. |

## Branches of Government

| | Legislative | Executive | Judicial |
|---|---|---|---|
| **Duties** | • Pass laws<br>• Vote on taxes | • Enforce laws<br>• Sign or refuse laws | • Decide if laws follow the Constitution<br>• Decide what laws mean |
| **Federal Leaders** | Congress | President | Supreme Court Justice |
| **California Leaders** | State Legislature | Governor | California Supreme Court Justice |

# 4 ☑ Assessment

🎮 **GAMES**

Play the vocabulary game.

## Vocabulary and Key Ideas  🦶 HSS 3.1, 3.4.1

The United States Constitution is the plan for our national government. **Complete** each sentence with one of these three words: legislative, judicial, executive.

1. The _____ branch decides if laws follow the Constitution.

2. The _____ branch makes the laws.

3. The _____ branch enforces the laws.

4. Use this data to **draw** bars in the bar graph.

   • San Diego has more than 1 million people but less than 2 million people.

   • San Francisco has a little less than 1 million people.

   • Los Angeles has almost 4 million people.

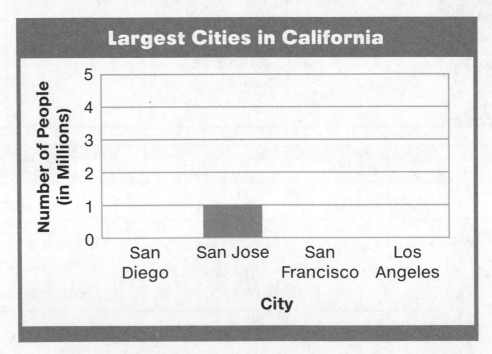

**Largest Cities in California**

Number of People (in Millions)

City

**Interpret a Graph** Use the information on the graph. What are the two cities with the most people?

_____

5. **Compare and Contrast** Tell how the governor of California is similar to and different from the president of the United States.

_____

_____

_____

6. **Sequence** Fill in the letter next to the event that happened first.

Ⓐ California becomes a state.

Ⓑ The United States Constitution is created.

Ⓒ The United States government recognizes that some American Indian groups are sovereign.

Ⓓ The California Constitution sets up a plan for state government.

7. **Analyze** Why is it important for a state like California to have its own flag and state symbols?

_____

_____

_____

8. **Revisit the Big Question** Why do we have government?

_____

_____

_____

9. **Writer's Workshop: Write Explanatory Text** On a sheet of paper, **write** a paragraph. Explain how and why we celebrate one of our patriotic holidays.

## Analyze Primary Sources  HSS 3.4.1

The President shall be Commander in Chief of the Army and Navy of the United States, . . .

—The United States Constitution Article II, Section 2

**10.** A commander is a leader. What do you think this title means that the president should do?

_____

_____

_____

_____

_____

## Summarize  HSS 3.4.1 Analysis HI.1

**11.** How do citizens contribute to the government?

_____

_____

_____

_____

_____

_____

# Quest Findings

INTERACTIVITY

Use this activity to help you prepare to present.

## Present a Local Government Job

In this chapter, you have read about the levels and branches of government. Now you are ready to prepare and give your presentation about a local government worker. Convince others that you know all about the job!

### 1 Job Title

What is the title of the job you chose? Write it here.

_____

### 2 Research

Find out more about the job. What tasks does someone who works at this job perform? What training is needed? What qualities should the person have? (For example, does the person need to be fair? Does the person need to be a good leader?)

### 3 Take Notes

List 2 duties that are important for this job. Then list 2 skills needed.

_____

_____

### 4 Present

On note cards, write what to say about the job. Remember, you will be presenting to first graders, so practice how to be clear. If you like, wear a costume to look like a worker who has the job.

GO ONLINE FOR
DIGITAL RESOURCES

▶ VIDEO

👆 INTERACTIVITY

🔊 AUDIO

🎮 GAMES

☑ ASSESSMENT

📖 ETEXT

## The BIG Question

# How can I participate?

▶ VIDEO

## JumPstart Activity

 INTERACTIVITY

One way to take part in your community is to be nice to others. Work with a partner and act out a time when you were nice to someone. Perhaps you helped someone with a problem or said something nice. Discuss with your partner how being nice to someone makes you feel and how it feels when someone is nice to you.

HSS 3.4, 3.4.1, 3.4.2, 3.4.6 **Analysis** RE.1, RE.3 **ELA** RI.3.1, RI.3.2, RI.3.4, RI.3.7, RI.3.9, RF.3.3.a, RF.3.4, L.3.4.b, W.3.2, SL.3.1

# Rap About It!

 AUDIO

# Citizenship Is Simple

Preview the chapter **vocabulary** as you sing the rap:

Citizenship is simple
As **citizens** of the United States
**Obey** the rules and **laws**
It's a **responsibility** we take.

You also have **rights**
To cast a vote and even to speak up
Freedoms of all kinds
All of them granted by the Bill of Rights.

Citizenship is simple
Sometimes the laws can fall behind the times
And **heroes** have to say,
"Hey! That really ought to be a crime!"

Take part, join a cause
Being a good citizen's the way to be.

# Vote or Volunteer?

It is important for all of us to take an active part in our community. People can do that in different ways. One way is by voting for our elected officials. Another way is by volunteering. Which way do you think helps a community more?

## **Quest** Kick Off

Hello there! I'm Benjamin Franklin. In this great nation, voting and volunteering are very important. But I can't decide which is more important to a community. Can you? Have a discussion to figure it out.

## 1 Ask Questions

Why should people vote? How is voting important? Why should people volunteer? Who does that help?

........................................................................

........................................................................

........................................................................

........................................................................

# 2 Plan

What facts do you need to know that will support your opinion?

....................................................................................

....................................................................................

....................................................................................

....................................................................................

**INTERACTIVITY**

Complete the activities to get started on your discussion.

VOTE FOR ME

COMMUNITY GARDEN

# 3 Look for *Quest* Connections

Turn to the next page to begin looking for Quest Connections that will help you prepare for your discussion.

BOOK MOBILE

# 4 *Quest* Findings
# Conduct a Discussion

Use the Quest Findings page at the end of the chapter to help you lead your discussion.

# The Reasons for Rules and Laws

👆 **INTERACTIVITY**

Participate in a class discussion to preview the content of this lesson.

## Vocabulary

obey

citizen

citizenship

responsibility

right

law

fine

## Academic Vocabulary

promote

enforce

consequence

**Unlock The BIG Question**

I will know why we have rules and laws and what happens when they are not followed.

### Jumpstart Activity

Work with a partner. Think of a classroom rule. Talk with your partner about what might happen if that rule is not followed.

People set rules to keep us safe and to help us. Different places have different rules. For example, in school, you should not run in the hallway. At home, you might have a rule to brush your teeth before going to bed. In your community, using a crosswalk during traffic is an important rule. In order for rules to work, people have to **obey**, or follow, them.

When you obey rules at school, you are being a good citizen.

# Citizenship

**HSS** 3.4, 3.4.1
**ELA** RI.3.1, RI.3.7

A **citizen** is a member of a community, state, or nation. Obeying rules is one part of good citizenship. **Citizenship** refers to the character and behavior of a citizen. For example, when you obey the rules of your classroom, you are showing good citizenship. Your school, city or town, state, and nation all value good citizenship. A great way to be a good citizen is to follow the rules of your community.

Good citizenship can change over time, such as when new rules are made. When people obey the new rules, they are **promoting** good citizenship.

**Academic Vocabulary**

**promote** • *v.*, to encourage or help

Most of the time, citizens follow rules because they feel it is their responsibility to do so. A **responsibility**, or duty, is something that a person should do. For example, many citizens feel it is their responsibility to help other people. They might do that by coaching a youth sports team, or helping people learn how to read.

1. ☑ **Reading Check** **Identify** and draw a picture of a rule you follow in your daily life.

This person is protesting an environmental issue. The Bill of Rights protects the right to protest.

## Academic Vocabulary

**enforce** • *v.*, to make sure people obey laws and rules

## Rights and Laws

Just as citizens have responsibilities, they also have rights. **Rights** are basic ideas or truths that people value. The United States government protects these rights with the Constitution and the Bill of Rights.

You have already read that the Constitution provides a system of government that makes, approves, and **enforces** the nation's laws. A **law** is an official rule. Laws help to keep communities orderly and safe. For example, it is against the law to drive through a red stoplight.

The Bill of Rights, the first ten amendments to the Constitution, protects basic rights for American citizens. Some of the rights include freedom of speech and freedom of religion. Freedom of the press gives citizens the right to hear news that is not controlled by the government. The Bill of Rights also gives people the freedom to gather and peacefully protest a law they disagree with.

The First Amendment of the Bill of Rights explains many of these rights:

**Primary Source**

Congress shall make no law respecting an establishment of religion, or prohibiting the free exercise thereof; or abridging the freedom of speech, or of the press; or the right of the people peaceably to assemble, and to petition the government for a redress of grievances.

—The Bill of Rights, Amendment I, 1791

Some laws protect the right to vote. For example, people can vote in an election even if they are out of town on the day of an election. Citizens vote to elect leaders who make laws. Voting is both a right and a responsibility.

**Quest Connection**

Why do we vote for our elected officials?

👆 **INTERACTIVITY**

Explore some of the reasons for voting.

2. ☑ **Reading Check** **Describe** to a partner how this image shows good citizenship.

People vote to choose their leaders.

# Consequences of Breaking Rules and Laws

## Academic Vocabulary

consequence • *n.*, a result of an event

**3.** ☑ **Reading Check**
**Underline** some consequences for breaking rules and laws.

If people do not obey rules and laws, there can be **consequences**. The consequences of violating, or breaking, a rule are usually not as bad as the consequences of breaking a law. When you break a classroom rule, for example, you might not be allowed to play outside.

When someone breaks a law, the consequences vary. Violating a traffic law, for example, usually means having to pay money, called a **fine**. Other times, the consequences can be more serious. Some people even go to jail for breaking a law. Lawmakers hope that the consequences of breaking a law will stop people from doing so.

There is a law that says cars must stop at stop signs. There are consequences to breaking that law.

**4. Summarize** Give three examples of rights that citizens have.

_____

_____

_____

**5. Cause and Effect** What happens when you do not follow a rule or a law? Fill in the chart to **identify** the consequences of each.

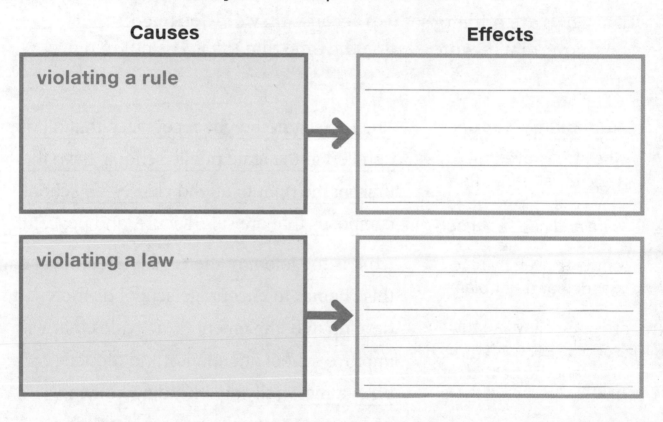

| Causes | Effects |
|--------|---------|
| violating a rule | |
| violating a law | |

**6. Understand the** *Quest* **Connections** Explain whether this statement is true or false: If we do not like a law, we can vote for different officials who can then change or replace it.

_____

_____

# California's Anti-Bullying Law

In 1985, California's state government passed a law to prevent the bullying of students in school. Bullying is when a student teases or hurts another student. Bullying violates good school citizenship. Students who are bullied have a more difficult time learning compared to students who are not bullied. Bullying has consequences. Students who bully may be suspended from school. That means they are not allowed to attend school for a period of time. More serious bullying can result in a student being expelled from, or kicked out of, school.

Laws are primary sources because they are documents that a government writes during the time that the law is put in place.

## Vocabulary Support

The state government believes all students have the right to go to safe and happy schools.

crimes driven by race, gender, or other bias

The state laws about schools are each given a number to help identify them.

**pupil** • *n.,* a student
**inalienable** • *adj.,* not able to be taken away
**enact** • *v.,* to make happen officially
**implement** • *v.,* to put into action

The Legislature hereby recognizes that all pupils enrolled in the state public schools have the inalienable right to attend classes on school campuses that are safe, secure, and peaceful ...

(d) It is the intent of the Legislature in enacting this chapter to encourage school districts ... to develop and implement ... activities that will improve school attendance and reduce ... hate crimes, bullying, including bullying committed personally or by means of an electronic act . . .

—California Education Code §32261

# Close Reading

**HSS** 3.4, 3.4.1
**ELA** RI.3.1

**1.** What kinds of schools do students have a right to attend? **Identify** and circle those qualities.

**2. Summarize** the intent, or goal, of the law in your own words.

_____

_____

_____

_____

## Wrap It Up

How does the law promote both rights and responsibilities?

_____

_____

_____

_____

_____

The opposite of bullying is working together with others, even if they are different than you in some way.

# 2 Being a Good Citizen

**Unlock The BIG Question**

I will know how to be a good citizen.

## Vocabulary

public virtue
deed
role model
volunteer
civic
tax
activist
cyberbullying

## Academic Vocabulary

require
issue
aid

### JumPstart Activity

As a class, think of ways people can be good citizens. When you have an idea, raise your hand. When your teacher selects you, stand and say your idea. The teacher will then write each idea on the board.

Good citizenship can happen anywhere. You can be a good citizen at home, at school, and in your community. As you have read, part of being a good citizen is obeying laws and rules. Responsibilities, like voting and helping other people, are also part of good citizenship.

When people practice good citizenship, it promotes public virtue. **Public virtue** is the goodness in all citizens and the willingness to work for the good of a community or nation. Public virtue is important. It means that people can get along with one another, so long as they are kind, honest, and respectful.

# In the Classroom

HSS 3.4.2 ELA RI.3.1, RI.3.2, RI.3.4, RI.3.7, RF.3.3.a, L.3.4.b

One place you can be a good citizen is in your classroom. First, you must follow the rules your teacher has made. That includes raising your hand before you speak, not talking too loudly, and not interrupting your classmates. You should always return things that are loaned to you. It is also a good idea to be a good sport, whether you win or lose a game.

In addition to obeying class rules, you can also do good deeds. A **deed** is an action. Doing good deeds promotes good citizenship and can improve your classroom. For example, you may want to help a classmate with her homework. Or, you could stay after school and help your teacher organize your classroom library.

When you do good deeds, you are acting as a role model. A **role model** is someone whose good behavior sets an example for others. Participating in your classroom in a positive way is a great way to be a good role model.

These students practice good citizenship at school by gathering canned food for those in need.

1. ✓ **Reading Check** **Identify** and underline ways to be a good citizen in the classroom.

# In Your Community

**Quest** Connection

What kind of volunteering do you think you might enjoy doing? Explain.

**INTERACTIVITY**

Take a closer look at different ways to volunteer.

## Academic Vocabulary

**require** • *v.*, to need

Good deeds are not limited to your classroom. You can also perform good deeds in your community. The public virtue of a community depends on people helping each other. For example, you and an adult might check in on an elderly neighbor. You could offer to help someone by raking leaves or walking the person's dog. A friend may need plants watered or mail collected while being out of town.

Some people in the community have jobs that **require** them to perform good deeds. Police officers keep people safe and direct traffic. Firefighters put out fires and respond to accidents. Medical staff help people when they get hurt or very sick.

Some citizens volunteer in their communities. To **volunteer** means to work or give help without being paid. Examples of volunteering include reading to children, working at a food bank, or cleaning up a park.

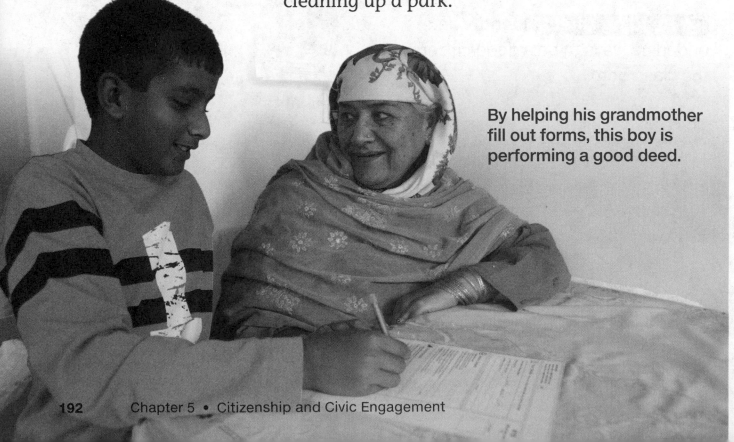

By helping his grandmother fill out forms, this boy is performing a good deed.

This organization, called the Alameda Food Bank, prepares a Thanksgiving meal for needy families in Alameda, California.

## Civic Engagement

Engaging, or participating, in civic life is another way to be a good citizen. **Civic** refers to the rights and responsibilities of citizens. Civic engagement includes voting and volunteering. It also includes paying taxes. A **tax** is money that the government collects. The government uses taxes to pay for community needs like schools, highways, and the police department.

Some people become very active in civic life. People who work to fix problems they see in society are called **activists**. Activists work hard for a certain cause, such as voting rights or the homeless. Large organizations can act as activists, too. California has many different civic organizations that work for different causes.

2. ☑ **Reading Check** Write how the photos on this page show good citizenship.

_____

_____

_____

The American Red Cross provides help to people in need in other countries.

## Citizens of the 21st Century

Civic engagement is changing in the 21st century. Technology has connected the world and made it easier to communicate. Citizens must understand what it means to be a good citizen in a digital world.

Voting remains an important right in civic life. Technology gives us more information about elections than ever before. Voters should learn about the **issues** before they vote. A responsible voter knows the facts and votes wisely.

Being a citizen today means learning how issues outside of your community affect you. For example, a flood in a faraway country could affect the price of goods sold in the United States. People living in that flooded country are likely to need **aid** from citizens all over the world.

### Academic Vocabulary

**issue** • *n.*, an important public matter

**aid** • *n.*, help or support

The Internet has helped to make the world interconnected. People from different places can communicate online. It is important to be a good digital citizen. That means not being rude or disrespectful to others. You should also not be a cyberbully. **Cyberbullying** is sending mean messages online.

3. ☑ **Reading Check** **Identify** one way that civic engagement has changed in the 21st century.

_____

_____

## ☑ Lesson 2 Check    ⓘ **HSS** 3.4.2 **ELA** RI.3.1, RI.3.2, RI.3.7

**INTERACTIVITY**

Check your understanding of the key ideas of this lesson.

4. **Main Idea and Details** **Describe** the role of a good citizen.

_____

_____

_____

_____

5. **Identify** an example of how you can participate in the civic life of your community.

_____

_____

6. **Understand the** *Quest* **Connections** Who in a community is helped by the work that volunteers do?

_____

_____

**Word Wise**

**Prefixes** A prefix is added to the beginning of a word. It changes that word's meaning. The prefix *inter-* means "between." What do you think *interconnected* means?

# Ask and Answer Questions

One way to understand something you read is to ask and answer questions about the text. The kinds of questions you ask can vary. You may ask questions that can be answered by the text. Or, you might ask questions that can be answered by your own knowledge. Other times you might be curious about ideas in the text. You may need to do research to find an answer.

Read the paragraph below and think of some questions you may have. Is there anything you do not understand? What are you curious about? Do you understand the meaning of all the words?

You are being a good citizen when you plant a tree. Trees help communities in many ways. They make communities more beautiful. They also give birds and squirrels a place to live. They provide shade and help cool off streets in the summer. Trees are also good for the environment because they supply oxygen to the air.

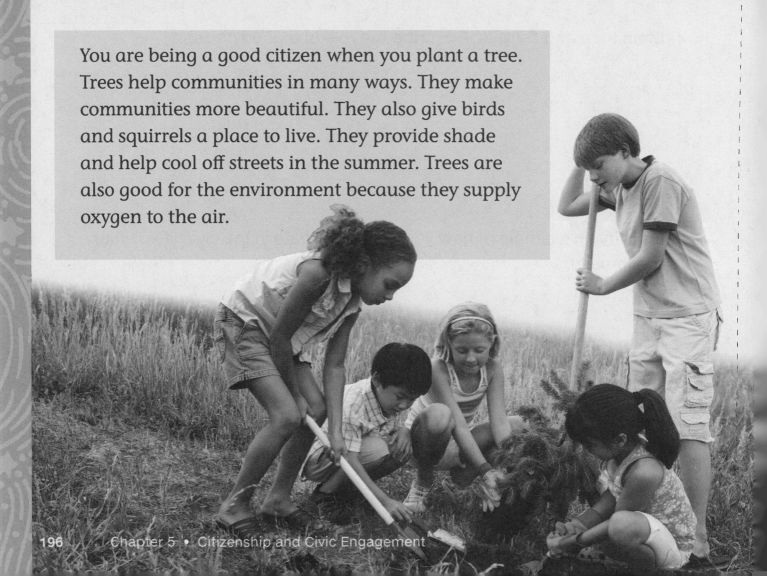

**1.** Use the first two rows of the graphic organizer to answer the questions about the paragraph you read about planting trees. You may need to do research. In the third row, ask and answer your own question about the paragraph.

**INTERACTIVITY**

Review and practice what you learned about asking and answering questions.

| Questions | Answers |
| --- | --- |
| What is one way trees make a community better? | ➡ |
| What is oxygen? | ➡ |
| | ➡ |

**2.** Go back to Lesson 2 and reread the section titled "Citizens of the 21st Century." Write a question that you have about the text. Answer it using the text, an online resource, or your own knowledge.

# American Heroes

**INTERACTIVITY**

Participate in a class discussion to preview the content of this lesson.

## Vocabulary

hero

independence

risk

civil war

slavery

abolitionist

civil rights

delegate

## Academic Vocabulary

despite

secure

**Unlock The BIG Question**

I will know about the lives of certain American heroes.

### JumpStart Activity

When have you ever been brave? Talk with a partner and share stories of a time when you were brave.

Throughout American history, certain people have worked to protect our rights and freedoms. Many Americans call these people heroes. A **hero** is someone who has done special deeds and is a role model for others.

George Washington and Thomas Jefferson are among others who appear on Mount Rushmore because they were American heroes.

# The Founding Fathers

HSS 3.4.6 **ELA** RI.3.1, RI.3.2, RI.3.7

People refer to the group of men who worked to shape the United States in its early years as the "Founding Fathers." Long ago, Great Britain ruled what is now the United States. Many Americans wanted independence from Britain. **Independence** means being free from the control or rule of someone else. Each of the Founding Fathers played an important role in making the United States a free, independent country.

In 1776, a group of American leaders—the Continental Congress—decided what to do about British rule. Among them was Thomas Jefferson. He helped write the Declaration of Independence. That document is the formal statement of freedom from British rule. When Jefferson and the Congress wrote and sent the Declaration to the British government, they were taking a risk. A **risk** is a dangerous chance. At that time, not everyone wanted to be free from British rule, and the British were firm about keeping control over America. The British and Americans were at war.

George Washington was the American military leader during the Revolutionary War. He was an excellent general and took many risks during the war. His leadership helped win the war.

After the war, the United States needed a constitution. Americans turned to many important leaders, including James Madison, to write that document. Madison was an important thinker. He helped plan the Constitution and the Bill of Rights. He has become known as the "Father of the Constitution" for his role. Both Washington and Madison went on to serve as presidents of the United States.

1. ☑ **Reading Check**
**Identify** and underline in the text one thing that each Founding Father accomplished for the United States.

Anne Hutchinson was told to leave Massachusetts.

## Anne Hutchinson and Freedom of Religion

Some American heroes are known for standing up for what they believed in. Anne Hutchinson lived in England in the 1600s. She was not allowed to practice her religion there. She decided to move to Boston, Massachusetts, along with others who shared her beliefs.

In America, she began to form her own ideas about religion. Because her thoughts were different from the official religion, she risked her own safety. Later, religious leaders forced her to leave Massachusetts. She moved to an area that became the state of Rhode Island.

Freedom of religion has been important in America since early times. Other Americans have stood up for their religious rights. The idea was so important that freedom of religion became a key part of the Bill of Rights. This freedom is still important today.

# Abraham Lincoln Ended Slavery

Abraham Lincoln was president of the United States during the Civil War. A **civil war** is fought between groups of people who live in the same country. The American Civil War was fought in the 1860s between southern states and mostly northern states. At the time, slavery was allowed in many states. **Slavery** was the practice of buying, selling, and owning people. The southern states put enslaved African Americans to work on their land. Many people in the northern states were against slavery. As a result of this disagreement, the southern states joined together and broke away from the country. The Civil War began shortly after.

President Lincoln wrote a document called the Emancipation Proclamation. His purpose was to free all enslaved African Americans living in the southern states. Many southerners believed it was their right to own slaves. This made it risky for Lincoln to issue the Proclamation. Slavery came to an official end when the northern states won the war in 1865.

### Quest Connection

How do you think people who voted for Lincoln affected the issue of slavery?

### INTERACTIVITY

Learn more about Abraham Lincoln and slavery.

Abraham Lincoln

### Primary Source

All persons held as slaves within any State ... in rebellion against the United States, shall be then ... and forever free.

—Abraham Lincoln, the Emancipation Proclamation, 1863

2. ☑ **Reading Check** Turn to a partner, and **explain** how Abraham Lincoln helped free enslaved African Americans.

## Clara Barton Aided Soldiers

Clara Barton worked as a nurse during the Civil War. She also brought soldiers medicine and supplies on the battlefield. Later in life, she started an organization called the Red Cross. The Red Cross cares for soldiers and their families. It also helps people who are the victims of floods and other natural disasters.

Clara Barton

## Frederick Douglass Spoke Out Against Slavery

Frederick Douglass was an abolitionist. An **abolitionist** was someone who worked to abolish, or get rid of, slavery. Frederick Douglass was born a slave in Maryland. He escaped to freedom as a young man and became a writer and speaker. Douglass spoke out about ending slavery. He traveled and spoke to people all over the United States. He was often attacked for his antislavery views. **Despite** the risk to his personal safety, Douglass continued to speak out.

Douglass's book, *Life and Times of Frederick Douglass,* is an important story of his escape from slavery. He also wrote an antislavery newspaper called the *North Star*. By writing and speaking out against slavery, Douglass helped change others' opinions about slavery.

Frederick Douglass

### Academic Vocabulary

**despite** • *prep.*, without being affected by

# Harriet Tubman and the Underground Railroad

Like Douglass, Harriet Tubman was an American hero born into slavery in Maryland. In the years before the Civil War, she escaped to Pennsylvania. There, she started working to help other enslaved African Americans become free.

Harriet Tubman worked with other abolitionists in the Underground Railroad. This was not an actual railroad. It was a secret system that helped enslaved African Americans living in southern states escape slavery. Tubman and other abolitionists risked their lives to **secure** others' freedom.

**Academic Vocabulary**

**secure** • *v.*, to make something safe and certain

3. ☑ **Reading Check** **Write** how Harriet Tubman worked to improve the lives of others.

_____

_____

The Underground Railroad helped enslaved African Americans escape to freedom.

## Martin Luther King, Jr. Worked for Equal Rights

Well after the Civil War, the struggle for African American civil rights continued. **Civil rights** are the rights of all citizens to be treated equally under the law. Even though slavery ended, African Americans did not have full civil rights. They had to go to schools that were separate from white people. They had to eat in separate areas in restaurants. Many were not allowed to vote.

Martin Luther King, Jr. gave his "I Have a Dream" speech in 1963.

Students celebrate Martin Luther King, Jr. Day at a parade.

Dr. Martin Luther King, Jr. believed that these rules were unfair. He gave speeches and organized peaceful protests in favor of civil rights. Some disagreed strongly with King. He and other activists faced violence. They risked their lives for their beliefs.

In 1963, King gave a speech declaring, "I have a dream." His dream, he said, was for children to be judged by who they are, and not by their skin color. As a result of the work of King and other leaders, two major civil rights laws were passed in 1964 and 1965.

Sadly, King was shot and killed in 1968. Years later, the U.S. government created a federal holiday to celebrate his life. The third Monday of each January, which is near King's birthday, is Martin Luther King, Jr. Day.

4. ☑ **Reading Check**
**Cause and Effect**
**Identify** and underline one effect of Martin Luther King, Jr.'s efforts to secure civil rights.

Eleanor Roosevelt was a delegate to the United Nations.

## Eleanor Roosevelt, Peace Leader

Eleanor Roosevelt loved solving problems and helping people. She was the wife of President Franklin D. Roosevelt. He served from 1933 to 1945. Eleanor Roosevelt fought for human rights all over the world, especially for women, children, and African Americans. In 1945, an international peace organization called the United Nations was formed. Eleanor Roosevelt was chosen as an American delegate. A **delegate** is a person chosen to act for others. She helped create the Universal Declaration of Human Rights. This document said that all people in the world had human rights.

5. **☑ Reading Check** **Describe** how Eleanor Roosevelt fought for human rights.

_____

_____

_____

INTERACTIVITY

Check your understanding of the key ideas of this lesson.

**☑ Lesson 3 Check** **ⓗ HSS** 3.4.6 **ELA** RI.3.1, RI.3.2, RI.3.7

6. **Main Idea and Details Identify** the risks George Washington took. Fill in the chart with supporting details.

**Main Idea**
George Washington took risks.

7. **Describe** why Frederick Douglass is considered to be a hero.

_____

_____

8. **Understand the** *Quest* **Connections** If people had not voted for Abraham Lincoln to be president, what might have happened to enslaved African Americans?

_____

# Distinguish Fact from Fiction

The American heroes you have read about so far were real people. The details you have learned about them are facts. Facts are statements that can be proven true. You can look in an encyclopedia, for example, to find out if a fact is true.

There are also American heroes who are fictional. That means that a writer made them up. Writers tell stories about these fictional heroes to teach about the time and place when they lived. It is important to distinguish, or know the difference between, fact and fiction. To do this, look for information that seems unbelievable.

Study the images and statements about Pecos Bill and Benjamin Franklin below.

Pecos Bill is a fictional hero. Stories about Pecos Bill describe his life in the American West. It is impossible that he used a rattlesnake as a rope!

Benjamin Franklin was a real American hero. He signed the Declaration of Independence and the Constitution.

# Your Turn!

**INTERACTIVITY**

Review and practice what you learned about distinguishing fact from fiction.

1. The following statements refer to Pecos Bill or Benjamin Franklin. Read each statement. Write "fact" or "fiction" on the lines to identify whether each sentence seems to be a fact or seems to be stretching the truth.

_____ He traveled to France many times.

_____ He was raised by a pack of wolves.

_____ He owned a printing shop in Philadelphia.

_____ In 1742, he invented a stove that allowed people to heat their homes more safely.

_____ One day when he was bored, he dug the Rio Grande.

2. **Explain** why you identified each statement as fact or fiction. What evidence in the text led you to your conclusion?

_____

_____

_____

_____

3. **Explain** why it is important to know if a statement about an American hero is fact or fiction.

_____

_____

_____

_____

# California Heroes

**INTERACTIVITY**

Participate in a class discussion to preview the content of this lesson.

## Vocabulary

union
strike
boycott
discrimination
stereotype
advocate
movement
emergency

## Academic Vocabulary

conditions
diverse

## Academic Vocabulary

**conditions** • *n.*, the circumstances affecting the way people live or work

**Unlock The BIG Question**

I will know about the lives of certain California heroes.

**JumPstart Activity**

Talk with your partner about who your heroes are. Which are real people? Which are fictional? Tell about the ways they are brave.

In addition to the American heroes you have read about, California has its own heroes. Not all heroes are famous or even well known, though. There are many heroes you have never heard of doing good deeds in their communities every day. In this lesson, you will learn about some of California's well-known heroes, and some that might be new to you.

## Fighting for Workers

César Chávez worked in California to help people who worked on farms. Chávez, a Mexican American, had been a farmworker himself. He knew the **conditions** that they worked under. For example, farmworkers' pay was poor. They worked long hours each day. Another Latino activist named Dolores Huerta helped Chávez.

Chávez and Huerta organized the workers by forming a union. A **union** is a group of workers who join together to gain more rights.

HSS 3.4.6 ELA RI.3.1, RI.3.2, RI.3.7

In 1965, Chávez and Huerta joined a strike that was started by another union leader named Larry Itliong. During a **strike**, workers refuse to do their jobs until their working conditions change for the better. Itliong and many of the workers in his union were Filipino. This means they came from the Philippines. The unions of Chávez and Itliong joined together to form the United Farm Workers, or UFW. Later, the UFW started a boycott. A **boycott** is when people refuse to buy, sell, or use something in order to make a point. The UFW wanted people across the nation to stop buying grapes. The boycott worked. Farm owners agreed to raise workers' pay. In 2014, the U.S. government created César Chávez Day, a holiday each March 31 to honor Chávez.

1. ☑**Reading Check**
**Discuss** with a partner why César Chávez, Dolores Huerta, and Larry Itliong might be considered heroes.

Dolores Huerta and César Chávez worked together to help farmworkers in California.

## Supporting Many Different Communities

Many other Californians worked hard to make changes in their communities. Charlotta Bass was a civil rights activist in Los Angeles. She worked to improve the lives of African Americans. In the 1920s, she formed a group that fought discrimination. **Discrimination** happens when people are treated differently because of their race, gender, age, or other characteristic. At that time, African Americans faced much discrimination. Bass started her own newspaper, the *California Eagle*, to promote African American rights.

Rupert and Jeannette Costo were American Indians who worked to improve education in their community. Rupert was Cahuilla and Jeannette was Cherokee. Together, they founded a program at the University of California to study American Indians. The program also fights stereotypes. A **stereotype** is an unfair and overly simple idea about a group of people. The Costos gave their personal collection of Indian books and paintings to the university.

Fred Korematsu is a role model for Asian Americans. During World War II in the 1940s, the United States was at war with Japan. Many Japanese Americans were forced to move to special camps. Korematsu refused to go. He was put in jail and forced into a camp. The Supreme Court supported this decision. However, in 1983 a federal court overturned this ruling. In 1998, he was awarded a Presidential Medal of Freedom for fighting against this discrimination.

Fred Korematsu

Harvey Milk was a political leader and a gay activist in the 1970s. Gay men are attracted to other men. Milk was elected to a local government office in San Francisco in 1977. He was one of the first elected officials in history to tell the public that he was gay. Milk worked hard to protect gay and lesbian rights. Lesbians are women who are attracted to other women. Milk's work also made it easier for gay, lesbian, bisexual (those attracted to both men and women), and transgender groups to stand up for their rights.

**Harvey Milk**

Chaz Bono is a transgender activist. The word *gender* refers to whether someone is male or female. Transgender people feel that their gender is the opposite of what it was at birth. Bono was born female, but always felt male. He changed his gender and today lives as a man. Bono and other activists fight against discrimination and stereotypes of their community.

Annette Funicello was a famous child actress who appeared in films and television shows. Later, she had an illness called multiple sclerosis that caused her to use a wheelchair. Funicello used her fame to bring attention to multiple sclerosis and other diseases like it.

2. ☑ **Reading Check** **Describe** the accomplishments of Rupert and Jeannette Costo that help make them California heroes.

_____

_____

_____

**Annette Funicello**

Billie Jean King was a great tennis player and is a leader in the women's movement.

## Women's Rights

Many Californians have worked to create opportunities for women and girls. Billie Jean King is one of the greatest female athletes of all time. Born in Long Beach, King won many professional tennis tournaments. She went on to be an advocate for the women's movement. An **advocate** is someone who fights on behalf of a cause. A **movement** is a group of people who work together to take action to achieve a goal. King helped to create a separate tennis tour for women. She believes in equal pay for female athletes. She is also a lesbian.

In 1973, King won a famous tennis match against a male tennis player. Millions of Americans watched on television as King beat Bobby Riggs. If she had lost, it could have been a setback for the women's movement.

### Word Wise

**Compound words** are words made from two different words. Find the word *setback*. To *set* is to put something in place. *Back* means the same as the word *reverse*. What do you think a *setback* is?

Sharon Hoshida is an activist in two communities. She is a past president of the Santa Barbara Women's Political Committee. She was also recognized by the Asian & Pacific Islander American Legislative Caucus for her activism. She helps others learn about the culture and history of these groups.

3. ☑Reading Check In what ways is Billie Jean King a hero of the women's movement?

_____

_____

## Serving Communities and Families

Every community has people who risk their lives to protect others. When a community has an **emergency**, or a sudden and urgent problem, police, firefighters, and medical workers arrive quickly. These groups are called first responders. First responders are heroes because they risk their own lives to save the lives of others. The United States also has a large military. Often the military helps communities during emergencies. They also serve to protect the country.

Families in a community need advocates, too. Sometimes families need help when they do not have enough money. Other times, a family needs help when someone becomes sick. Many organizations exist just to help families. Others work to help children. Sometimes children are not able to protect themselves, so advocates do it for them.

First responders, such as police officers and medical workers, come together to help during emergencies.

## Working for Better Schools

Some of California's heroes work with students and try to improve schools. Jaime Escalante was born in Bolivia in South America and studied to be a teacher. When he moved to Southern California, he taught math at a high school that had mostly Mexican American students. He helped his students learn calculus, a very difficult kind of math. His students succeeded and Escalante became a well-known and respected teacher. His story was turned into a movie that made him even more famous.

Rona T. Halualani is of Hawaiian heritage. She studies the history of native Hawaiians in California. She also works to support Asian and Pacific Islander American students at the state's schools. Her goal is to make California's schools more **diverse**.

Alice Waters is a world-famous chef who believes in making school lunches healthier and tastier. She started a program called the Edible Schoolyard. In this program, students learn how to garden, and to grow and cook healthy food. Waters also teaches schools how to use farm-fresh local foods in their lunches.

The Edible Schoolyard has improved students' lives. Because the school lunches are healthier, students behave better at school. They also learn to apply math and social studies skills in the garden.

4. ☑ **Reading Check** **Identify** and underline one detail that supports the following main idea: Jaime Escalante helped people.

Jaime Escalante

### Academic Vocabulary

**diverse** • *adj.*, made up of different groups of people

Alice Waters's Edible Schoolyard program teaches students how to eat healthy foods.

## ✓ Lesson 4 Check

HSS 3.4.6 **ELA** RI.3.1, RI.3.2, RI.3.7

5. **Main Idea and Details Identify** one Californian who worked to improve the lives of students and **explain** the person's contribution.

_____

_____

6. **Compare** How have people helped Asian Americans in California?

_____

_____

_____

_____

7. How might Charlotta Bass's newspaper have helped the African American community?

_____

_____

## ★ Citizenship

**Quality:**
Problem Solving

# Sylvia Mendez
## Ending Segregation in Public Schools

When Sylvia Mendez was a little girl, there was one elementary school she wanted to attend more than any other. There was a problem, however. She was not allowed to go to that school. She was only allowed to go to a school for Mexican American girls and boys. Back in 1945, schools in Orange County were segregated, which meant they were separated by race. White children went to certain schools, and Mexican American children went to other schools. The schools for Mexican American children were not as nice as the other schools.

Sylvia's parents thought this was unfair. They believed that all children should be treated equally. They fought to allow Sylvia to go to her favorite school. In 1947, the Mendez family won a federal court case that allowed Sylvia to attend whatever school she wanted. The Mendez family's victory set an important example for other schools in the United States. By 1954, it was against the law in the United States to separate schools by race.

## Find Out More

**1.** What problem did Sylvia Mendez and her family solve?

_____

_____

_____

**2.** Research someone in your community who has been honored as a problem solver. Learn how the person improved the safety, welfare, and happiness of others.

Use these graphics to review some of the key terms, people, and ideas from this chapter.

| | Example From Chapter | People and Groups From Chapter Who Illustrated This |
| --- | --- | --- |
| **Why do we follow rules and laws?** | They keep our communities orderly and safe. | First responders help keep our communities orderly and safe by making sure rules and laws are followed.  |
| **How can we be good citizens at school?** | Follow classroom rules; help fellow students. | Jaime Escalante worked to help Mexican American students learn math.  |
| **How can we be good citizens in our community?** | Volunteer, do good deeds, be a role model, and engage in civic life. | People in the community and organizations such as the Red Cross help those in need.  |
| **How can we be good citizens in the 21ˢᵗ century?** | Be a good citizen in the digital world; no cyberbullying; help people in other countries. | Eleanor Roosevelt fought for the human rights of people all over the world.  |

**GAMES**

Play the vocabulary game.

## Vocabulary and Key Ideas

🔔 **HSS** 3.4.2, 3.4.6 **ELA** RI.3.1, RI.3.4, RI.3.7

> law, civil rights, volunteer, risk

1. Fill in the blank with the correct word from the word bank.

   a. to work without being paid _____

   b. an official rule _____

   c. rights of all citizens to be treated equally under

   the law _____

   d. a dangerous chance _____

> abolitionist, advocate, Civil War, Emancipation Proclamation

2. **Identify** Fill in the blanks: Frederick Douglass was an

   _____ for enslaved African Americans. Like Harriet

   Tubman, he was an _____. That meant he wanted

   to get rid of slavery. An important step towards that goal came

   when Abraham Lincoln wrote the _____

   _____. Slavery was finally abolished when the

   northern states won the _____.

3. **Define** Fill in the circle next to the best answer.
   Which of the following shows good citizenship
   in today's world?

   Ⓐ Volunteering          Ⓒ Violating rules

   Ⓑ Cyberbullying          Ⓓ Being an abolitionist

4. **Identify** Study the image. For which group of Americans did this person work to protect rights?

_____

5. **Main Idea and Details** How did what happened to Anne Hutchinson relate to the idea of freedom of religion?

_____

_____

_____

6. **Cause and Effect** What are the consequences of breaking a law or violating a rule?

_____

_____

_____

_____

7. **Revisit the Big Question Describe** in detail two ways that people can participate in their community.

_____

_____

_____

_____

8. **Writer's Workshop: Write Informative Text** What problem in your community do you think needs to be solved? On a separate sheet of paper, identify a problem and the kinds of things you can do to solve it.

## Analyze Primary Sources

HSS 3.4.6 ELA RI.3.1

We do not have to become heroes overnight. Just a step at a time, meeting each thing that comes up, seeing it is not as dreadful as it appeared, discovering we have the strength to stare it down.

—Eleanor Roosevelt, *You Learn by Living*, 1960

**9.** What do you think Eleanor Roosevelt meant when she wrote "we do not have to become heroes overnight"?

_____

_____

_____

_____

## Distinguish Fact from Fiction

Analysis RE.3 ELA RI.3.1, RI.3.9

**10.** Read the two texts. Then label which one you think is fact and which is fiction. Explain how you can tell the difference on the lines below.

_____   _____

> George Washington was the first president of the United States. This is one of the many reasons he is called the "father" of his country.

> Paul Bunyan was a giant lumberjack. When he was born, five storks delivered him to his parents. He had a blue ox named Babe.

_____

_____

_____

_____

# Quest Findings

## Discuss Voting and Volunteering

You have read the lessons in this chapter and now you are ready to have your discussion. Remember that you are going to discuss whether voting or volunteering is more helpful to your community.

 **INTERACTIVITY**

Use this activity to help you prepare your discussion.

### 1 Prepare to Discuss

Choose two facts that support each side of the discussion. Write them down on a separate piece of paper. Choose what you think is more important: voting or volunteering.

### 2 Write Your Opinion

Use your notes and your answers to the chapter's Quest Connections to prepare for your group discussion. Be prepared to use what you've written to support your opinion.

### 3 Have Your Discussion

Gather with your small group. Begin by discussing the importance of voting. Then talk about how volunteering helps others. Let all the students in your group have a chance to share their opinions.

### 4 Conclude

After your discussion, sum up what conclusions your group made. What did your group decide between voting and volunteering? Did your own opinion change or stay the same?

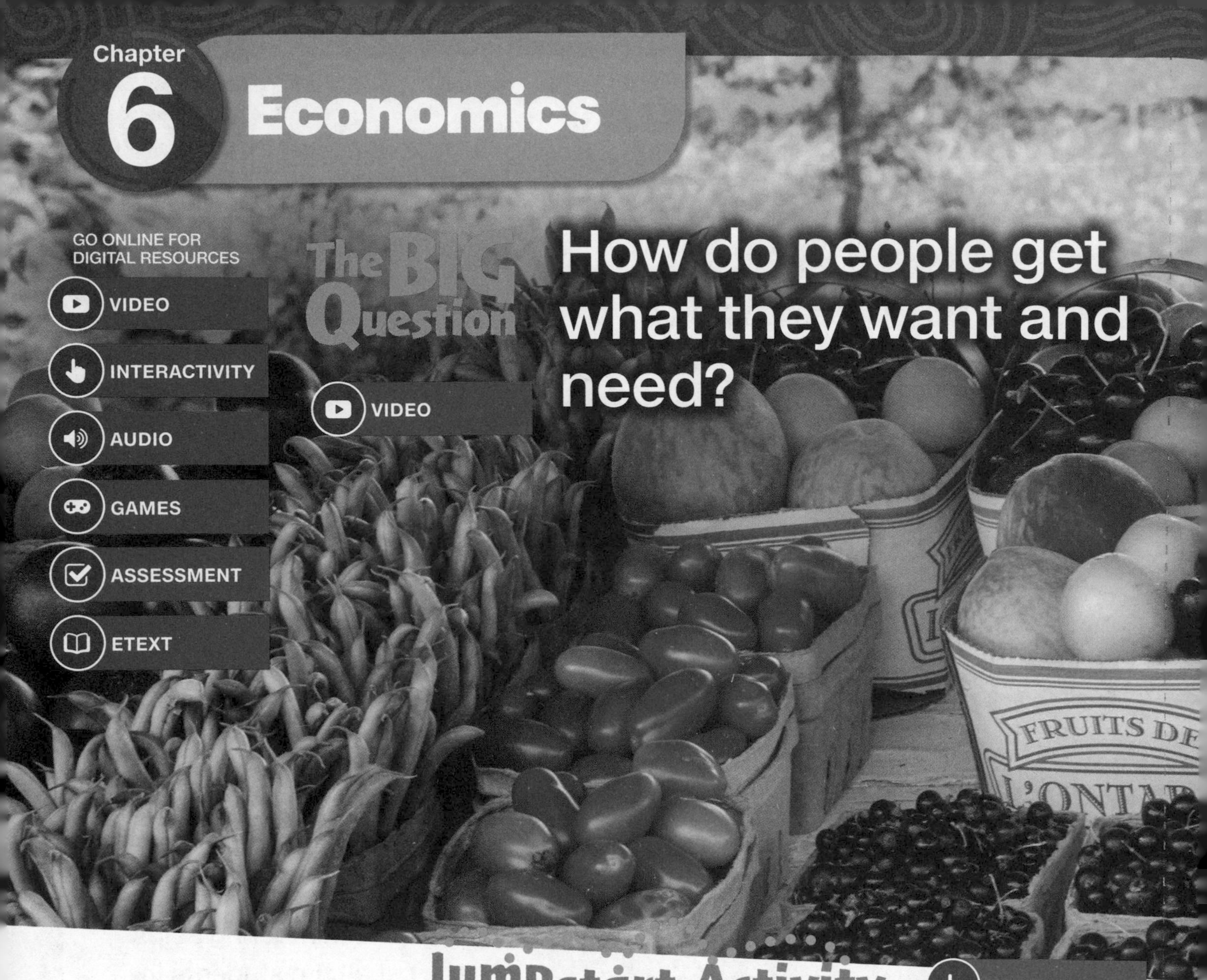

GO ONLINE FOR
DIGITAL RESOURCES

▶ VIDEO

👆 INTERACTIVITY

🔊 AUDIO

🎮 GAMES

☑ ASSESSMENT

📖 ETEXT

The BIG
Question

▶ VIDEO

# How do people get what they want and need?

FRUITS DE
L'ONTA

## JumpStart Activity

👆 INTERACTIVITY

Write five things that are valuable. Include two that do not cost money. Share your list with a partner. On the board, put your two lists in the order in which you think is most important. Talk about your reasons.

_____

_____

_____

_____

♪ **Rap** About It! ♪

🔊 AUDIO

# What You Need, What You Want

Preview the chapter **vocabulary** as you sing the rap:

We all have some **needs**

We can't live without these items.

We all have some **wants**

Like them but can live without them.

Needs and wants can be **goods**

Like a home, some food, or a purse.

**Services** help others

Like teaching or being a nurse.

What are goods made of?

Mostly **natural resources**.

How are the goods made?

By people, **human resources**.

Plus machines and tools

Those are **capital resources**.

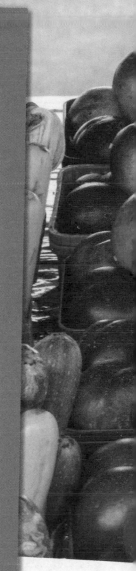

# Quest

**Project-Based Learning**

# Resources All Around Us

You know a lot about economics already. You know that people make, spend, and save money. You can save money for something you want. You may do chores or other work to make some money. You are using items right now that were made with resources. Let's find out more about resources.

## Quest Kick Off

Your quest is to make a poster showing three types of resources needed to sell lemonade. Add definitions to explain the types of resources. Include labels to tell possible uses for the resources.

## 1 Ask Questions

What resources do you use to make lemonade?
What resources do you use to sell lemonade?

......................................................................................

......................................................................................

## 2 Plan

Talk with your teacher and others about where you can find pictures of different resources. Write some things you can include on your poster.

INTERACTIVITY

Learn more about the resources you need to make lemonade.

.......................................................................

.......................................................................

.......................................................................

.......................................................................

.......................................................................

## 3 Look for Quest Connections

Turn to the next page to begin looking for Quest Connections that will help you make your poster.

## 4 Quest Findings
## Create Your Poster

Use the Quest Findings page at the end of the chapter to help you make your resources poster.

# Goods and Services

INTERACTIVITY

Participate in a class discussion to preview the content of this lesson.

**Unlock The BIG Question**

I will know how goods and services have changed over time and where goods are produced.

## Vocabulary

goods
services
consumer
local
producer
import
export

## Academic Vocabulary

rely
purchase

## JumpStart Activity

You are going on a label hunt. Look for labels that tell where a product is made. List the places you find.

_____

_____

## Academic Vocabulary

**rely** • *v.*, to depend on, to trust

You see people spend and earn money every day. You can spend money to buy goods. Your teacher earns money by providing a service. **Goods** are items you can see, like pencils or cars. Businesses sell goods for people to use. **Services** are work that people do, such as fixing a car or cutting your hair. You are a **consumer**, or user, of goods and services.

## Early Economies

The early settlers in California had to **rely** on themselves to provide everything they needed. They had to grow their own food, build their own homes, and mend their own clothes. They had to use what they found nearby.

As settlements grew, people traded or earned money to get what they needed. They bought **local** goods, or things made near where they were sold. For example, suppose a family grew extra beans. They might trade or sell the beans to someone who had fruit or knew how to repair a wagon wheel. As time went on, entrepreneurs built businesses to provide goods or services for growing towns. Many California businesses that started long ago are still in business today. They helped shaped other businesses.

1. ☑ **Reading Check** Use Evidence from Text
Underline ways the economies of later settlements and towns changed from the economies of the early settlers.

Pasadena, California, in the 1880s

## Quest Connection

Think about some products that are produced near where you live. What resources are used to make them?

### 🖐 INTERACTIVITY

Take a closer look at some California resources.

## Producing and Buying Local Goods

In the mid-1850s, families who came to California from China settled in Point Alones, near Monterey. They fished in the waters offshore. Since there were many sardines and shrimp, a fishing industry began. People built factories to prepare the fish for sale.

**Producers**, the makers of goods, often build their businesses near the things they need to make the goods. Why? Being close to the resources saves money shipping the resources to other places. If they save money, the goods cost less to sell.

Sardines dry in the sun on a wharf in Monterey, California, in the early 1900s.

As you have read, settlers had only local products to choose from. Today, we have choices from near and far. Even so, many people still try to buy products that are produced nearby. They might do this for several reasons. Perhaps they like to support small businesses that people in their community own. They might like to save the cost of shipping goods from far away. They may feel that food produced closer is fresher. In some ways, buying locally produced goods is like returning to an earlier time.

Strawberries ripen in a field near Dinuba, California.

2. ☑ **Reading Check** **Identify** and add details to the diagram to support the main idea.

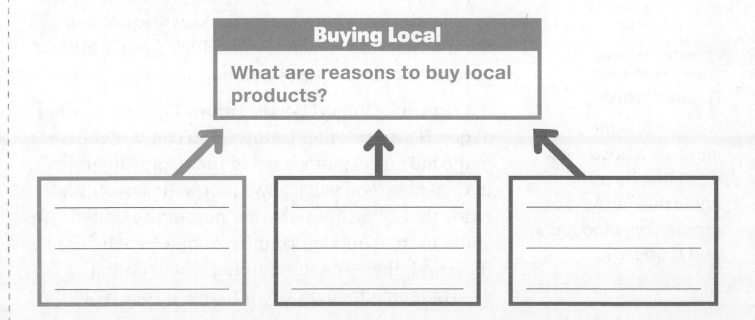

**Buying Local**

What are reasons to buy local products?

Freight containers on a ship in Los Angeles Harbor

## Goods From Far Away

Long ago, traveling in a horse-pulled wagon to get supplies could take a day or longer. When settlers got to the store, they would have only a few choices of what to buy. Today, you can drive or walk to a nearby store in minutes. You can also shop on the Internet. You can choose products from local producers or from places around the world.

A store may import goods. **Import** means to bring in goods from another country. You can buy cheese made in France, pants sewn in India, or fruit grown in Colombia. You will likely eat or wear something today that came from another part of the United States or from another country. Somewhere in the world, there is a third grader who is eating or wearing something grown or made in your region.

**Word Wise**

**Related words**

A *product* is the same as a *good.* How does that help you know the meaning of *production*, *producer*, and *produce*?

Producers may get, or secure, new customers if they export their products to faraway places. **Export** means to send goods out to another country. Having new consumers increases the amount of money a business makes. Consumers often like to try new products or **purchase** products that are not made near them. Even though oranges do not grow in Alaska, a child in Alaska can drink orange juice for breakfast. That orange juice may have been made in California. The next time you are in a store, look to see where products are grown or made.

**Academic Vocabulary**

**purchase** • *v.*, to buy with money

3. ☑ **Reading Check** **Talk with a partner** about why you would buy or sell products from far away.

**INTERACTIVITY**

Check your understanding of the key ideas of this lesson.

☑ **Lesson 1 Check** 🛈 **HSS** 3.3.2, 3.5.1, 3.5.2

4. **Explain** how shopping would be different if you were an early settler in California.

_____

_____

_____

5. **Identify** and circle the word to complete each sentence.

An (import export) is a product brought into a country for sale.

An (import export) is a product sent out of a country for sale.

6. **Quest** Connections In this lesson, you thought about products made near you and the resources used. Write other things that might be needed to make those products. (Hint: Think about workers or machines.)

_____

_____

# Advertisement From Early California

A primary source may be just text, like a letter or diary. A primary source might also be just a picture, like a painting or photograph. The advertisement on this page is from the early 1900s. It contains both text and a picture. It is important to look at both to understand the information.

Think about what you already know about advertisements you see every day. Ads are designed to sell you something and make you feel good about it. The ad on this page is a colorful label that went on the sides of fruit boxes. The label tries to make you think good things about the product.

San Jose, California,
pear label from the 1930s

**Fun Fact**
The first pear orchards were started in California during the Gold Rush.

# Close Reading

1. **Identify** and circle parts of the advertisement that tell about or show what is being sold.

2. **Identify** and write words from the advertisement that **describe** the product.

_____

_____

## Wrap It Up

Look at the advertisement from today. **Compare** it with the early advertisement. How are the two ads alike? How are they different?

_____

_____

_____

_____

FARM FRESH **VEGETABLES**

ORGANIC
Natural 100%

**INTERACTIVITY**

Participate in a class discussion to preview the content of this lesson.

**Unlock The BIG Question**

I will know the three types of resources used to create a product.

## Vocabulary

human resource
capital resource

## Academic Vocabulary

sufficient
technology

### JumpStart Activity

In small groups, select one of these products: a car, desk, book, carton of milk, tube of toothpaste, or loaf of bread. Your group will then list resources needed to make that product. The resources should include materials, people, and tools needed.

A logging truck drives past Mount Shasta in northern California.

What is needed to make a product? Many of the objects we use each day take many steps to create. In this lesson, you will learn about resources that producers need.

## Natural Resources

The California Indians, and the settlers who came after them, used the natural resources of California. These resources helped them meet their needs for food, shelter, and clothing. Natural resources are items found in nature that people use. They include trees, water, minerals, and soil. We still use natural resources to meet our needs. Farmers use water and soil to raise crops. A factory uses wood from trees to make furniture. To get to school, a school bus needs gasoline from oil found underground.

1. ☑ **Reading Check** **Explain** what a natural resource is.

_____

_____

# Human Resources

How did California Indians know how to make pots or use the skins of deer? How did settlers know how to herd cattle, plant crops, or heal a cough? They learned from their parents or other members of a group. Knowing how to make or do something is an important resource. **Human resources** are people's talents and skills.

Just having trees is not **sufficient** if you want to make a table. You also need the skill to cut the tree into lumber. You need to make the pieces of wood fit together to make a table.

Without the human resources of cooks, you would not get a hot bowl of vegetable soup. A skilled scientist helps make certain medicine is safe and can help heal a cut.

**Academic Vocabulary**

sufficient • *adj.*, enough

## Milk: From Farm to Store

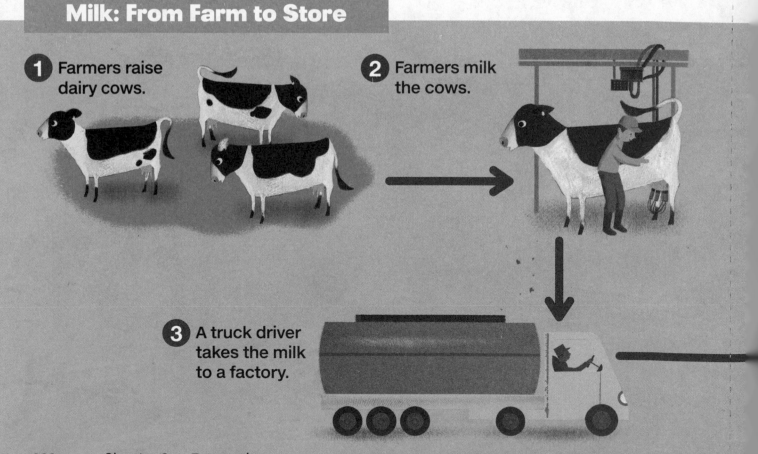

**1** Farmers raise dairy cows.

**2** Farmers milk the cows.

**3** A truck driver takes the milk to a factory.

Look at the diagram showing how milk is made. It shows that many people work together to get milk to stores. For any product, there might be people who designed it, worked in a factory, tested the product for safety, wrote ads for the product, and brought the product to a store. There were likely many more people (human resources) involved in making the product and getting it to the consumer.

We can plant trees to grow more. What can we do to increase our human resources? You are doing something right now that increases your value as a human resource. You are learning. Learning, trying new things, and observing others are ways we each can become more valuable human resources.

2. ✓ **Reading Check** **Use Evidence From Text** Underline details in the text that show how human resources are needed to get goods to a consumer.

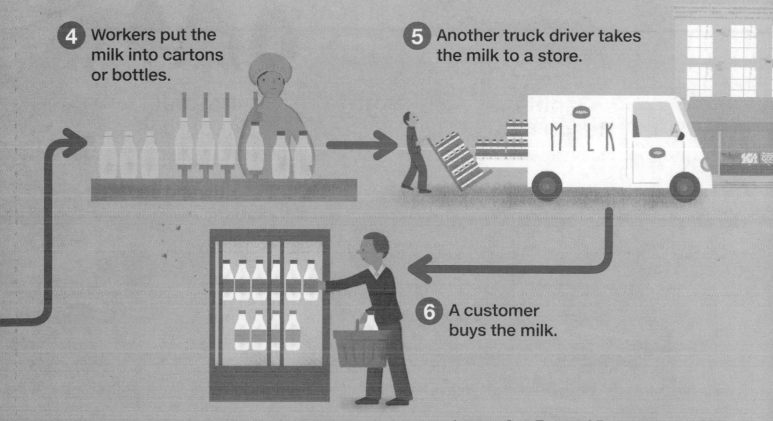

4 Workers put the milk into cartons or bottles.

5 Another truck driver takes the milk to a store.

6 A customer buys the milk.

## Capital Resources

There is another resource that people need to create products. **Capital resources** are human-made items used to make other goods or provide services. Some California Indians made fish weirs to catch fish. Settlers used plows to help with planting. A barber uses scissors to cut hair. Tools and buildings are capital resources.

Think about milk again. What capital resources are used to get the milk from the cow to the store? There are barns, milking machines, tanks, bottles, trucks, and the refrigerator at the grocery store. You can probably think of others. The early settlers may have used only their hands and a bucket to get milk. Times have changed!

3. ☑ **Reading Check Compare and Contrast** Fill in the diagram to **compare and contrast** capital resources and natural resources. In the center, **describe** how they are alike.

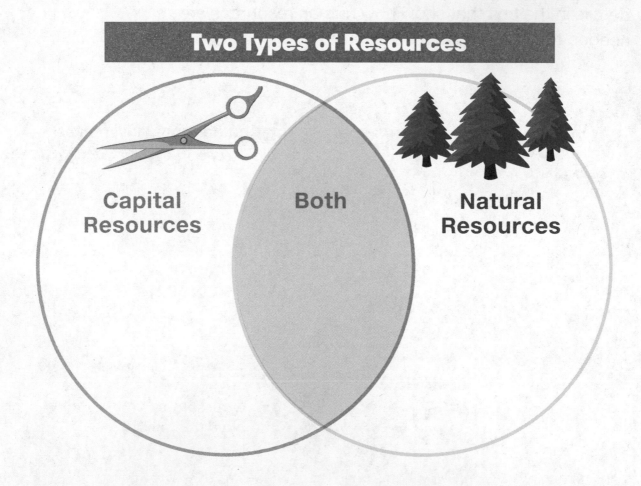

### Two Types of Resources

Capital Resources

Both

Natural Resources

This hand-powered dental drill was used long ago. Today, dental drills are powered by electricity.

Some of our tools and capital resources have changed over time. None of us would want to go to a dentist who uses tools from a hundred years ago! As time passes, **technology** advances. For example, it used to take a long time to place metal letters to print one page of a newspaper. Now a news story can be delivered to someone's phone or tablet very fast. Computers are an important capital resource. They are used in most businesses today.

**Academic Vocabulary**

**technology** • *n.*, the use of science to solve problems and make things work better

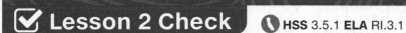

**INTERACTIVITY**

Check your understanding of the key ideas of this lesson.

✔ **Lesson 2 Check** 🕐 **HSS** 3.5.1 **ELA** RI.3.1

4. **Identify** Soil, water, forests, and minerals are examples of what type of resource?

_____

5. **Explain** two ways people can become more valuable human resources.

_____

_____

6. **Identify** and list one natural resource, one human resource, and one capital resource used to make a salad.

_____

_____

**INTERACTIVITY**

Review and practice what you learned about summarizing.

# Summarize

When you summarize you tell the most important parts. Have you explained a book or movie to a friend? There is no time and no need to tell every detail. You have to summarize and just tell the main idea and most important points.

Read about the restaurant. If the chef told a friend about a day at the restaurant, how would the chef summarize the day?

People in the restaurant work very hard. Everyone has a job to do. Chef Angela arrives at the restaurant at 6 A.M. She turns on the ovens and heats up the grill. She mixes pancake batter for breakfast, and chops fruit. She checks that all of her cooking supplies and tools are nearby. The first customer arrives. Chef Angela is ready to cook!

By 7 A.M. the restaurant is very busy. The seats are filling up, and the servers have all arrived. They make hot drinks, and fill people's cups. They take breakfast orders from customers, and give the orders to the cooks. They carry plates of hot and cold food to people. Later, they take away the empty plates from tables and bring customers the bill. Servers have no time to rest because breakfast is a busy time.

# Your Turn!

**1.** What are the main ideas and details of the paragraphs describing the restaurant? **Fill in** the organizer showing the main idea and details from the first paragraph. Use the box labeled "Summary" to **write** a short statement that summarizes the paragraph. Use your own words to sum up what you have read.

| MAIN IDEA | DETAILS |
|---|---|
| _____ | _____ |

**SUMMARY**

_____

**2.** Read the second paragraph. **Underline** the main idea and important details. Then **write** a sentence or two that summarizes that paragraph.

_____

# 3 Economic Choices

Unlock
The **BIG**
Question

I will know how economic choices are made.

## Vocabulary

trade-off
cost
opportunity cost
benefit
need
want

## Academic Vocabulary

adjust
responsible
option

### JumpStart Activity

Stand with a partner. Play a game of "You Choose." Think of two things your partner may want, such as a video game or a fun toy. Have your partner say which of the two he or she would rather have. Then switch. Think of at least five pairs of things.

We may wish to have unlimited resources, but none of us do. People, families, communities, and even states and countries have to work with the resources they have. Limited resources cause us to make careful choices about goods and services we use. Sometimes we have to **adjust** what we expect to get.

HSS 3.5, 3.5.3
Analysis HI.4 ELA RI.3.2

**Academic Vocabulary**

**adjust** • *v.*, to change or shift

## Why We Have to Choose

When settlers were deciding if and where to move, they had to weigh the good and bad things. For example, they might strike it rich looking for gold, or they might lose everything. Today, communities might have to choose to use money to build a new school or repair pipes. There might not be enough money to do both. People have to make economic choices, too. For example, suppose you must decide whether to buy soccer shoes or a soccer ball. You cannot do both. Whatever you choose, that choice is a **trade-off**. In a trade-off, you give up one thing for another.

1. ☑ Reading Check **Summarize** Why does everyone have to make economic choices?

_____

_____

_____

A family compares bicycles to decide which one to buy.

# Possible Costs

How much does it cost? You have probably asked that question. **Cost** is the price needed to get something else. The cost of something is more than just the price on the tag. There may be other costs. For example, a new kitten may cost $40. There are other costs to think about, however. There is the cost to feed it. There might also be costs if the kitten scratches a chair or sofa. It will also cost time to take care of the kitten. The kitten costs more than the $40 to buy it.

An **opportunity cost** is what you have to give up to have something else. Suppose you have $10. You can spend that money on a movie ticket or on a collar for your dog. You do not have enough money for both. If you do one, you cannot do the other. The one you cannot do is called the opportunity cost.

2. ☑ **Reading Check**
**Main Idea and Details** Add details to the graphic organizer that support the main idea.

## Cost of a Pet

**Main Idea**
The cost of a pet is more than just the price to buy it.

| Detail | Detail | Detail |
| --- | --- | --- |
| | | |

## Possible Benefits

If there is a cost to something, why would you buy it? There needs to be a benefit of a good or service. A **benefit** is a useful result. A benefit can mean you get something you need or want. The benefit of having a kitten is that it is fun to play with, it helps you learn to be **responsible**, and you feel good about giving it a home. One benefit of paying a person to fix your broken bicycle is that you can ride it again. The benefit of buying a sandwich is that it removes your hunger. A benefit may be something that is helpful. It may be something that makes you feel good.

This produce costs money. But it has other costs, too. It costs the time it takes to go to the store. It may also cost gasoline and wear and tear on a car.

### Academic Vocabulary

**responsible** • *adj.*, able to be trusted to do what is right

3. ☑ **Reading Check** **Define** What is a benefit?

_____

_____

# Making Choices

When making a good choice, you need to see if the benefits are greater than the costs. Here are some steps to help when trying to make a good choice.

1. List your **options**, or choices that can be made.

2. Identify the costs to each option.

3. Identify the possible benefits to each option.

Here is how a town might study the decision between updating a library or updating a school.

| Options | Update the Library | Update the School |
|---------|--------------------|--------------------|
| Costs | • $8 million dollars<br>• Takes one year | • $16 million dollars<br>• Takes two years |
| Benefits | • Makes people want to move to community<br>• A place to go that is free<br>• Fixes an old library that has many problems<br>• Provides resources and enjoyment for everyone | • Helps with crowding<br>• Provides space if more students move to town<br>• Is modern; uses new technology<br>• Provides resources and enjoyment for students |

You make economic choices each day. To make a good choice, ask questions. Is it something you need? A **need** is something you must have to live. Is it something you want? A **want** is something you would like to have but do not need. Do you give up something to save money for something else? Do you do extra chores to earn money for something you want? At the store, do you ask a parent for a new eraser or your favorite snack? Your choices tell a lot about what is important to you.

**Quest** Connections

With a partner, think of some of the natural, human, and capital resources needed to build a new school.

4. ☑ Reading Check **Opinion** Look at the chart. **Turn and talk** with a partner. What decision do you think the town should make based on the costs and benefits? Circle the benefits that you think are most important. Underline the most important cost.

👆 **INTERACTIVITY**

Take a closer look at natural, human, and capital resources.

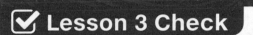
☑ **Lesson 3 Check**   🛈 **HSS** 3.5.3 **Analysis** HI.1

👆 **INTERACTIVITY**

Check your understanding of the key ideas of this lesson.

5. **Summarize** why people and communities have to make economic choices.

_____

_____

6. **Identify** and circle the correct word to complete the sentence.

The (cost  benefit) of a good or service is the price you have to pay.

7. 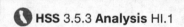 **Quest** Connections What capital resources do you use in your classroom each day to get your education?

_____

_____

_____

## Analyze Costs and Benefits

When making an important decision, first weigh the costs and the benefits. For example, think about the costs and benefits to a family during the 1860s. They want to decide if they should move to California or stay in Missouri. In Missouri, they live on their parents' land. Read to learn about the costs and benefits of each option.

| Options | Move to California | Stay in Missouri |
|---|---|---|
| Costs | • Buy a wagon and supplies<br>• Trip takes four months<br>• No income during trip<br>• Dangerous journey<br>• Moving far from family<br>• Future unknown | • Land belongs to parents<br>• Share all farm money with parents<br>• Difficult winters<br>• Little money from farm<br>• Hard to earn a living<br>• Small plot of land |
| Benefits | • Better farmland<br>• Mild winters<br>• Own the land<br>• Adventure<br>• More future possibilities | • Support of family<br>• Easy to stay<br>• Known future<br>• Nearby school<br>• Already have farm and house |

## Your Turn!

HSS 3.5, 3.5.3 **Analysis** HI.4

1. **Identify** and circle the one cost of moving to California that you think would be the biggest problem.
2. **Explain** why the benefits are different for each option.

______________________________

______________________________

______________________________

**INTERACTIVITY**

Review and practice what you learned about analyzing costs and benefits.

3. Create your own cost-benefit chart about an economic choice you can make. **Compare** two choices for how to spend, save, or donate some money.

| **Options** | | |
|---|---|---|
| **Costs** | | |
| **Benefits** | | |

# Human Capital and Your Future

## Vocabulary

invest
human capital
occupation

## Academic Vocabulary

prepare
fund

Jobs such as a veterinarian, electrician, and farmer use different skills.

**Unlock The BIG Question**

I will know how I can prepare for my future with my work today.

### JUMPstart Activity

Think of a job you might like to do when you grow up. Work with a partner. Take turns acting out skills needed for that job.

Do you enjoy working with numbers and shapes? Studying math and science may lead to becoming an architect or a game creator. Do you enjoy learning about people? Studying history, the arts, and reading may lead to becoming a historian or an entertainer. What do you enjoy?

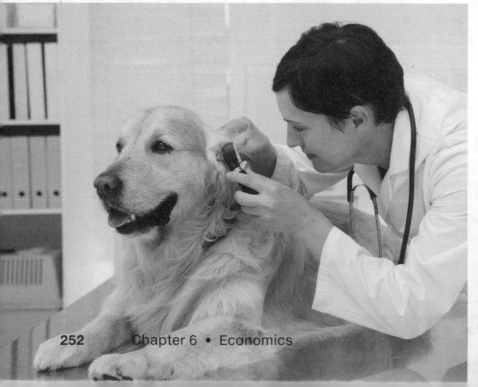

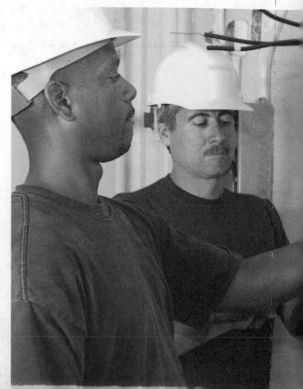

# Planning Ahead

Each day you learn is a day you invest in your future. **Invest** means to spend now in the hope of future reward. The time and effort you put into learning now will reward you as you get older. Every doctor, teacher, electrician, singer, or other adult learned while in school. Even if you do not know what adult job you might like, you can begin to **prepare** now. You can grow your human capital. Your **human capital** is your skills, knowledge, and experiences. You can develop good habits now. These habits will help you be a learner your whole life.

## Academic Vocabulary

**prepare** • *v.*, to get ready

1. ☑ **Reading Check** **Explain** how working and studying today is an investment in your future.

_____

_____

_____

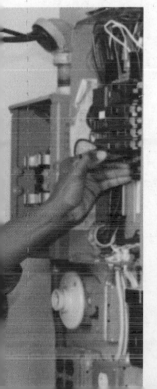

Taxpayers may pay for school buses to take students to school.

**Academic Vocabulary**

fund • v., to pay for

## Education Matters

Education helps prepare you for the future. You work in school. This work helps you learn skills and habits that help you as an adult. Educated people make good citizens. They have the knowledge for a good work and family life.

Americans believe in the importance of education. They pay for every child in the United States to go to school. Taxpayers **fund** your education. They pay for the school building, your teacher, the playground, and your books. They believe in you, and they believe in the value of a good education.

2. ☑ **Reading Check** **Cause and Effect** What is the effect of citizens believing in the value of a good education?

_____

_____

# What Does It Take to Succeed on the Job?

Success means many different things to people. For some, success is doing what you enjoy and making a difference. Others like earning enough money to own a home or raise a family. Most would agree that doing well on the job makes people successful. You can learn how to do well on the job by talking to people about how they prepared for work. Shop owners might tell you how they use art to present their goods. Nurses might tell you how they use science to help those who are sick. Truck drivers might tell you how they use geography to deliver goods.

A student talks to a peace officer to find out more about his job.

3. ☑ **Reading Check** **Ask Questions** What questions would you ask an adult to learn about how to do well on the job?

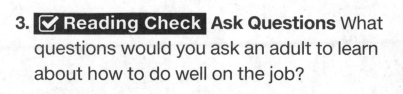

_____

_____

_____

_____

_____

_____

## Big Dreams Plus Hard Work

### Word Wise

**Parts of Speech**
*Volunteer* can be used as a noun, a verb, or an adjective. How is it used in this sentence: We would like to *volunteer* to help with the clean up.

A big dream can lead to a future occupation. An **occupation** is a job or work. A big dream might also lead to rewarding volunteer work. Helping others can be a way to make a difference. Whether the work is paid work or volunteer work, we all want to do work that is worth doing.

### Primary Source

Far and away the best prize that life offers is the chance to work hard at work worth doing.

—President Theodore Roosevelt, Address to the New York State Agricultural Association, 1903

How is this boy working hard at something worth doing?

**4.** ☑ **Reading Check** **Opinion** Who do you think
Roosevelt was talking to? What kind of hard,
rewarding work might they do?

_____

_____

_____

_____

INTERACTIVITY

Check your understanding
of the key ideas of this
lesson.

☑ **Lesson 4 Check** 🕐 **HSS** 3.5.4

**5. Identify** and circle the correct word.
His (occupation volunteer) is a chef, but he also helps as a (occupation
volunteer) at the food bank.

**6. Explain** how your education is an investment in your future.

_____

_____

_____

**7.** How does the work you do in school improve your human capital?
**Describe** ways your skills, knowledge, and experiences have grown in
school this year.

_____

_____

_____

_____

★ **Citizenship**

**Quality:
Determination**

# Jerry Yang
## A Leader in Technology

Jerry Yang moved from Taiwan to the United States when he was about ten. Jerry says that the only word he understood when he got to California was *shoe*. He studied hard and became a very good student. He graduated with the highest grades in his high school. He was also voted class president.

Jerry Yang was interested in computers and the Internet. He and a college friend, David Filo, started a Web site called *Jerry and David's Guide to the World Wide Web*. They started a company based on a search engine, which helps users search the Internet for information.

Mr. Yang is often called one of the top innovators in the world. He continues to work with technology companies by providing funding through his latest company.

### Find Out More

**1.** How did Jerry Yang show determination?

_____

_____

_____

**2. Research** Go online to find out the names of three search engines.

_____

_____

_____

# Visual Review

Use these graphics to review some of the key terms and ideas from this chapter.

**EXPORTS**
Goods that are sent out of a country to be sold in a different country.

**IMPORTS**
Goods that come into a country from a different country.

## Three Types of Resources

| | Natural Resources | Human Resources | Capital Resources |
|---|---|---|---|
| **Definitions** | items found in nature that people use | talents and skills that people have and use | human-made items used to make goods or provide services |
| **Examples** | forests, water, minerals, soil, gasoline, oil | skills to do a job, such as repairing a car or treating an illness | computers, buildings, tools, machines |

GAMES

Play the vocabulary game.

## Vocabulary and Key Ideas
HSS 3.5.1

**Identify** and circle the correct word to complete each sentence.

1. A person who creates products is called a _____. producer
consumer

2. Trees and water are _____. natural resources
capital resources

3. Equipment and buildings are _____. human resources
capital resources

## Critical Thinking and Writing
HSS 3.5, 3.5.1, 3.5.2, 3.5.3
**Analysis** CST.3

4. **Summarize** How has the way people use resources changed over time?

_____

_____

_____

_____

5. **Explain** why people need to make trade-offs when making economic decisions.

_____

_____

_____

_____

6. **Cost-Benefit Analysis** Ella's family made a cost-benefit chart to help them decide between adopting a puppy or an adult dog.

| Options | Adopt a Puppy | Adopt an Adult Dog |
|---|---|---|
| Costs | • $200 fee<br>• Training tools<br>• Time spent training<br>• Food and supplies | • $100 fee<br>• Unknown past<br>• Food and supplies |
| Benefits | • Very cute<br>• Known past | • Very cute<br>• Already trained |

**Explain** why Ella's family decided to adopt an adult dog.

_____

_____

_____

_____

7. **Revisit the Big Question** How do people get what they want and need?

_____

_____

_____

_____

8. **Writer's Workshop: Write a Narrative Text** On separate paper, write a short story about a person who has to decide between buying something now or saving for something to buy in the future. Include the costs and benefits involved with the decision.

9. **Describe** the photograph using the words *import* and *export*. What questions do you have about this photo?

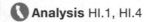

_____

_____

_____

_____

**Summarize**   💧 **Analysis** HI.1, HI.4

10. **Summarize** the difference between a cost and a benefit.

_____

_____

_____

_____

# Quest Findings

## Resources All Around

You have read about many resources people use. Now it's time to show what you have learned. Make a poster showing the resources needed to make and sell lemonade.

INTERACTIVITY
Use this activity to help you make your poster.

### 1 Prepare Your Poster

Make headings for each of the three types of resources. Next to each heading give a short definition of that type of resource.

### 2 Gather the Pictures

Look for pictures of natural resources, human resources, and capital resources that could be used to make lemonade. Look in old magazines, newspapers, and on the Internet. Figure out the group where each picture should be placed. Leave space for the labels. Do not paste on your pictures yet.

### 3 Share With the Class

With your poster flat on your desk and the pictures where you want them, show your poster to the class. Everyone will look at each poster to help make sure the pictures are in the correct groups. If any are not in the right place, move them.

### 4 Add Details

Complete your poster by pasting on the pictures. Add labels telling why each picture is an example of that resource. Hang up your poster for everyone to see!

# The Declaration of Independence

**In Congress, July 4, 1776**
**The Unanimous Declaration of the Thirteen**
**United States of America**

The first part of the Declaration of Independence is called the Preamble. A preamble is an introduction, or the part that comes before the main message. The Preamble states why the Declaration was written.

The second paragraph lists the basic rights that all people should have. The founders called these **unalienable** rights, meaning that these rights cannot be taken or given away. If a government cannot protect these rights, the people must change the government or create a new one.

1. According to the Declaration, what are three "unalienable rights"? Circle these words in the text.

The third paragraph introduces the List of Grievances. Each part of this list begins with the words, "He has...." These words refer to King George III's actions in the colonies. To prove that the king had abused his power over the colonies, this list of 27 complaints described how the British government and the king had treated the colonists.

When in the Course of human events it becomes necessary for one people to dissolve the political bands which have connected them with another, and to assume among the powers of the earth, the separate and equal station to which the Laws of nature and of nature's God entitle them, a decent respect to the opinions of mankind requires that they should declare the causes which impel them to the separation.

We hold these truths to be self-evident, that all men are created equal, that they are endowed by their Creator with certain unalienable Rights, that among these are Life, Liberty and the Pursuit of Happiness. That to secure these rights, Governments are instituted among Men, deriving their just powers from the consent of the governed; That whenever any Form of Government becomes destructive of these ends it is the Right of the People to alter or to abolish it, and to institute new Government, laying its foundation on such principles and organizing its powers in such form, as to them shall seem most likely to effect their Safety and Happiness. Prudence, indeed, will dictate that Governments long established should not be changed for light and transient causes; and accordingly all experience hath shown, that mankind are more disposed to suffer, while evils are sufferable, than to right themselves by abolishing the forms to which they are accustomed. But when a long train of abuses and usurpations, pursuing invariably the same Object evinces a design to reduce them under absolute Despotism, it is their right, it is their duty, to throw off such Government, and to provide new Guards for their future security.

Such has been the patient sufferance of these Colonies; and such is now the necessity which constrains them to alter their former Systems of Government. The history of the present King of Great Britain is a history of repeated injuries and usurpations, all having in direct object the establishment of an absolute Tyranny over these States. To prove this, let Facts be submitted to a candid world.

He has refused his Assent to Laws, the most wholesome and necessary for the public good.

He has forbidden his Governors to pass Laws of immediate and pressing importance, unless suspended in their operation till his

Assent should be obtained; and when so suspended, he has utterly neglected to attend to them.

He has refused to pass other Laws for the accommodation of large districts of people, unless those people would relinquish the right of Representation in the Legislature, a right inestimable to them and formidable to tyrants only.

He has called together legislative bodies at places unusual, uncomfortable, and distant from the depository of their Public Records, for the sole purpose of fatiguing them into compliance with his measures.

He has dissolved Representative Houses repeatedly, for opposing with manly firmness his invasions on the rights of the people.

He has refused for a long time, after such dissolutions, to cause others to be elected; whereby the Legislative powers, incapable of Annihilation, have returned to the People at large for their exercise; the State remaining in the mean time exposed to all the dangers of invasions from without, and convulsions within.

He has endeavored to prevent the population of these States; for that purpose obstructing the Laws for Naturalization of Foreigners; refusing to pass others to encourage their migration hither, and raising the conditions of new Appropriations of Lands.

He has obstructed the Administration of Justice, by refusing his Assent to Laws for establishing Judiciary powers.

He has made Judges dependent on his Will alone for the tenure of their offices, and the amount and payment of their salaries.

He has erected a multitude of New Offices, and sent hither swarms of Officers to harass our people and eat out their substance.

He has kept among us in time of peace, Standing Armies, without the Consent of our legislatures.

He has affected to render the Military independent of, and superior to, the Civil Power.

He has combined with others to subject us to a jurisdiction foreign to our constitutions, and unacknowledged by our laws; giving his Assent to their Acts of pretended Legislation:

For quartering large bodies of armed troops among us;

For protecting them, by a mock Trial, from punishment for any Murders which they should commit on the Inhabitants of these States;

In the List of Grievances, the colonists complain that they have no say in choosing the laws that govern them. They say that King George III is not concerned about their safety and happiness. They list the times when the king denied them the right to representation. The colonists also state that the king has interfered with judges, with the court system, and with foreigners who want to become citizens.

2. There are many words in the Declaration that may be unfamiliar to you. Circle three words you do not know. Look the words up in the dictionary. Write one word and its meaning on the lines below.

_____

_____

_____

_____

_____

_____

_____

This page continues the colonists' long List of Grievances.

3. In your own words, briefly sum up three grievances.

_____

_____

_____

4. Match each word from the Declaration with its meaning. Use a dictionary if you need help with a word.

| | |
|---|---|
| abolishing | tried to achieve |
| plundered | changing |
| suspending | doing away with |
| altering | stopping for a time |
| endeavored | robbed |

**Statement of Independence**
After listing their many grievances, the signers begin their statement of independence. Because the king has refused to correct the problems, he is an unfair ruler. Therefore, he is not fit to rule the free people of America.

For cutting off our Trade with all parts of the world;

For imposing Taxes on us without our Consent;

For depriving us, in many cases, of the benefits of Trial by Jury;

For transporting us beyond Seas to be tried for pretended offenses;

For abolishing the free System of English Laws in a neighboring Province, establishing therein an Arbitrary government, and enlarging its Boundaries so as to render it at once an example and fit instrument for introducing the same absolute rule into these Colonies;

For taking away our Charters, abolishing our most valuable Laws, and altering fundamentally the Forms of our Governments;

For suspending our own Legislatures, and declaring themselves invested with Power to legislate for us in all cases whatsoever.

He has abdicated Government here, by declaring us out of his Protection, and waging War against us.

He has plundered our seas, ravaged our Coasts, burned our towns, and destroyed the lives of our people.

He is at this time transporting large Armies of foreign mercenaries to complete the works of death, desolation and tyranny, already begun with circumstances of Cruelty and perfidy scarcely paralleled in the most barbarous ages, and totally unworthy the Head of a civilized nation.

He has constrained our fellow Citizens taken Captive on the high Seas to bear Arms against their Country, to become the executioners of their friends and Brethren, or to fall themselves by their Hands.

He has excited domestic insurrections amongst us, and has endeavored to bring on the inhabitants of our frontiers the merciless Indian Savages whose known rule of warfare, is an undistinguished destruction of all ages, sexes, and conditions.

In every stage of these Oppressions We have Petitioned for Redress in the most humble terms. Our repeated Petitions have been answered only by repeated injury. A Prince, whose character is thus marked by every act which may define a Tyrant, is unfit to be the ruler of a free People.

Nor have We been wanting in attentions to our British brethren. We have warned them from time to time of attempts by their legislature to extend an unwarrantable jurisdiction over us. We have reminded them of the circumstances of our emigration and settlement here. We have appealed to their native justice and magnanimity, and we have conjured them by the ties of our common kindred to disavow these usurpations, which, would inevitably interrupt our connections and correspondence. They too have been deaf to the voice of justice and of consanguinity. We must, therefore, acquiesce in the necessity, which denounces our Separation, and hold them, as we hold the rest of mankind, Enemies in War, in Peace Friends.

We, therefore, the Representatives of the United States of America, in General Congress, Assembled, appealing to the Supreme Judge of the world for the rectitude of our intentions, do, in the Name, and by the Authority of the good People of these Colonies, solemnly publish and declare, That these United Colonies are, and of right ought to be Free and Independent States; that they are Absolved from all Allegiance to the British Crown, and that all political connection between them and the State of Great Britain, is and ought to be totally dissolved, and that as Free and Independent States, they have full Power to levy War, conclude Peace, contract Alliances, establish Commerce, and to do all other Acts and Things which Independent States may of right do. And for the support of this Declaration, with a firm reliance on the protection of Divine Providence, we mutually pledge to each other our Lives, our Fortunes, and our sacred Honor.

**New Hampshire:**
Josiah Bartlett
William Whipple
Matthew Thornton

**Massachusetts Bay:**
John Hancock
Samuel Adams
John Adams
Robert Treat Paine
Elbridge Gerry

**Rhode Island:**
Stephan Hopkins
William Ellery

**Connecticut:**
Roger Sherman
Samuel Huntington
William Williams
Oliver Wolcott

**New York:**
William Floyd
Philip Livingston
Francis Lewis
Lewis Morris

**New Jersey:**
Richard Stockton
John Witherspoon
Francis Hopkinson
John Hart
Abraham Clark

**Delaware:**
Caesar Rodney
George Read
Thomas M'Kean

**Maryland:**
Samuel Chase
William Paca
Thomas Stone
Charles Carroll of
    Carrollton

**Virginia:**
George Wythe
Richard Henry Lee
Thomas Jefferson
Benjamin Harrison
Thomas Nelson, Jr.
Francis Lightfoot Lee
Carter Braxton

**Pennsylvania:**
Robert Morris
Benjamin Rush
Benjamin Franklin
John Morton
George Clymer
James Smith
George Taylor
James Wilson
George Ross

**North Carolina:**
William Hooper
Joseph Hewes
John Penn

**South Carolina:**
Edward Rutledge
Thomas Heyward, Jr.
Thomas Lynch, Jr.
Arthur Middleton

**Georgia:**
Button Gwinnett
Lyman Hall
George Walton

In this paragraph, the signers point out that they have asked the British people for help many times. The colonists hoped the British would listen to them because they have so much in common. The British people, however, paid no attention to their demand for justice. This is another reason for why the colonies must break away from Great Britain.

In the last paragraph, the members of the Continental Congress declare that the thirteen colonies are no longer colonies. They are now a free nation with no ties to Great Britain. The United States now has all the powers of other independent countries.

5. List three powers that the signers claim the new nation now has.

_____

_____

_____

_____

6. The signers promised to support the Declaration of Independence and each other with their lives, their fortunes, and their honor. On a separate sheet of paper, tell what you think this means. Then explain why it was a brave thing to do.

# United States Constitution

This **Preamble** gives the reasons for writing and having a Constitution. The Constitution will form a stronger and more united nation. It will lead to peace, justice, and liberty and will defend American citizens. Finally, it will improve the lives of people.

## Section 1. Congress
The legislative branch of government makes the country's laws. Called the Congress, it has two parts, or houses: the House of Representatives and the Senate.

## Section 2. The House of Representatives
Members of the House of Representatives are elected every two years. Representatives must be 25 years old and United States citizens. They must also live in the states that elect them.

The number of Representatives for each state is based on the population, or number of people who live there.

1. Why do some states have more Representatives in Congress than other states?

_____

_____

_____

_____

Over the years, the Constitution has been altered, or changed. These altered parts are shown here in gray type.

## PREAMBLE

We the People of the United States, in Order to form a more perfect Union, establish Justice, insure domestic Tranquility, provide for the common defense, promote the general Welfare, and secure the Blessings of Liberty to ourselves and our Posterity, do ordain and establish this Constitution for the United States of America.

## ARTICLE I

### Section 1.
All legislative Powers herein granted shall be vested in a Congress of the United States, which shall consist of a Senate and House of Representatives.

### Section 2.
1. The House of Representatives shall be composed of Members chosen every second Year by the People of the several States, and the Electors in each State shall have the Qualifications requisite for Electors of the most numerous Branch of the State Legislature.
2. No Person shall be a Representative who shall not have attained to the age of twenty-five Years, and been seven Years a Citizen of the United States, and who shall not, when elected, be an Inhabitant of that State in which he shall be chosen.
3. Representatives and direct Taxes shall be apportioned among the several States which may be included within this Union, according to their respective Numbers, which shall be determined by adding to the whole Number of free Persons, including those bound to Service for a Term of Years and excluding Indians not taxed, three fifths of all other Persons. The actual Enumeration shall be made within three Years after the first Meeting of the Congress of the United States, and within every subsequent Term of ten Years, in such Manner as they shall by Law direct. The Number of Representatives shall not exceed one for every thirty Thousand, but each State shall have at Least one Representative; and, until such enumeration shall be made, the State of New Hampshire shall be entitled to choose three, Massachusetts eight, Rhode Island and Providence Plantations one, Connecticut five, New York six, New Jersey four, Pennsylvania eight, Delaware one, Maryland six, Virginia ten, North Carolina five, South Carolina five, and Georgia three.

4. When vacancies happen in the Representation from any State, the Executive Authority thereof shall issue Writs of Election to fill such Vacancies.
5. The House of Representatives shall choose their Speaker and other Officers; and shall have the sole Power of Impeachment.

## Section 3.

1. The Senate of the United States shall be composed of two Senators from each State chosen by the Legislature thereof for six Years; and each Senator shall have one Vote.
2. Immediately after they shall be assembled in Consequences of the first Election, they shall be divided, as equally as may be, into three Classes. The Seats of the Senators of the first Class shall be vacated at the Expiration of the second Year; of the second Class, at the Expiration of the fourth Year; and of the third Class, at the Expiration of the sixth Year; so that one-third may be chosen every second Year; and if Vacancies happen by Resignation, or otherwise, during the Recess of the Legislature of any State, the Executive thereof may make temporary Appointments until the next Meeting of the Legislature, which shall then fill such Vacancies.
3. No Person shall be a Senator who shall not have attained to the Age of thirty Years, and been nine Years a Citizen of the United States, and who shall not, when elected, be an Inhabitant of that State for which he shall be chosen.
4. The Vice President of the United States shall be President of the Senate but shall have no Vote, unless they be equally divided.
5. The Senate shall choose their other Officers, and also a President pro tempore, in the Absence of the Vice President, or when he shall exercise the Office of President of the United States.
6. The Senate shall have the sole Power to try all Impeachments. When sitting for that Purpose, they shall be on Oath or Affirmation. When the President of the United States is tried, the Chief Justice shall preside: And no Person shall be convicted without the Concurrence of two thirds of the Members present.
7. Judgment in Cases of Impeachment shall not extend further than to removal from Office, and disqualification to hold and enjoy any Office of honor, Trust, or Profit under the United States: but the Party convicted shall nevertheless be liable and subject to Indictment, Trial, Judgment and Punishment, according to Law.

A state governor calls a special election to fill an empty seat in the House of Representatives.

Members of the House of Representatives choose their own leaders. They also have the power to impeach, or accuse, government officials of crimes.

**Section 3. Senate**
Each state has two Senators. A Senator serves a six-year term.

At first, each state legislature elected its two Senators. The Seventeenth Amendment changed that. Today, the voters of each state elect their Senators.

Senators must be 30 years old and United States citizens. They must also live in the states they represent.

**2.** How is the length of a Senator's term different from a Representative's term?

_____

_____

The Vice President is the officer in charge of the Senate but only votes to break a tie. When the Vice President is absent, a temporary leader (President Pro Tempore) leads the Senate.

The Senate holds impeachment trials. When the President is impeached, the Chief Justice of the Supreme Court is the judge. A two-thirds vote is needed to convict. Once convicted, an official can be removed from office. Other courts of law can impose other punishments.

## Section 4. Elections and Meetings of Congress

The state legislatures determine the times, places, and method of holding elections for senators and representatives.

## Section 5. Rules for Congress

The Senate and House of Representatives judge the fairness of the elections and the qualifications of its own members. At least half of the members must be present to do business. Each house may determine the rules of its proceedings and punish its member for disorderly behavior. Each house of Congress shall keep a record of its proceedings and from time to time publish the record.

**3.** Why is it important for Congress to publish a record of what they do?

_____

_____

_____

_____

## Section 6. Rights and Restrictions of Members of Congress

The Senators and Representatives shall receive payment for their services to be paid out of the Treasury of the United States. Members of Congress cannot be arrested during their attendance at the session of Congress, except for a very serious crime, and they cannot be arrested for anything they say in Congress. No person can have a government job while serving as a member of Congress.

## Section 4.

1. The Times, Places and Manner of holding Elections for Senators and Representatives, shall be prescribed in each State by the Legislature thereof; but the Congress may at any time by law make or alter such Regulations, except as to the Places of choosing Senators.

2. The Congress shall assemble at least once in every Year, and such Meeting shall be on the first Monday in December, unless they shall by Law appoint a different Day.

## Section 5.

1. Each House shall be the Judge of the Elections, Returns and Qualifications of its own Members, and a Majority of each shall constitute a Quorum to do Business; but a smaller Number may adjourn from day to day, and may be authorized to compel the Attendance of absent Members, in such Manner, and under such Penalties, as each House may provide.

2. Each House may determine the Rules of its Proceedings, punish its Members for disorderly Behavior, and, with the Concurrence of two thirds, expel a Member.

3. Each House shall keep a Journal of its Proceedings, and from time to time publish the same, excepting such Parts as may in their Judgment require Secrecy; and the Yeas and Nays of the Members of either House on any question shall, at the Desire of one fifth of those Present, be entered on the Journal.

4. Neither House, during the Session of Congress, shall, without the Consent of the other, adjourn for more than three days, nor to any other Place than that in which the two Houses shall be sitting.

## Section 6.

1. The Senators and Representatives shall receive a Compensation for their Services, to be ascertained by Law, and paid out of the Treasury of the United States. They shall in all Cases, except Treason, Felony, and Breach of the Peace, be privileged from Arrest during their Attendance at the Session of their respective Houses, and in going to and returning from the same; and for any Speech or Debate in either House, they shall not be questioned in any other Place.

2. No Senator or Representative shall, during the Time for which he was elected, be appointed to any civil Office under the Authority of the United States, which shall have been created, or the Emoluments whereof shall have been increased during such time; and no Person holding any Office under the United States, shall be a Member of either House during his Continuance in Office.

# Section 7.

1. All Bills for raising Revenue shall originate in the House of Representatives; but the Senate may propose or concur with amendments as on other Bills.

2. Every Bill which shall have passed the House of Representatives and the Senate, shall, before it become a law, be presented to the President of the United States: If he approve, he shall sign it, but if not he shall return it, with his Objections to that House in which it shall have originated, who shall enter the Objections at large on their Journal, and proceed to reconsider it. If after such Reconsideration two thirds of the House shall agree to pass the Bill, it shall be sent, together with the Objections, to the other House, by which it shall likewise be reconsidered, and if approved by two thirds of that House, it shall become a Law. But in all such Cases the Votes of both Houses shall be determined by Yeas and Nays, and the Names of the Persons voting for and against the Bill shall be entered on the Journal of each House respectively. If any Bill shall not be returned by the President within ten Days (Sunday excepted) after it shall have been presented to him, the Same shall be a law, in like Manner as if he had signed it, unless the Congress by their Adjournment, prevent its Return, in which Case it shall not be a Law.

3. Every Order, Resolution, or Vote to which the Concurrence of the Senate and House of Representatives may be necessary (except on a question of adjournment) shall be presented to the President of the United States; and before the Same shall take Effect, shall be approved by him, or, being disapproved by him, shall be repassed by two thirds of the Senate and House of Representatives, according to the Rules and Limitations prescribed in the Case of a Bill.

# Section 8.

The Congress shall have Power

1. To lay and collect Taxes, Duties, Imposts and Excises to pay the Debts and provide for the common Defense and general Welfare of the United States; but all Duties, Imposts and Excises, shall be uniform throughout the United States;

2. To borrow Money on the credit of the United States;

3. To regulate Commerce with foreign Nations, and among the several States, and with the Indian Tribes;

4. To establish an uniform Rule of Naturalization, and uniform Laws on the subject of Bankruptcies throughout the United States;

## Section 7. How Laws are Made

All bills for raising money shall begin in the House of Representatives. The Senate may suggest or agree with amendments to these tax bills, as with other bills.

Every bill which has passed the House of Representatives and the Senate must be presented to the President of the United States before it becomes a law. If the President approves of the bill, the President shall sign it. If the President does not approve, then the bill may be vetoed. The President then sends it back to the house in which it began, with an explanation of the objections. That house writes the objections on their record and begins to reconsider it. If two thirds of each house agrees to pass the bill, it shall become a law. If any bill is neither signed nor vetoed by the President within ten days, (except for Sundays) after it has been sent to the President, the bill shall be a law. If Congress adjourns before ten days have passed, the bill does not become a law.

## Section 8. Powers of Congress

Among the powers of Congress listed in Section 8 are:

- establish and collect taxes on imported and exported goods and on goods sold within the country. Congress also shall pay the debts and provide for the defense and general welfare of the United States. All federal taxes shall be the same throughout the United States.
- borrow money on the credit of the United States;
- make laws about trade with other countries, among the states, and with the American Indian tribes;
- establish one procedure by which a person from another country can become a legal citizen of the United States;
- protect the works of scientists, artists, authors, and inventors;
- create federal courts lower than the Supreme Court;

- declare war;
- establish and support an army and navy;
- organize and train a National Guard and call them up in times of emergency;
- govern the capital and military sites of the United States; and
- make all laws necessary to carry out the powers of Congress.

**4.** The last clause of Section 8 is called "the elastic clause" because it stretches the power of Congress. Why do you think it was added to the Constitution?

_____

_____

_____

_____

_____

_____

_____

5. To coin Money, regulate the Value thereof, and of foreign Coin, and fix the Standard of Weights and Measures;

6. To provide for the Punishment of counterfeiting the Securities and current Coin of the United States;

7. To establish Post Offices and post Roads;

8. To promote the Progress of Science and useful Arts, by securing, for limited Times to Authors and Inventors the exclusive Right to their respective Writings and Discoveries;

9. To constitute Tribunals inferior to the supreme Court;

10. To define and punish Piracies and Felonies committed on the high Seas, and Offences against the Law of nations;

11. To declare War, grant Letters of Marque and Reprisal, and make Rules concerning Captures on Land and Water;

12. To raise and support Armies; but no Appropriation of Money to that Use shall be for a longer Term than two Years;

13. To provide and maintain a Navy;

14. To make Rules for the Government and Regulation of the land and naval Forces;

15. To provide for calling forth the Militia to execute the Laws of the Union, suppress Insurrections and repel Invasions;

16. To provide for organizing, arming, and disciplining the Militia, and for governing such Part of them as may be employed in the Service of the United States, reserving to the States respectively the Appointment of the Officers, and the Authority of training the Militia according to the discipline prescribed by Congress;

17. To exercise exclusive Legislation in all Cases whatsoever, over such District (not exceeding ten Miles square) as may, by Cession of Particular States, and the Acceptance of Congress, become the Seat of the Government of the United States, and to exercise like Authority over all Places purchased by the Consent of the Legislature of the State in which the Same shall be, for the Erection of Forts, Magazines, Arsenals, Dockyards and other needful Buildings;—And

18. To make all Laws which shall be necessary and proper for carrying into Execution the foregoing Powers and all other Powers vested by this Constitution in the Government of the United States, or in any Department or Officer thereof.

## Section 9.

1. The Migration or Importation of such Persons as any of the States now existing shall think proper to admit, shall not be prohibited by the Congress prior to the Year one thousand eight hundred and eight, but a Tax or duty may be imposed on such Importation, not exceeding ten dollars for each Person.

2. The Privilege of the Writ of Habeas Corpus shall not be suspended, unless when in Cases of Rebellion or Invasion the public safety may require it.

3. No Bill of Attainder or ex post facto Law shall be passed.

4. No Capitation, or other direct, Tax shall be laid, unless in Proportion to the Census of Enumeration herein before directed to be taken.

5. No Tax or Duty shall be laid on Articles exported from any State.

6. No Preference shall be given by any Regulation of Commerce or Revenue to the Ports of one State over those of another: nor shall Vessels bound to, or from, one State, be obliged to enter, clear or pay Duties in another.

7. No Money shall be drawn from the Treasury, but in Consequence of Appropriations made by Law; and a regular Statement and Account of the Receipts and Expenditures of all public Money shall be published from time to time.

8. No Title of Nobility shall be granted by the United States: And no Person holding any Office of Profit or Trust under them, shall, without the Consent of the Congress, accept of any present, Emolument, Office, or Title, of any kind whatever, from any King, Prince, or foreign State.

## Section 10.

1. No State shall enter into any Treaty, Alliance, or Confederation; grant Letters of Marque and Reprisal; coin Money; emit Bills of Credit; make any Thing but gold and silver Coin a Tender in Payment of Debts; pass any Bill of Attainder, ex post facto Law, or Law impairing the Obligation of Contracts, or grant any Title of Nobility.

2. No State shall, without the Consent of the Congress, lay any Imposts or Duties on Imports or Exports, except what may be absolutely necessary for executing its inspection Laws; and the net Produce of all Duties and Imposts, laid by any State on Imports or Exports, shall be for the Use of the Treasury of the United States; and all such Laws shall be subject to the Revision and Control of the Congress.

**Section 9: Powers Denied to Congress**

Congress cannot
- stop slaves from being brought into the United States until 1808;
- arrest and jail people without charging them with a crime, except during an emergency;
- punish a person without a trial; punish a person for something that was not a crime when he or she did it;
- pass a direct tax, such as an income tax, unless it is in proportion to the population;
- tax goods sent out of a state;
- give the seaports of one state an advantage over another state's ports; let one state tax the ships of another state;
- spend money without passing a law to make it legal; spend money without keeping good records;
- give titles, such as king and queen, to anyone; allow federal workers to accept gifts or titles from foreign governments.

5. Why do you think the writers included the last clause of Section 9?

_____

_____

_____

_____

_____

_____

**Section 10: Powers Denied to the States**

After listing what Congress is not allowed to do, the Constitution tells what powers are denied to the states.

State governments do not have the power to
- make treaties with foreign countries; print money; do anything that Section 9 of the Constitution says the federal government cannot;
- tax goods sent into or out of a state unless Congress agrees;
- keep armed forces or go to war; make agreements with other states or foreign governments unless Congress agrees.

**6.** What problems might arise if one state went to war with a foreign country?

_____

_____

_____

_____

Article 2 describes the executive branch.

**Section 1. Office of President and Vice President**

The President has power to execute, or carry out, the laws of the United States.

Electors from each state choose the President. Today, these electors are called the Electoral College and are chosen by the voters.

Before 1804, the person with the most electoral votes became President. The person with the next-highest number became Vice President. The Twelfth Amendment changed this way of electing Presidents.

3. No State shall, without the Consent of Congress, lay any Duty of Tonnage, keep Troops, or Ships of War in time of Peace, enter into any Agreement or Compact with another State, or with a foreign Power, or engage in War, unless actually invaded, or in such imminent Danger as will not admit of delay.

## ARTICLE II

# Section 1.

1. The executive Power shall be vested in a President of the United States of America. He shall hold his Office during the Term of four Years, and, together with the Vice President, chosen for the same Term, be elected as follows:

2. Each State shall appoint, in such Manner as the Legislature thereof may direct, a Number of Electors, equal to the whole Number of Senators and Representatives to which the State may be entitled in the Congress: but no Senator or Representative, or Person holding an Office of Trust or Profit, under the United States, shall be appointed an Elector.

3. The Electors shall meet in their respective States, and vote by Ballot for two Persons, of whom one at least shall not be an Inhabitant of the same State with themselves. And they shall make a List of all the Persons voted for, and of the Number of Votes for each; which List they shall sign and certify, and transmit sealed to the Seat of the Government of the United States, directed to the President of the Senate. The President of the Senate shall, in the Presence of the Senate and House of Representatives, open all the Certificates, and the Votes shall then be counted. The Person having the greatest Number of Votes shall be the President, if such Number be a majority of the whole Number of Electors appointed; and if there be more than one who have such Majority, and have an equal Number of Votes, then, the House of Representatives shall immediately choose by Ballot one of them for President; and if no Person have a Majority, then from the five highest on the List the said House shall in like Manner choose the President. But in choosing the President, the Votes shall be taken by States, the Representatives from each State having one Vote; a quorum for this Purpose shall consist of a Member or Members from two thirds of the States, and a Majority of all the States shall be necessary to a Choice. In every Case, after the Choice of the President, the Person having the greatest Number of Votes of the Electors shall be the Vice President. But if there should remain two or more who have equal Votes, the Senate shall choose from them by Ballot the Vice President.

4. The Congress may determine the Time of choosing the Electors, and the Day on which they shall give their Votes; which Day shall be the same throughout the United States.

5. No Person except a natural born Citizen, or a Citizen of the United States, at the time of the Adoption of this Constitution, shall be eligible to the Office of President; neither shall any person be eligible to that Office who shall not have attained to the Age of thirty-five Years, and been fourteen Years a Resident within the United States.

6. In Case of the Removal of the President from Office, or of his Death, Resignation, or Inability to discharge the Powers and Duties of the said Office, the Same shall devolve on the Vice President, and the Congress may by Law provide for the Case of Removal, Death, Resignation or Inability, both of the President and Vice President, declaring what Officer shall then act as President, and such Officer shall act accordingly, until the Disability be removed, or a President shall be elected.

7. The President shall, at stated Times, receive for his Services, a Compensation, which shall neither be increased nor diminished during the Period for which he shall have been elected, and he shall not receive within that Period any other Emolument from the United States, or any of them.

8. Before he enter on the Execution of his Office, he shall take the following Oath or Affirmation: "I do solemnly swear (or affirm) that I will faithfully execute the Office of President of the United States, and will to the best of my Ability, preserve, protect and defend the Constitution of the United States."

## Section 2.

1. The President shall be Commander in Chief of the Army and Navy of the United States, and of the Militia of the several States, when called into the actual Service of the United States; he may require the Opinion, in writing, of the principal Officer in each of the executive Departments, upon any Subject relating to the Duties of their respective Offices, and he shall have Power to Grant Reprieves and Pardons for Offences against the United States, except in Cases of Impeachment.

Congress decides when electors are chosen and when they vote for President. Americans now vote for the electors on Election Day, the Tuesday after the first Monday in November.

To become President, a person must be born in the United States and be a citizen. Presidents also have to be at least 35 years old and have lived in the United States for at least 14 years.

If a President dies or leaves office for any reason, the Vice President becomes President. If there is no Vice President, Congress decides on the next President. (In 1967, the Twenty-fifth Amendment changed how these offices are filled.)

**7.** Why is it important to agree on how to replace the President or Vice President if one should die or leave office?

_____

_____

_____

_____

The President's salary cannot be raised or lowered while he is in office. The President cannot accept other money or gifts while in office. Before taking office, the President must swear to preserve, protect, and defend the Constitution.

### Section 2. Powers of the President

The President controls the armed forces and National Guard, and can ask for advice of those who run government departments. (These advisers to the President are members of the Cabinet.) The President can pardon, or free, people convicted of federal crimes.

The President can make treaties, but two thirds of the Senate must approve them. The President, with Senate approval, can name Supreme Court judges, ambassadors, and other important officials.

**8.** What is the Senate's ability to approve or reject treaties an example of?

_____

_____

**Section 3. Duties of the President**

From time to time, the President must talk to Congress about the condition of the nation. (Today, we call this speech the State of the Union address. It is given once a year in late January.) In an emergency, the President can call on Congress to meet. The President also meets with foreign leaders, makes sure the nation's laws are carried out, and signs the orders of military officers.

**Section 4. Removal From Office**

The President, Vice President, and other high officials can be impeached. If proved guilty, they are removed from office.

2. He shall have Power, by and with the Advice and Consent of the Senate, to make Treaties, provided two thirds of the Senators present concur; and he shall nominate, and by and with the Advice and Consent of the Senate, shall appoint Ambassadors, other public Ministers and Consuls, Judges of the supreme Court, and all other Officers of the United States, whose Appointments are not herein otherwise provided for, and which shall be established by Law: but the Congress may by Law vest the Appointment of such inferior Officers, as they think proper, in the President alone, in the Courts of Law, or in the Heads of Departments.

3. The President shall have Power to fill up all Vacancies that may happen during the Recess of the Senate, by granting Commissions which shall expire at the End of their next Session.

## Section 3.

He shall from time to time give to the Congress Information of the State of the Union, and recommend to their Consideration such Measures as he shall judge necessary and expedient; he may, on extraordinary Occasions, convene both Houses, or either of them, and in Case of Disagreement between them, with Respect to the Time of Adjournment, he may adjourn them to such Time as he shall think proper; he shall receive Ambassadors and other public Ministers; he shall take Care that the Laws be faithfully executed, and shall Commission all the Officers of the United States.

## Section 4.

The President, Vice President and all Civil Officers of the United States, shall be removed from Office on Impeachment for and Conviction of, Treason, Bribery, or other high Crimes and Misdemeanors.

## ARTICLE III

### Section 1.

The judicial Power of the United States, shall be vested in one supreme Court, and in such inferior Courts as the Congress may from time to time ordain and establish. The Judges, both of the supreme and inferior Courts, shall hold their Offices during good Behavior, and shall, at stated Times, receive for their Services, a Compensation, which shall not be diminished during their Continuance in Office.

### Section 2.

1. The judicial Power shall extend to all Cases, in Law and Equity, arising under this Constitution, the Laws of the United States, and Treaties made, or which shall be made, under their Authority;— to all Cases affecting Ambassadors, other public ministers, and Consuls;— to all Cases of Admiralty and maritime Jurisdiction;— to Controversies to which the United States shall be a Party;— to Controversies between two or more States;— between a State and Citizens of another State;— between Citizens of different States;— between Citizens of the same State claiming Lands under Grants of different States, and between a State, or the Citizens thereof, and foreign States, Citizens, or Subjects.

2. In all Cases affecting Ambassadors, other public Ministers and Consuls, and those in which a State shall be a Party, the supreme Court shall have original Jurisdiction. In all the other Cases before mentioned, the supreme Court shall have appellate Jurisdiction, both as to Law and Fact, with such Exceptions, and under such Regulations as the Congress shall make.

3. The trial of all Crimes, except in Cases of Impeachment, shall be by Jury; and such Trial shall be held in the State where the said Crimes shall have been committed; but when not committed within any State, the Trial shall be at such Place or Places as the Congress may by Law have directed.

Article 3 deals with the judicial branch.

**Section 1. Federal Courts**
The judges of the Supreme Court and other federal courts have the power to make decisions in courts of law. If they act properly, federal judges hold their offices for life.

**9.** Do you think it's a good idea that federal judges hold their offices for life? Why?

_____

_____

_____

_____

_____

_____

**Section 2. Powers of Federal Courts**
Federal Courts have legal power over
- laws made under the Constitution
- treaties made with foreign nations
- cases occurring at sea
- cases involving the federal government
- cases involving states or citizens of different states
- cases involving foreign citizens or governments

Only the Supreme Court can judge cases involving ambassadors, government officials, or states. Other cases begin in lower courts, but they can be appealed, or reviewed, by the Supreme Court. In criminal cases other than impeachment, trials are held in the state in which the crime took place. A jury decides the case.

### Section 3. Treason

Treason is waging war against the United States or helping its enemies. To be found guilty of treason, a person must confess to the crime; or, two people must have seen the crime committed.

**10.** Name the three branches of federal government described in Articles 1-3.

_____

_____

_____

Congress decides the punishment for a traitor. The traitor's family cannot be punished if innocent.

Article 4 deals with relationships between the states.

### Section 1. Recognition by Each State

Each state must respect the laws and court decisions of the other states.

### Section 2. Rights of Citizens in Other States

Citizens keep all their rights when visiting other states.

A person charged with a crime who flees to another state must be returned to the state in which the crime took place.

A slave who escapes to another state must be returned to his or her owner. (The Thirteenth Amendment outlawed slavery.)

### Section 3. New States

Congress may let new states join the United States. New states cannot be formed from the land of existing states unless Congress approves.

Congress has the power to make laws to govern territories of the United States.

## Section 3.

1. Treason against the United States shall consist only in levying War against them, or in adhering to their Enemies, giving them Aid and Comfort. No Person shall be convicted of Treason unless on the Testimony of two Witnesses to the same overt Act, or on Confession in open Court.
2. The Congress shall have Power to declare the Punishment of Treason, but no Attainder of Treason shall work Corruption of Blood, or Forfeiture except during the Life of the Person attainted.

### ARTICLE IV

## Section 1.

Full Faith and Credit shall be given in each State to the public Acts, Records, and judicial Proceedings of every other State. And the Congress may by general Laws prescribe the Manner in which such Acts, Records and Proceedings shall be proved, and the Effect thereof.

## Section 2.

1. The Citizens of each State shall be entitled to all Privileges and Immunities of Citizens in the several States.
2. A Person charged in any State with Treason, Felony, or other Crime, who shall flee from justice, and be found in another State, shall on Demand of the executive Authority of the State from which he fled, be delivered up, to be removed to the State having Jurisdiction of the Crime.
3. No Person held to Service or Labor in one State, under the Laws thereof, escaping into another, shall, in Consequence of any Law or Regulation therein, be discharged from Service or Labor, but shall be delivered up on Claim of the Party to whom such Service or Labor may be due.

## Section 3.

1. New States may be admitted by the Congress into this Union; but no new State shall be formed or erected within the Jurisdiction of any other State; nor any State be formed by the Junction of two or more States, or Parts of States, without the Consent of the Legislatures of the States concerned as well as of the Congress.

2. The Congress shall have Power to dispose of and make all needful Rules and Regulations respecting the Territory or other Property belonging to the United States; and nothing in this Constitution shall be so construed as to Prejudice any Claims of the United States, or of any particular State.

## Section 4.

The United States shall guarantee to every State in this Union a Republican Form of Government, and shall protect each of them against Invasion; and on Application of the Legislature, or of the Executive (when the Legislature cannot be convened) against domestic Violence.

## ARTICLE V

The Congress, whenever two thirds of both Houses shall deem it necessary, shall propose Amendments to this Constitution, or, on the Application of the Legislatures of two thirds of the several States, shall call a Convention for proposing Amendments, which, in either Case, shall be valid to all Intents and Purposes, as Part of this Constitution, when ratified by the Legislatures of three fourths of the several States, or by Conventions in three fourths thereof, as the one or the other Mode of Ratification may be proposed by the Congress; Provided that no Amendment which may be made prior to the Year One thousand eight hundred and eight shall in any Manner affect the first and fourth Clauses in the Ninth section of the first Article; and that no State, without its Consent, shall be deprived of its equal Suffrage in the Senate.

## ARTICLE VI

## Section 1.

All Debts contracted and Engagements entered into, before the Adoption of this Constitution, shall be as valid against the United States under this Constitution, as under the Confederation.

## Section 2.

This Constitution, and the Laws of the United States which shall be made in Pursuance thereof; and all Treaties made, or which shall be made, under the Authority of the United States, shall be the supreme Law of the Land; and the Judges in every State shall be bound thereby, anything in the constitution or Laws of any State to the Contrary notwithstanding.

**Section 4. Guarantees to the States**

The federal government guarantees that each state has the right to elect its leaders. The federal government will also protect the states from invasion and violent disorders.

11. There were only thirteen states when the Constitution was written. Do you think the framers expected the United States to grow in size? Why?

_____

_____

_____

_____

_____

Article 5 describes the two ways the Constitution can be amended. Two thirds of the Senate and House of Representatives can suggest an amendment, or two thirds of the state legislatures can have a special convention to suggest an amendment. Once an amendment has been suggested, three fourths of the state legislatures or three fourths of the special conventions must approve the amendment.

Article 6 deals with national law and the national debt. The federal government promises to pay all its debts and keep all agreements made under the Articles of Confederation.

The Constitution and federal laws are the highest laws in the land. If state laws disagree with them, the federal laws must be obeyed.

## Section 3. Supporting the Constitution

Federal and state officials must promise to support the Constitution. A person's religion cannot disqualify him or her from holding office. Nine of the thirteen states must approve the Constitution for it to become the law of the land.

Article 7 deals with ratifying the Constitution. On September 17, 1787, twelve years after the Declaration of Independence, everyone at the Constitutional Convention agreed that the Constitution was complete.

The delegates to the Constitutional Convention signed their names below the Constitution to show they approved of it.

**12.** "The power under the Constitution will always be in the people," wrote George Washington in 1787. Explain what you think he meant.

_____

_____

_____

_____

_____

_____

## Section 3.

The Senators and Representatives before mentioned, and the Members of the several State legislatures, and all executive and judicial Officers, both of the United States and of the several States, shall be bound by Oath or Affirmation, to support this Constitution; but no religious Test shall ever be required as a Qualification to any Office or public Trust under the United States.

### ARTICLE VII

The ratification of the Conventions of nine States, shall be sufficient for the Establishment of this Constitution between the States so ratifying the same.

Done in Convention by the Unanimous Consent of the States present the Seventeenth Day of September in the Year of our Lord one thousand seven hundred and Eighty-seven and of the Independence of the United States of America the twelfth. In witness whereof We have hereunto subscribed our Names.

**Attest:**
William Jackson,
*Secretary*
George Washington,
*President and Deputy from Virginia*

**New Hampshire**
John Langdon
Nicholas Gilman

**Massachusetts**
Nathaniel Gorham
Rufus King

**Connecticut**
William Samuel
 Johnson
Roger Sherman

**New York**
Alexander Hamilton

**New Jersey**
William Livingston
David Brearley
William Paterson
Jonathan Dayton

**Pennsylvania**
Benjamin Franklin
Thomas Mifflin
Robert Morris
George Clymer
Thomas FitzSimons
Jared Ingersoll
James Wilson
Gouverneur Morris

**Delaware**
George Read
Gunning Bedford, Jr.
John Dickinson
Richard Bassett
Jacob Broom

**Maryland**
James McHenry
Dan of St. Thomas
 Jenifer
Daniel Carroll

**Virginia**
John Blair
James Madison, Jr.

**North Carolina**
William Blount
Richard Dobbs
 Spaight
Hugh Williamson

**South Carolina**
John Rutledge
Charles
 Cotesworth Pinckney
Charles Pinckney
Pierce Butler

**Georgia**
William Few
Abraham Baldwin

## AMENDMENTS
### Amendment 1

Congress shall make no law respecting an establishment of religion, or prohibiting the free exercise thereof, or abridging the freedom of speech, or of the press; or the right of the people peaceably to assemble, and to petition the Government for a redress of grievances.

### Amendment 2

A well-regulated Militia being necessary to the security of a free State, the right of the people to keep and bear Arms, shall not be infringed.

### Amendment 3

No Soldier shall, in time of peace be quartered in any house, without the consent of the Owner, nor, in time of war, but in a manner to be prescribed by law.

### Amendment 4

The right of the people to be secure in their persons, houses, papers, and effects, against unreasonable searches and seizures, shall not be violated, and no Warrants shall issue, but upon probable cause, supported by Oath or affirmation, and particularly describing the place to be searched, and the persons or things to be seized.

### Amendment 5

No person shall be held to answer for a capital, or otherwise infamous crime, unless on a presentment or indictment of a Grand Jury, except in cases arising in the land or naval forces, or in the Militia, when in actual service in time of War, or public danger; nor shall any person be subject for the same offence to be twice put in jeopardy of life or limb; nor shall be compelled in any criminal case to be a witness against himself, nor be deprived of life, liberty, or property, without due process of law; nor shall private property be taken for public use, without just compensation.

The first ten amendments to the Constitution are called the Bill of Rights.

**First Amendment—1791**
**Freedom of Religion and Speech**
Government cannot promote religion or set up an official religion or stop people from practicing a religion. Government cannot stop people or newspapers from saying what they want. People can gather peacefully to complain to the government.

**Second Amendment—1791**
**Right to Have Firearms**
People have the right to own and carry guns.

**Third Amendment—1791**
**Right Not to House Soldiers**
During peacetime, citizens do not have to house soldiers.

**Fourth Amendment—1791**
**Search and Arrest Warrant**
People or homes cannot be searched without reason. A search warrant is needed to search a house.

**Fifth Amendment—1791**
**Rights of People Accused of Crimes**
Only a grand jury can accuse people of a serious crime. No one can be tried twice for the same crime if found not guilty. People cannot be forced to testify against themselves.

**13.** Write the amendment number that protects each right.

_____ to speak freely

_____ to be protected against unreasonable searches

_____ to not be put on trial twice for the same crime

## Sixth Amendment—1791
### Right to a Jury Trial
People have the right to a fast trial by a jury and to hear the charges and evidence against them. They also have the right to a lawyer and to call witnesses in their own defense.

## Seventh Amendment—1791
### Right to a Jury Trial in a Civil Case
In a civil, or noncriminal case, a person also has the right to a trial by jury.

## Eighth Amendment—1791
### Protection From Unfair Punishment
A person accused of a crime cannot be forced to pay a very high bail. A person convicted of a crime cannot be asked to pay an unfairly high fine or be punished in a cruel or unusual way.

## Ninth Amendment—1791
### Other Rights
People have other rights that are not specifically mentioned in the Constitution.

## Tenth Amendment—1791
### Powers of the States and the People
Some powers are not given to the federal government or denied to states. These rights belong to the states or to the people.

## Eleventh Amendment—1795
### Limits on Rights to Sue States
People from another state or foreign country cannot sue a state.

## Amendment 6
In all criminal prosecutions, the accused shall enjoy the right to a speedy and public trial, by an impartial jury of the State and district wherein the crime shall have been committed, which district shall have been previously ascertained by law, and to be informed of the nature and cause of the accusation; to be confronted with the witnesses against him; to have compulsory process for obtaining witnesses in his favor, and to have the Assistance of Counsel for his defense.

## Amendment 7
In Suits at common law, where the value in controversy shall exceed twenty dollars, the right of trial by jury shall be preserved, and no fact tried by a jury, shall be otherwise re-examined in any Court of the United States, than according to the rules of the common law.

## Amendment 8
Excessive bail shall not be required, nor excessive fines imposed, nor cruel and unusual punishment inflicted.

## Amendment 9
The enumeration in the Constitution, of certain rights, shall not be construed to deny or disparage others retained by the people.

## Amendment 10
The powers not delegated to the United States by the Constitution, nor prohibited by it to the States, are reserved to the States respectively, or to the people.

## Amendment 11
The Judicial power of the United States shall not be construed to extend to any suit in law or equity, commenced or prosecuted against one of the United States by Citizens of another State, or by Citizens or Subjects of any Foreign State.

## Amendment 12

The Electors shall meet in their respective States and vote by ballot for President and Vice President, one of whom, at least, shall not be an inhabitant of the same State with themselves; they shall name in their ballots the person voted for as President, and in distinct ballots the person voted for as Vice President, and they shall make distinct lists of all persons voted for as President, and of all persons voted for as Vice President, and of the number of votes for each, which lists they shall sign and certify, and transmit sealed to the seat of the government of the United States, directed to the President of the Senate;— The President of the Senate shall, in the presence of the Senate and the House of Representatives, open all the certificates and the votes shall then be counted;— the person having the greatest Number of votes for President shall be the President, if such number be a majority of the whole number of Electors appointed; and if no person have such a majority, then, from the persons having the highest numbers not exceeding three on the list of those voted for as President, the House of Representatives shall choose immediately, by ballot, the President. But in choosing the President, the votes shall be taken by States, the representation from each State having one vote; a quorum for this purpose shall consist of a member or members from two thirds of the States, and a majority of all the States shall be necessary to a choice. And if the House of Representatives shall not choose a President whenever the right of choice shall devolve upon them, before the fourth day of March next following, then the Vice President shall act as President, as in case of death or other constitutional disability of the President. The person having the greatest number of votes as Vice President, shall be the Vice President, if such number be a majority of the whole number of Electors appointed, and if no person have a majority, then from the two highest numbers on the list, the Senate shall choose the Vice President; a quorum for the purpose shall consist of two thirds of the whole number of Senators, a majority of the whole number shall be necessary to a choice. But no person constitutionally ineligible to the office of President shall be eligible to that of Vice-President of the United States.

**Twelfth Amendment—1804**
**Election of President and Vice President**

This amendment changed the way the Electoral College chooses the President and Vice President. Before this amendment, candidates for President and Vice President ran separately, and each elector had two votes—one for President and one for Vice President. The candidate receiving the most votes became President, and the runner-up became Vice President.

Under this amendment, a candidate for President and a candidate for Vice President must run together. Each elector has only one vote, and the pair of candidates that receives more than half the electoral votes become the President and Vice President. If no one receives a majority of the electoral votes, the House of Representatives votes for the President from a list of the top three vote getters. In this situation, each state has one vote, and the candidate must receive more than half of the votes to become President.

If the Representatives fail to elect a President by March 4 (later changed to January 20), the Vice President serves as President. If no candidate receives at least half the electoral votes for Vice President, the names of the two top vote getters are sent to the Senate. The Senators then vote on the names, and the person receiving more than half the votes becomes Vice President.

### Thirteenth Amendment—1865
### Abolition of Slavery

The United States outlaws slavery. Congress can pass any laws that are needed to carry out this amendment.

### Fourteenth Amendment—1868
### Rights of Citizens

People born in the United States are citizens of both the United States and of the state in which they live. States must treat their citizens equally. States cannot deny their citizens the rights outlined in the Bill of Rights.

This section of the amendment made former slaves citizens of both the United States and their home state.

Based on its population, each state has a certain number of Representatives in Congress. The number of Representatives from a state might be lowered, however, if the state does not let certain citizens vote.

This section tried to force states in the South to let former slaves vote.

**14.** Why would a state not want to have its number of Representatives in Congress cut?

_____

_____

_____

_____

### Amendment 13

Section 1. Neither slavery nor involuntary servitude, except as a punishment for crime whereof the party shall have been duly convicted, shall exist within the United States, or any place subject to their jurisdiction.

Section 2. Congress shall have power to enforce this article by appropriate legislation.

### Amendment 14

Section 1. All persons born or naturalized in the United States and subject to the jurisdiction thereof, are citizens of the United States and of the State wherein they reside. No State shall make or enforce any law which shall abridge the privileges or immunities of citizens of the United States; nor shall any State deprive any person of life, liberty, or property, without due process of law; nor deny to any person within its jurisdiction the equal protection of the laws.

Section 2. Representatives shall be apportioned among the several States according to their respective numbers, counting the whole number of persons in each State, excluding Indians not taxed. But when the right to vote at any election for the choice of electors for President and Vice President of the United States, Representatives in Congress, the Executive and Judicial officers of a State, or the members of the Legislature thereof, is denied to any of the male inhabitants of such State, being twenty-one years of age and citizens of the United States, or in any way abridged, except for participation in rebellion, or other crime, the basis of representation therein shall be reduced in the proportion which the number of such male citizens shall bear to the whole number of male citizens twenty-one years of age in such State.

Section 3. No person shall be a Senator or Representative in Congress, or elector of President and Vice President, or hold any office, civil or military, under the United States, or under any State, who, having previously taken an oath, as a member of Congress, or as an officer of the United States, or as a member of any State legislature, or as an executive or judicial officer of any State, to support the Constitution of the United States, shall have engaged in insurrection or rebellion against the same, or given aid or comfort to the enemies thereof. But Congress may, by a vote of two thirds of each House, remove such disability.

Section 4. The validity of the public debt of the United States, authorized by law, including debts incurred for payment of pensions and bounties for services in suppressing insurrection or rebellion, shall not be questioned. But neither the United States nor any State shall assume or pay any debt or obligation incurred in aid of insurrection or rebellion against the United States, or any claim for the loss or emancipation of any slave; but all such debts, obligations and claims shall be held illegal and void.

Section 5. The Congress shall have power to enforce, by appropriate legislation, the provisions of this article.

## Amendment 15

Section 1. The right of citizens of the United States to vote shall not be denied or abridged by the United States or by any State on account of race, color, or previous condition of servitude.

Section 2. The Congress shall have power to enforce this article by appropriate legislation.

Officials who took part in the Civil War against the United States cannot hold federal or state office. Congress can remove this provision by a two-thirds vote.

The United States will pay back the money it borrowed to fight the Civil War. The money that the South borrowed to fight the Civil War will not be paid back to lenders. The former owners of slaves will not be paid for the slaves that were set free. Congress can pass any necessary laws to enforce this article.

**15.** List two ways in which the Fourteenth Amendment tended to punish those who rebelled against the United States.

_____

_____

_____

_____

_____

_____

_____

_____

**Fifteenth Amendment—1870 Voting Rights**
The federal and state government cannot stop people from voting based on race or color. Former slaves must be allowed to vote.

## Sixteenth Amendment—1913
### Income Tax
Congress has the power to collect an income tax regardless of the population of a state. (Originally, Section 9 of Article 1 had denied this power to Congress.)

## Seventeenth Amendment—1913
### Direct Election of Senators
The voters of each state will elect their Senators directly. (Originally, Article 1, Section 3 said state legislatures would elect Senators.)

A state can hold a special election to fill an empty Senate seat. Until then, the governor can appoint a Senator to fill an empty seat.

## Eighteenth Amendment—1919
### Prohibition
Making, importing, or selling alcoholic drinks is illegal in the United States. This was called Prohibition because the amendment prohibited, or outlawed, alcohol.

Congress and the states can make any laws to prohibit alcohol.

This amendment becomes part of the Constitution if it is approved within seven years.

This amendment was repealed, or cancelled, in 1933 by the Twenty-first Amendment.

**16.** Write the amendment number that did each of the following:

_____ let the Federal Government collect income tax

_____ guaranteed voting rights for African Americans

_____ outlawed the sale of alcohol

_____ abolished slavery

_____ let voters elect their Senators

## Amendment 16
The Congress shall have power to lay and collect taxes on incomes, from whatever source derived, without apportionment among the several States, and without regard to any census or enumeration.

## Amendment 17
The Senate of the United States shall be composed of two Senators from each State, elected by the people thereof, for six years; and each Senator shall have one vote. The electors in each State shall have the qualifications requisite for electors of the most numerous branch of the State legislatures.

When vacancies happen in the representation of any State in the Senate, the executive authority of such State shall issue writs of election to fill such vacancies: Provided, That the legislature of any State may empower the executive thereof to make temporary appointments until the people fill the vacancies by election as the legislature may direct.

This amendment shall not be so construed as to affect the election or term of any Senator chosen before it becomes valid as part of the Constitution.

## Amendment 18
Section 1. After one year from the ratification of this article the manufacture, sale, or transportation of intoxicating liquors within, the importation thereof into, or the exportation thereof from the United States and all territory subject to the jurisdiction thereof for beverage purposes is hereby prohibited.

Section 2. The Congress and the several States shall have concurrent power to enforce this article by appropriate legislation.

Section 3. This article shall be inoperative unless it shall have been ratified as an amendment to the Constitution by the legislatures of the several States, as provided in the Constitution, within seven years of the date of the submission hereof to the States by Congress.

## Amendment 19

The right of citizens of the United States to vote shall not be denied or abridged by the United States or by any State on account of sex.

Congress shall have power to enforce this article by appropriate legislation.

## Amendment 20

Section 1. The terms of the President and Vice President shall end at noon on the 20th day of January, and the terms of Senators and Representatives at noon on the 3d day of January, of the years in which such terms would have ended if this article had not been ratified; and the terms of their successors shall then begin.

Section 2. The Congress shall assemble at least once in every year, and such meeting shall begin at noon on the 3d day of January, unless they shall by law appoint a different day.

Section 3. If, at the time fixed for the beginning of the term of the President, the President elect shall have died, the Vice President elect shall become President. If a President shall not have been chosen before the time fixed for the beginning of his term, or if the President-elect shall have failed to qualify, then the Vice President elect shall act as President until a President shall have qualified; and the Congress may by law provide for the case wherein neither a President elect nor a Vice President elect shall have qualified, declaring who shall then act as President, or the manner in which one who is to act shall be selected, and such person shall act accordingly until a President or Vice President shall have qualified.

Section 4. The Congress may by law provide for the case of the death of any of the persons from whom the House of Representatives may choose a President whenever the right of choice shall have devolved upon them, and for the case of the death of any of the persons from whom the Senate may choose a Vice President whenever the right of choice shall have devolved upon them.

Section 5. Sections 1 and 2 shall take effect on the 15th day of October following the ratification of this article.

Section 6. This article shall be inoperative unless it shall have been ratified as an amendment to the Constitution by the legislatures of three fourths of the several States within seven years from the date of its submission.

**Twenty-first Amendment—1933**
**Repeal of Prohibition**
The Eighteenth Amendment, which outlawed alcohol, is no longer in effect.

Any state may pass laws to prohibit alcohol.

**17. How long was the Eighteenth Amendment in effect in the United States?**

_____

**Twenty-second Amendment—1951**
**Limit on Terms of the President**
A President can only be elected to the office for two terms (eight years). If a President serves more than two years of the last President's term, then the President may only be re-elected once.

**18. Do you think a President should be limited to just two terms in office? Why or why not?**

_____

_____

_____

_____

_____

_____

## Amendment 21

Section 1. The eighteenth article of amendment to the Constitution of the United States is hereby repealed.

Section 2. The transportation or importation into any State, Territory, or possession of the United States for delivery or use therein of intoxicating liquors, in violation of the laws thereof, is hereby prohibited.

Section 3. This article shall be inoperative unless it shall have been ratified as an amendment to the Constitution by conventions in the several States, as provided in the Constitution, within seven years from the date of the submission hereof to the States by the Congress.

## Amendment 22

Section 1. No person shall be elected to the office of the President more than twice, and no person who has held the office of President, or acted as President, for more than two years of a term to which some other person was elected President shall be elected to the office of the President more than once. But this Article shall not apply to any person holding the office of President, when this Article was proposed by the Congress, and shall not prevent any person who may be holding the office of President, or acting as President, during the term within which this Article becomes operative from holding the office of President or acting as President during the remainder of such term.

Section 2. This article shall be inoperative unless it shall have been ratified as an amendment to the Constitution by the legislatures of three fourths of the several states within seven years from the date of its submission to the States by the Congress.

## Amendment 23

Section 1. The District constituting the seat of Government of the United States shall appoint in such manner as the Congress may direct:

A number of electors of President and Vice President equal to the whole number of Senators and Representatives in Congress to which the District would be entitled if it were a State, but in no event more than the least populous State; they shall be in addition to those appointed by the States, they shall be considered, for the purposes of the election of President and Vice President, to be electors appointed by a State; and they shall meet in the District and perform such duties as provided by the twelfth article of amendment.

## Amendment 24

Section 1. The right of citizens of the United States to vote in any primary or other election for President or Vice President, for electors for President or Vice President, or for Senator or Representative in Congress, shall not be denied or abridged by the United States or any State by reason of failure to pay any poll tax or other tax.

Section 2. The Congress shall have power to enforce this article by appropriate legislation.

## Amendment 25

Section 1. In case of the removal of the President from office or of his death or resignation, the Vice President shall become President.

Section 2. Whenever there is a vacancy in the office of the Vice President, the President shall nominate a Vice President who shall take office upon confirmation by a majority vote of both Houses of Congress.

Section 3. Whenever the President transmits to the President pro tempore of the Senate and the Speaker of the House of Representatives his written declaration that he is unable to discharge the powers and duties of his office, and until he transmits to them a written declaration to the contrary, such powers and duties shall be discharged by the Vice President as Acting President.

### Twenty-third Amendment—1961 Presidential Elections for District of Columbia

People living in Washington, D.C., have the right to vote in presidential elections. Washington, D.C., can never have more electoral votes than the state with the smallest number of people.

### Twenty-fourth Amendment—1964 Outlawing of Poll Tax

No one can be stopped from voting in a federal election because he or she has not paid a poll tax or any other kind of tax.

Congress can make laws to carry out this amendment.

### Twenty-fifth Amendment—1967 Presidential Succession

If the President dies or resigns, the Vice President becomes President. If the office of Vice President is empty, the President appoints a new Vice President.

When the President is unable to carry out the duties of the office, Congress should be informed. The Vice President then serves as Acting President. The President may resume the duties of the office after informing Congress.

If the Vice President and half the President's top advisers, or Cabinet, inform Congress that the President cannot carry out his or her duties, the Vice President becomes Acting President. If the President informs Congress that he or she is able to carry out these duties, the President returns to office. However, after four days, if the Vice President and half the Cabinet again tell Congress that the President cannot carry out his or her duties, the President does not return to office. Instead, Congress must decide within 21 days whether the President is able to carry out his or her duties. If two thirds of Congress votes that the President cannot continue in office, the Vice President becomes Acting President. If two thirds do not vote in this way, the President remains in office.

People who are 18 years old have the right to vote in federal and state elections.

Congress can pass laws to carry out this amendment.

Over the years, amendments to the Constitution have improved our democracy by expanding voting rights to more and more citizens.

**19.** Write the number of the amendment that:

_____ gave votes to women

_____ gave votes to citizens in Washington, D.C.

_____ gave votes to 18-year-old people

_____ outlawed taxes that blocked voting

**Twenty-seventh Amendment—1992**
**Limits on Congressional Salary Changes**

Laws that increase the salaries of Senators and Representatives do not take effect immediately. They take effect after the next election of the House of Representatives.

Section 4. Whenever the Vice President and a majority of either the principal officers of the executive departments or of such other body as Congress may by law provide, transmit to the President pro tempore of the Senate and the Speaker of the House of Representatives their written declaration that the President is unable to discharge the powers and duties of his office, the Vice President shall immediately assume the powers and duties of the office as Acting President.

Thereafter, when the President transmits to the President pro tempore of the Senate and the Speaker of the House of Representatives his written declaration that no inability exists, he shall resume the powers and duties of his office unless the Vice President and a majority of either the principal officers of the executive department or of such other body as Congress may by law provide, transmit within four days to the President pro tempore of the Senate and the Speaker of the House of Representatives their written declaration that the President is unable to discharge the powers and duties of his office. Thereupon Congress shall decide the issue, assembling within forty-eight hours for that purpose if not in session. If the Congress, within twenty-one days after receipt of the latter written declaration, or, if Congress is not in session, within twenty-one days after Congress is required to assemble, determines by two-thirds vote of both Houses that the President is unable to discharge the powers and duties of his office, the Vice President shall continue to discharge the same as Acting President; otherwise, the President shall resume the powers and duties of his office.

## Amendment 26

Section 1. The right of citizens of the United States, who are eighteen years of age or older, to vote shall not be denied or abridged by the United States or by any State on account of age.

Section 2. The Congress shall have the power to enforce this article by appropriate legislation.

## Amendment 27

No law varying the compensation for the services of the Senators and Representatives, shall take effect, until an election of Representatives shall have intervened.

## The United States of America, Political

Washington
★ Olympia

★ Salem

Oregon

Montana
★ Helena

★ Boise
Idaho

North
Dakota
★ Bismarck

Minnesot

St. Paul

South Dakota
Pierre ★

Wyoming

Iow

Sacramento ★

Carson
City ★

Salt Lake ★
City

Cheyenne ★

Nebraska

Lincoln ★

Nevada

Utah

Denver ★

Colorado

Topeka ★

California

Kansas

M

Arizona

★ Phoenix

Santa Fe ★

New
Mexico

Oklahoma
★ Oklahoma
City

L
F

Texas

Austin ★

Alaska

Juneau ★

Honolulu ★

Hawaii

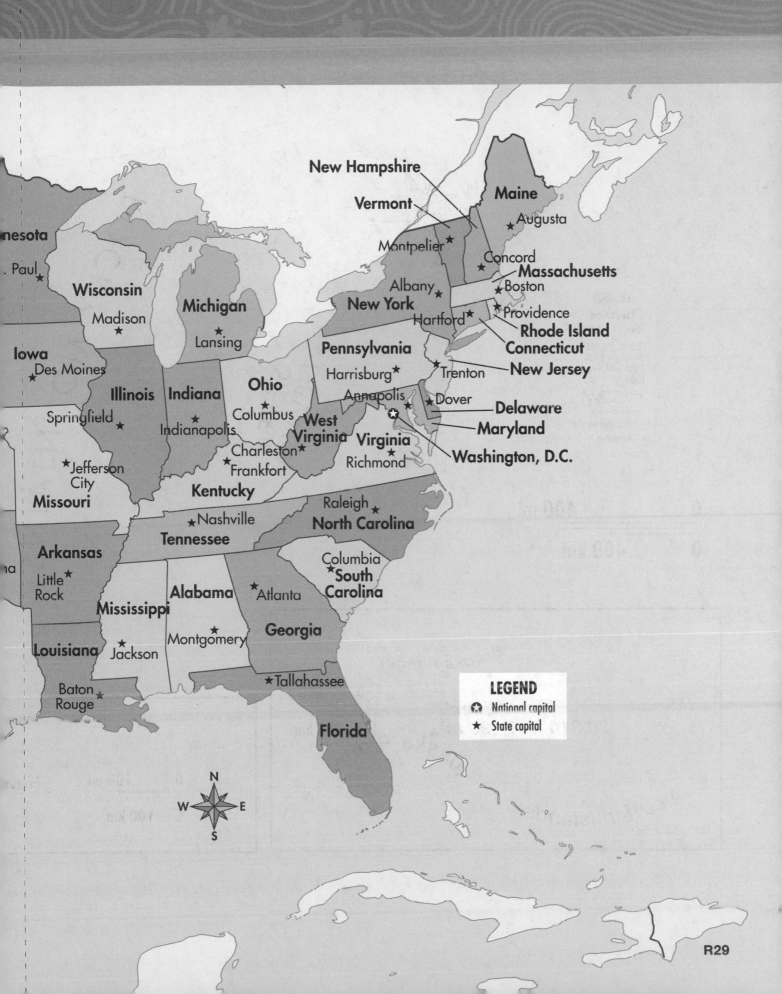

Minnesota

St. Paul

Wisconsin

Madison

Michigan

Lansing

Iowa

Des Moines

Illinois

Springfield

Indiana

Indianapolis

Ohio

Columbus

Jefferson City

Missouri

Kentucky

Frankfort

West Virginia

Charleston

Virginia

Richmond

Pennsylvania

Harrisburg

New York

Albany

Hartford

Trenton

Annapolis

Dover

Delaware

Maryland

Washington, D.C.

New Jersey

Connecticut

Rhode Island

Providence

Massachusetts

Boston

Concord

New Hampshire

Vermont

Montpelier

Maine

Augusta

Arkansas

Little Rock

Tennessee

Nashville

Raleigh

North Carolina

Columbia

South Carolina

Alabama

Atlanta

Montgomery

Georgia

Mississippi

Jackson

Louisiana

Baton Rouge

Tallahassee

Florida

**LEGEND**
✪ National capital
★ State capital

N
W E
S

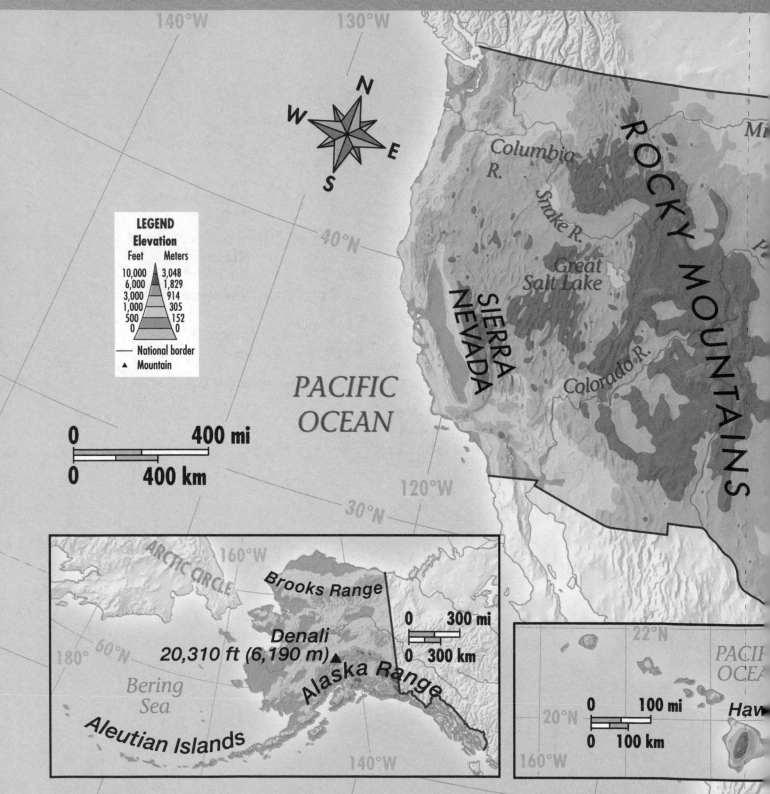

LEGEND
Elevation

| Feet | Meters |
| --- | --- |
| 10,000 | 3,048 |
| 6,000 | 1,829 |
| 3,000 | 914 |
| 1,000 | 305 |
| 500 | 152 |
| 0 | 0 |

— National border
▲ Mountain

PACIFIC OCEAN

Columbia R.

Snake R.

Great Salt Lake

Colorado R.

SIERRA NEVADA

ROCKY MOUNTAINS

0 __ 400 mi
0 __ 400 km

ARCTIC CIRCLE

Brooks Range

Denali
20,310 ft (6,190 m) ▲

Alaska Range

Bering Sea

Aleutian Islands

0 __ 300 mi
0 __ 300 km

0 __ 100 mi
0 __ 100 km

PACIFIC OCEAN

Hawa

Missouri R.

Lake Superior

Great Lakes

Lake Ontario

Lake Huron

Lake Michigan

Lake Erie

G R E A T   P L A I N S

Platte R.

CENTRAL PLAINS

Ohio R.

APPALACHIAN MOUNTAINS

Red R.

Mississippi R.

ATLANTIC OCEAN

C O A S T A L   P L A I N

80°W

70°W

Rio Grande

Gulf of Mexico

90°W

ACIFIC OCEAN

Hawaii

154°W

TROPIC OF CANCER

20°N

map area

# The World, Political

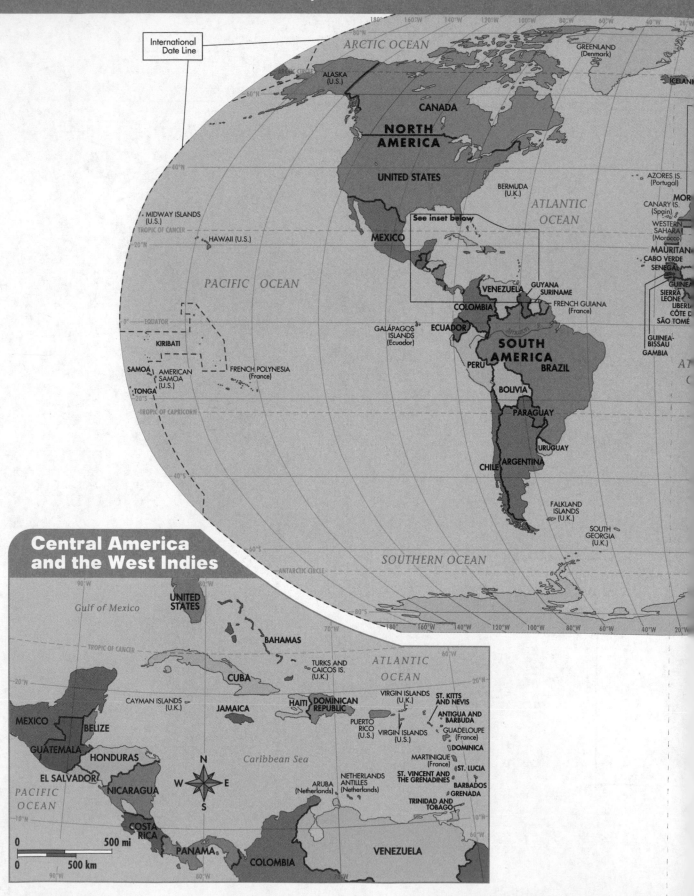

International Date Line

ARCTIC OCEAN

GREENLAND
(Denmark)

ICELAN

ALASKA
(U.S.)

CANADA

NORTH
AMERICA

UNITED STATES

BERMUDA
(U.K.)

ATLANTIC
OCEAN

AZORES IS.
(Portugal)

MOR

CANARY IS.
(Spain)

WESTERN
SAHARA
(Morocco)

See inset below

MIDWAY ISLANDS
(U.S.)

TROPIC OF CANCER

HAWAII (U.S.)

MEXICO

MAURITAN

CABO VERDE

SENEGAL

GUINEA

PACIFIC OCEAN

VENEZUELA

GUYANA
SURINAME

SIERRA
LEONE

LIBERI

CÔTE D

SÃO TOMÉ

COLOMBIA

FRENCH GUIANA
(France)

GALÁPAGOS
ISLANDS
(Ecuador)

ECUADOR

EQUATOR

GUINEA-
BISSAU

GAMBIA

KIRIBATI

SOUTH
AMERICA

Amazon

A

C

PERU

SAMOA

AMERICAN
SAMOA
(U.S.)

FRENCH POLYNESIA
(France)

BRAZIL

TONGA

BOLIVIA

TROPIC OF CAPRICORN

PARAGUAY

URUGUAY

CHILE

ARGENTINA

FALKLAND
ISLANDS
(U.K.)

SOUTH
GEORGIA
(U.K.)

SOUTHERN OCEAN

ANTARCTIC CIRCLE

## Central America and the West Indies

Gulf of Mexico

UNITED
STATES

BAHAMAS

TROPIC OF CANCER

TURKS AND
CAICOS IS.
(U.K.)

ATLANTIC
OCEAN

CUBA

VIRGIN ISLANDS
(U.K.)

ST. KITTS
AND NEVIS

CAYMAN ISLANDS
(U.K.)

JAMAICA

HAITI

DOMINICAN
REPUBLIC

ANTIGUA AND
BARBUDA

MEXICO

BELIZE

PUERTO
RICO
(U.S.)

VIRGIN ISLANDS
(U.S.)

GUADELOUPE
(France)

GUATEMALA

DOMINICA

HONDURAS

Caribbean Sea

MARTINIQUE
(France)

ST. LUCIA

EL SALVADOR

PACIFIC
OCEAN

NICARAGUA

ARUBA
(Netherlands)

NETHERLANDS
ANTILLES
(Netherlands)

ST. VINCENT AND
THE GRENADINES

BARBADOS

GRENADA

TRINIDAD AND
TOBAGO

COSTA
RICA

PANAMA

COLOMBIA

VENEZUELA

0        500 mi

0    500 km

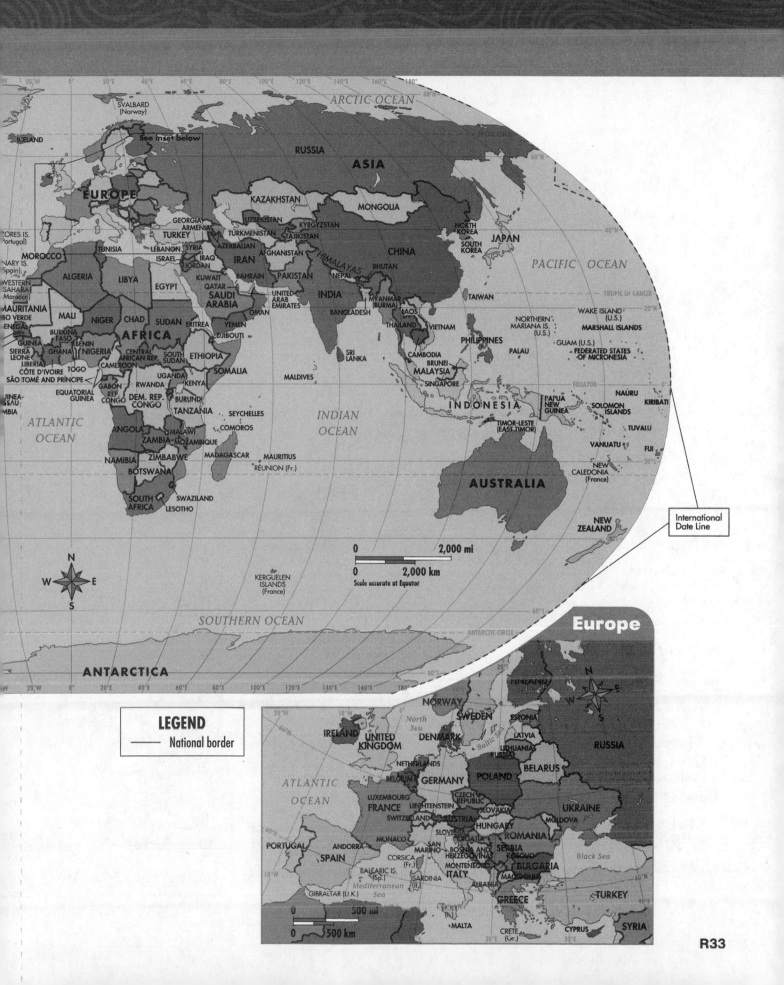

**ARCTIC OCEAN**

SVALBARD
(Norway)

ICELAND

See inset below

RUSSIA

ASIA

EUROPE

AZORES IS.
(Portugal)

GEORGIA
ARMENIA
TURKEY

KAZAKHSTAN

MONGOLIA

MOROCCO

CANARY IS.
(Spain)

TUNISIA

LEBANON
ISRAEL
JORDAN

SYRIA
IRAQ

UZBEKISTAN
TURKMENISTAN

KYRGYZSTAN
TAJIKISTAN

NORTH
KOREA

JAPAN

SOUTH
KOREA

**PACIFIC OCEAN**

WESTERN
SAHARA
(Morocco)

ALGERIA

LIBYA

EGYPT

IRAN

AFGHANISTAN

CHINA

KUWAIT
BAHRAIN
QATAR
UNITED
ARAB
EMIRATES

PAKISTAN

HIMALAYAS

BHUTAN
NEPAL

TAIWAN

TROPIC OF CANCER

MAURITANIA

CABO VERDE

SENEGAL

MALI

NIGER

CHAD

SUDAN

SAUDI
ARABIA

OMAN

INDIA

BANGLADESH

MYANMAR
(BURMA)

LAOS

VIETNAM

PHILIPPINES

WAKE ISLAND
(U.S.)

NORTHERN
MARIANA IS.
(U.S.)

MARSHALL ISLANDS

GUINEA
SIERRA
LEONE
LIBERIA
CÔTE D'IVOIRE

GUINEA-BISSAU
GAMBIA

BURKINA
FASO
GHANA
TOGO

BENIN
NIGERIA

AFRICA

CENTRAL
AFRICAN REP.
CAMEROON

ERITREA

DJIBOUTI

YEMEN

ETHIOPIA

SOUTH
SUDAN

THAILAND

CAMBODIA
BRUNEI
MALAYSIA

SRI
LANKA

MALDIVES

PALAU

GUAM (U.S.)

FEDERATED STATES
OF MICRONESIA

SÃO TOMÉ AND PRÍNCIPE

EQUATORIAL
GUINEA
GABON
CONGO

DEM. REP.
CONGO

UGANDA

RWANDA
BURUNDI

KENYA

SOMALIA

SINGAPORE

INDONESIA

PAPUA
NEW
GUINEA

SOLOMON
ISLANDS

EQUATOR

NAURU

KIRIBATI

**ATLANTIC
OCEAN**

ANGOLA

TANZANIA

ZAMBIA

MALAWI

MOZAMBIQUE

SEYCHELLES

COMOROS

**INDIAN
OCEAN**

TIMOR-LESTE
(EAST TIMOR)

TUVALU

VANUATU

FIJI

NAMIBIA
BOTSWANA

ZIMBABWE

MADAGASCAR

MAURITIUS

RÉUNION (Fr.)

**AUSTRALIA**

NEW
CALEDONIA
(France)

SOUTH
AFRICA

SWAZILAND

LESOTHO

International
Date Line

N
W    E
S

**2,000 mi**

0

0    **2,000 km**

Scale accurate at Equator

KERGUELEN
ISLANDS
(France)

NEW
ZEALAND

**SOUTHERN OCEAN**

ANTARCTIC CIRCLE

**ANTARCTICA**

See inset below

## LEGEND

— National border

## Europe

N
W    E
S

FINLAND

NORWAY

SWEDEN

ESTONIA

RUSSIA

IRELAND

UNITED
KINGDOM

North
Sea

DENMARK

Baltic Sea

LATVIA

LITHUANIA

RUSSIA

BELARUS

**ATLANTIC
OCEAN**

NETHERLANDS

BELGIUM

GERMANY

POLAND

LUXEMBOURG

FRANCE

LIECHTENSTEIN

SWITZERLAND

CZECH
REPUBLIC

AUSTRIA

SLOVAKIA

HUNGARY

UKRAINE

MOLDOVA

SLOVENIA

CROATIA

ROMANIA

PORTUGAL

ANDORRA

SPAIN

MONACO

SAN
MARINO

CORSICA
(Fr.)

BOSNIA AND
HERZEGOVINA

MONTENEGRO

SERBIA

KOSOVO

BULGARIA

Black Sea

BALEARIC IS.
(Sp.)

SARDINIA
(It.)

ITALY

MACEDONIA

ALBANIA

GIBRALTAR (U.K.)

Mediterranean
Sea

GREECE

TURKEY

**500 mi**

0

0    **500 km**

MALTA

CRETE
(Gr.)

CYPRUS

SYRIA

R33

# California, Political and Population

Oregon

Idaho

Alturas

Eureka

Redding

Chico    Quincy

Nevada

Utah

Santa Rosa

Napa    ★Sacramento

Stockton

San Francisco    Oakland    Modesto

San Jose    Merced

Fresno    Independence

Monterey

Visalia

Bakersfield

PACIFIC OCEAN

San Luis Obispo

Lancaster

Santa Barbara    Victorville

San Bernardino

Los Angeles    Anaheim    Palm Springs

Long Beach

Oceanside

El Centro

San Diego

Arizona

MEXICO

N
W    E
S

0         100 mi
0         100 km

## LEGEND
### Population Density

| Persons per square mile | per square kilometer |
| --- | --- |
| More than 5,000 | More than 1,900 |
| 1,000 to 5,000 | 400 to 1,900 |
| 500 to 1,000 | 200 to 400 |
| 50 to 500 | 20 to 200 |
| 1 to 50 | 1 to 20 |
| Less than 1 | Less than 1 |

★ State capital
● City

# California, Physical

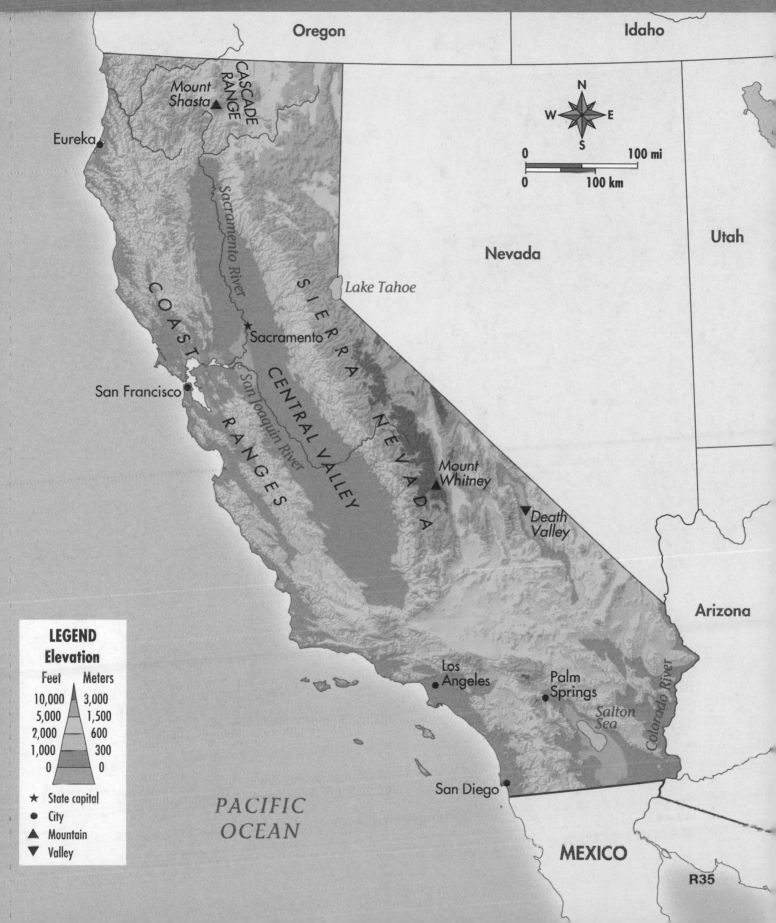

Oregon

Idaho

Nevada

Utah

Arizona

MEXICO

Mount Shasta ▲

CASCADE RANGE

Eureka •

Sacramento River

SIERRA NEVADA

Lake Tahoe

★ Sacramento

San Francisco •

San Joaquin River

CENTRAL VALLEY

COAST RANGES

Mount Whitney ▲

▼ Death Valley

Los Angeles •

Palm Springs •

Salton Sea

Colorado River

San Diego •

PACIFIC OCEAN

N
W    E
S

0          100 mi
0          100 km

## LEGEND

**Elevation**

| Feet | Meters |
|------|--------|
| 10,000 | 3,000 |
| 5,000 | 1,500 |
| 2,000 | 600 |
| 1,000 | 300 |
| 0 | 0 |

★ State capital
• City
▲ Mountain
▼ Valley

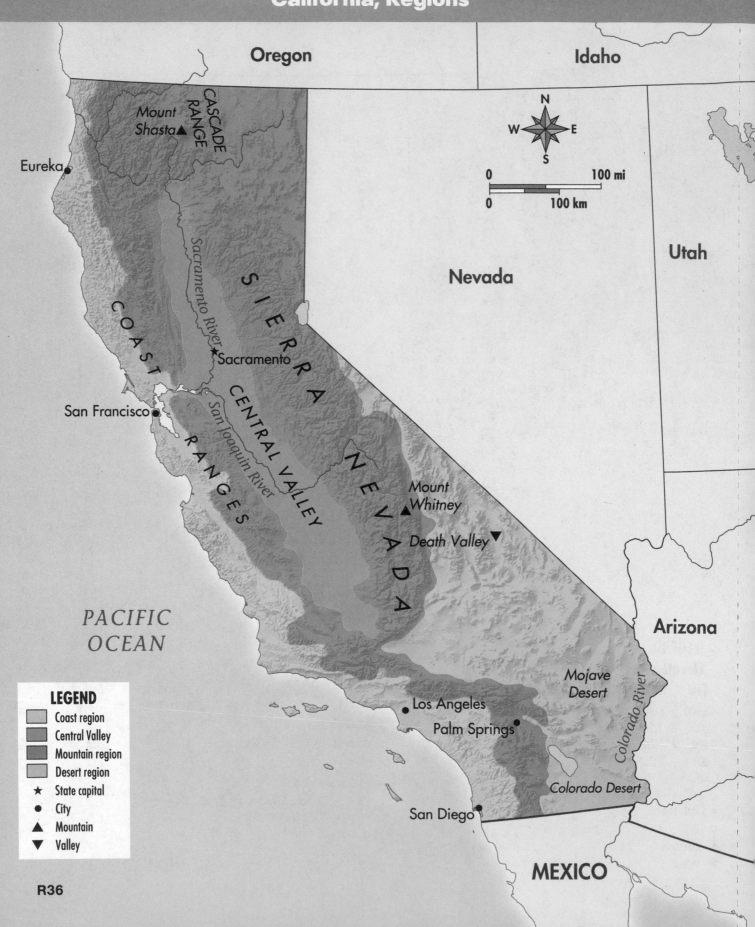

# California, Regions

Oregon

Idaho

Nevada

Utah

Arizona

MEXICO

Mount Shasta▲

CASCADE RANGE

Eureka

Sacramento River

S I E R R A

Sacramento★

San Francisco

C O A S T   R A N G E S

San Joaquin River

CENTRAL VALLEY

N E V A D A

Mount Whitney ▲

Death Valley ▼

PACIFIC OCEAN

Los Angeles

Palm Springs

Mojave Desert

Colorado River

Colorado Desert

San Diego

## LEGEND

- Coast region
- Central Valley
- Mountain region
- Desert region
- ★ State capital
- ● City
- ▲ Mountain
- ▼ Valley

N
W E
S

0 —— 100 mi
0 —— 100 km

# Glossary

## A

**abolitionist** (ab uh LIHSH un ihst) Someone who worked to abolish, or get rid of, slavery.

**absolute location** (AB suh loot loh KAY shun) The exact location of a place on Earth.

**activist** (AK tihv ihst) A person who is very active and engaged in civic life.

**adapt** (uh DAPT) To change to live in a new environment.

**adjust** (uh JUST) To change or shift.

**advocate** (AD vuh kiht) Someone who fights on behalf of a cause.

**agricultural region** (ag rih KUL chur ul REE jun) An area where certain types of crops are grown.

**aid** (ayd) Help or support.

**architecture** (AHR kuh tek chur) How a building is designed.

**area** (AIR ee uh) A part of a larger place.

**arrange** (uh RAYNJ) To plan or decide.

**artifact** (AHRT uh fakt) An object that was made and used by people.

## B

**bay** (bay) A body of water that is part of an ocean and partly surrounded by land.

**benefit** (BEN uh fiht) A useful result.

**biography** (by AH gruh fee) A story about a person's life that is written by someone else.

**boundary** (BOUN dree) A border or dividing line.

**boycott** (BOI kaht) When people refuse to buy, sell, or use something in order to make a point.

**breakwater** (BRAYK wawt ur) A wall or barrier that stops waves.

## C

**capital resource** (KAP ut ul REE sors) A human-made item used to make other goods or provide services.

**celebrity** (suh LEB ruh tee) A person who is famous.

**century** (SEN chuh ree) A period of time lasting 100 years.

**ceremony** (SAIR uh moh nee) A special activity done for an important reason.

**charter** (CHAHRT ur) A document, similar to a constitution, that outlines rules for a colony, city, or other group.

**citizen** (SIHT uh zun) A member of a community, state, or nation.

**citizenship** (SIHT uh zun shihp) The character and behavior of a citizen.

**civic** (SIHV ihk) Referring to the rights and responsibilities of citizens.

**civil rights** (SIHV ul ryts) The rights of all citizens to be treated equally under the law.

**civil war** (SIHV ul wor) A war fought between groups of people within one country.

**claim** (klaym) To say that land belongs to a certain country.

**climate** (KLY mut) The weather that a place has over a long period of time.

**common** (KAHM un) Not rare or unusual.

**community** (kuh MYOO nuh tee) A place where people live.

**compass rose** (KUM pus rohz) A map symbol that shows the cardinal directions of north, south, east, and west; may also show northwest, southwest, northeast, and southeast.

**conditions** (kun DIHSH unz) Existing circumstances.

**conflict** (KAHN flikt) A disagreement.

**Congress** (KAHN grus) The U.S. legislative group, which makes the laws.

**consequence** (KAHN sih kwens) The result or effect of an action.

**conserve** (kun SURV) To protect a resource.

**constitution** (kahn stuh TOO shuyn) A plan or set of rules that explains how a country will work.

**consumer** (kun SOOM ur) A user of goods or services.

**contribute** (kun TRIHB yoot) To give or help.

**convert** (kun VIHRT) To change; to take on a different religion, opinion, or political idea.

**cost** (kawst) The price needed to get something else.

**council** (KOUN sul) A group of local leaders.

**culture** (KUL chur) The arts, beliefs, behaviors, and ideas of a group of people.

**custom** (KUS tum) A way of doing something.

**cyberbullying** (SY bur bool ee ing) The act of sending mean messages online.

# D

**decade** (DEK ayd) A period of 10 years.

**deed** (deed) An action.

**delegate** (DEL uh giht) A person chosen to act for others.

**desert** (DEZ urt) An area of very dry land where few plants grow.

**despite** (dih SPYT) Without being affected by.

**develop** (dih VEL up) To create.

**discover** (dih SKUV ur) To find.

**discrimination** (dih skrihm ih NAY shun) Treating people differently because of their race, gender, age, or other characteristic.

**display** (dih SPLAY) To show off.

**diverse** (duh VURS) Made up of different groups of people.

**document** (DAHK yoo munt) A written record.

# E

**earthquake** (URTH kwayk) A sudden movement of Earth's upper layer.

**ecosystem** (EE koh sihs tum) All the living and nonliving things that interact in a certain place.

**elder** (EL dur) An older leader.

**electricity** (ee lek TRIHS ih tee) A type of power used to light bulbs and run machines.

**element** (EL uh munt) A part of something larger.

**elevation** (el uh VAY shun) The height of land above sea level.

**emergency** (ee MUR jun see) A sudden and urgent problem.

**energy** (EN ur jee) Usable power.

**enforce** (en FORS) To make sure people obey laws and rules.

**entrepreneur** (ahn truh pruh NOOR) Someone who sets up a business.

**environment** (en VY run munt) The natural world in which people, plants, and animals live.

**equator** (ee KWAYT ur) An imaginary line that extends around the center of Earth.

**ethnicity** (eth NIHS uh tee) People who share a common background or culture.

**executive** (eg ZEK yoo tihv) The branch of government that carries out laws.

**explorer** (ek SPLAWR ur) A person who goes to an unfamiliar area to learn about it.

**export** (eks PORT) To send goods to another country.

**eyewitness** (eye WIHT nihs) A person who was at an event.

# F

**feature** (FEE chur) An important or interesting part of something.

**federal** (FED ur ul) National.

**fine** (fyn) Money paid as a consequence.

**folklore** (FOHK lor) All the traditions, customs, beliefs, and stories of a group of people that are passed down by word of mouth.

**founded** (FOWN ded) Started.

**fund** (fund) To pay for.

**future** (FYOO chur) The time after now.

# G

**generation** (jen ur AY shun) The period of time between the birth of parents and the birth of their children.

**globe** (glohb) A model of Earth.

**good** (good) An item you can see, like a pencil or a car.

**governor** (GUV uh nur) The leader of the executive branch of a state's government.

# H

**hemisphere** (HEM ih sfeer) A half of Earth.

**heritage** (HAIR uh tihj) Traditions that are passed down from parent to child.

**hero** (HEER oh) Someone who has done special deeds and is a role model for others.

**high-tech** (hy tek) Using advanced technology and computers.

**human capital** (HYOO mun KAP ut ul) People's skills, knowledge, and experiences.

**human geography** (HYOO mun jee AHG ruh fee) The study of how people affect the Earth's surface.

**human resource** (HYOO mun REE sors) People's talents and skills.

**hunter-gatherer** (HUNT ur GATH ur ur) Early people who survived by hunting animals and gathering nuts and plants for food.

## I

**ideals** (eye DEELZ) Ideas that we hope will come true.

**identity** (eye DEN tuh tee) All the things that make people who they are.

**immigrant** (IHM uh grunt) A person who moves from one country to settle in a different country.

**import** (ihm PORT) To bring goods in from another country.

**independence** (ihn dee PEN dents) Freedom from the control or rule of someone else.

**influence** (IHN floo uns) When one thing affects another.

**interact** (ihn tur AKT) To act together.

**invest** (ihn VEST) To spend now in the hope of future reward.

**irrigate** (IHR uh gayt) To supply water to an area.

**issue** (IHSH oo) An important public matter.

## J

**job** (jahb) What a person is supposed to do; duty.

**judicial** (joo DIHSH ul) The branch of government that makes certain the laws follow what is in the U.S. Constitution.

## L

**landform** (LAND form) A natural part of Earth's surface.

**landmark** (LAND mahrk) An important building or monument.

**latitude** (LAT uh tood) Lines on a map or globe that measure distances north and south of the equator.

**law** (law) An official rule.

**legacy** (LEG uh see) Something handed down from the past.

**legislative** (LEJ ihs lay tihv) The branch of government that makes the laws.

**legislature** (LEJ ihs lay chur) The branch of government that makes the laws.

**local** (LOH kul) Nearby.

**longitude** (LAHN juh tood) Lines on a map or globe that measure distances east and west of the prime meridian.

## M

**map key** (map kee) A box that explains the meaning of the symbols on the map; also called map legend.

**map legend** (map LEJ und) A box that explains the meaning of the symbols on the map; also called map key.

**mayor** (MAY ur) The leader of a local government, usually a city.

**mineral** (MIHN ur ul) A resource that comes from under the ground.

**mission** (MIHSH un) A Spanish settlement built by the Catholic church.

**modify** (MAHD uh fy) To change.

**movement** (MOOV munt) A series of actions taken to achieve a goal.

**mudslide** (MUD slyd) The downward movement of a large amount of wet soil, often caused by flooding or rain.

## N

**natural resource** (NACH ur ul REE sors) An item found in nature that people use.

**need** (need) Something you must have to live.

**nonrenewable resource** (nahn rih NOO uh bul REE sors) A resource that cannot be replaced.

## O

**obey** (oh BAY) To follow a rule or law.

**obsidian** (ub SIHD ee un) A black glass-like material often used by American Indians to make tools.

**obtain** (ub TAYN) To acquire, or get.

**occupation** (ah kyuh PAY shun) A job.

**official** (uh FIHSH ul) Approved or recognized for use.

**opportunity cost** (ahp ur TOO nih tee kawst) Something you give up to have something else.

**option** (AHP shun) A choice.

**oral** (AWR ul) Spoken.

**oral history** (AWR ul HIHS tuh ree) Stories or songs passed down within a family.

**original** (uh RIHJ ih nul) The first.

## P

**participate** (pahr TIHS uh payt) To take part, be involved.

**past** (past) The time before now.

**physical geography** (FIHZ ih kul jee AHG ruh fee) The land, water, and other natural features of a place.

**physical map** (FIHZ ih kul map) A map that shows the landforms and bodies of water found in a place.

**political map** (puh LIHT ih kul map) A map that shows information such as state or national borders and cities.

**pop culture** (pahp KUL chur) Activities and products that target a wide audience.

**population map** (pahp yuh LAY shun map) A map that shows where people live.

**prepare** (pree PAIR) To get ready.

**present** (PREZ unt) Now.

**preserve** (PREE zurv) To save or keep.

**presidio** (prih SIHD ee oh) A fort that protected a mission.

**primary** (PRY mair ee) Most important.

**primary source** (PRY mair ee sors) A source that is written or made by a person at an event.

**prime meridian** (prym muh RIHD ee un) The line of longitude marked as 0°.

**process** (PRAH ses) To change something into another form.

**produce** (pruh DOOS) To make or create.

**producer** (pruh DOOS ur) A maker of goods or services.

**promote** (pruh MOHT) To encourage or help.

**property** (PRAHP ur tee) Something that belongs to, or is owned by, someone.

**public virtue** (PUB lihk VUR choo) The goodness that is in all citizens and the willingness to work for the good of a community or nation.

**pueblo** (PWEB loh) A settlement used mostly for farming.

**purchase** (PUR chuz) To buy with money.

## R

**rancho** (RAN choh) A large ranch.

**range** (raynj) A group of mountains.

**refine** (rih FYN) To take away the unwanted parts in something.

**region** (REE jun) A large area of land with similar features that is different from other areas.

**relative location** (REL uh tihv loh KAY shun) Where a place is in relation to another place.

**rely** (rih LY) To depend on, to trust.

**renewable resource** (rih NOO uh bul REE sors) A resource that can be replaced.

**require** (rih KWYR) To need.

**reservation** (rez ur VAY shun) An area of land controlled by an American Indian group.

**responsibility** (rih spahn suh BIHL ih tee) A duty that a person should do.

**responsible** (rih SPAHN suh bul) Able to be trusted to do what is right.

**right** (ryt) A basic idea or truth that people value.

**risk** (rihsk) A dangerous chance.

**role model** (rohl MAHD ul) Someone whose good behavior sets an example for others.

## S

**scale** (skayl) A symbol that represents distance on a map.

**seal** (seel) An official symbol of a place, group, or office.

**secondary source** (SEK un dair ee sors) A source that was written or made by someone who did not witness an event.

**secure** (sih KYOOR) To make something safe and certain.

**series** (SEE reez) A group of similar things next to one another.

**service** (SUR vihs) Work that people do.

**settle** (SET ul) To organize and live in a place.

**settlement** (SET ul munt) A place where people build a community.

**slavery** (SLAY vur ee) The practice of buying and selling people.

**sovereign** (SAHV run) Given the power to govern oneself.

**state seal** (stayt seel) The official symbol of California.

**stereotype** (STAIR ee uh typ) An unfair and overly simple idea about a group of people.

**strike** (stryk) Workers refusing to do their jobs until their working conditions change for the better.

**structure** (STRUK chur) A building.

**sufficient** (suh FIHSH unt) Enough.

**support** (suh PORT) To help by giving money to.

**symbol** (SIHM bul) Something that stands for something else; a marking or color that stands for something else on a map.

## T

**tax** (taks) Money that the government collects.

**technology** (tek NAHL uh jee) The use of science to solve problems and make things work better.

**title** (TYT ul) A line of text that tells what a map shows.

**tourism** (TOOR ihz um) The business of providing hotels, restaurants, and entertainment for people who are visiting.

**tourist** (TOOR ihst) A person who travels for pleasure.

**trade-off** (trayd awf) Giving up one thing for another.

**tradition** (truh DIHSH un) A way of life that is handed down over many years.

**translate** (TRANZ layt) To put words into a different language.

**treaty** (TREE tee) A written agreement.

**tribal government** (TRY bul GUV urn munt) An Indian government.

## U

**union** (YOON yun) A group of workers who join together to gain more rights.

## V

**valley** (VAL ee) An area of low land between mountains and hills.

**value** (VAL yoo) To think something is important.

**violate** (VY uh layt) To break or fail to follow a rule.

**volunteer** (vahl un TEER) A person who works or gives help without being paid.

**voyage** (VOI ihj) A trip.

## W

**want** (wahnt) Something you would like to have but do not need to live.

**wealth** (welth) A large amount of money or other items of value.

**weir** (weer) A dam built across a river by American Indians to catch fish.

**White House** (wyt hous) The place where the president of the United States lives and works.

# Glosario

## A

**abolitionist/abolicionista** Alguien que trabajó para abolir, es decir eliminar, la esclavitud.

**absolute location/ubicación absoluta** La ubicación exacta de un lugar en la Tierra.

**activist/activista** Persona que es muy activa en la vida civil y está comprometida con ella.

**adapt/adaptarse** Cambiar para vivir en un entorno nuevo.

**adjust/modificar** Cambiar o alterar.

**advocate/defensor** Alguien que lucha por una causa.

**agricultural region/región agrícola** Zona donde se produce cierto tipo de cultivos.

**aid/ayuda** Asistencia o apoyo.

**architecture/arquitectura** Cómo está diseñado un edificio.

**area/área** Una parte de un lugar más grande.

**arrange/organizar** Planificar o decidir.

**artifact/artefacto** Objeto que fue hecho y usado por personas.

## B

**bay/bahía** Masa de agua que es parte de un océano y está parcialmente rodeada de tierra.

**benefit/beneficio** Resultado útil.

**biography/biografía** El relato de la vida de una persona escrito por otra persona.

**boundary/límite** Frontera o línea divisoria.

**boycott/boicot** Cuando las personas deciden no comprar, vender o usar algo para apoyar una idea.

**breakwater/rompeolas** Muro o barrera que detiene a las olas.

## C

**capital resource/recurso de capital** Un artículo hecho por humanos que se usa para producir otros bienes o prestar servicios.

**celebrity/celebridad** Persona famosa.

**century/siglo** Período de tiempo de 100 años.

**ceremony/ceremonia** Actividad especial que se realiza por una razón importante.

**charter/carta** Documento similar a una constitución que establece las reglas para una colonia, una ciudad u otro grupo.

**citizen/ciudadano** Miembro de una comunidad, un estado o una nación.

**citizenship/ciudadanía** Carácter y conducta de un ciudadano.

**civic/cívico** Referido a los derechos y las responsabilidades de los ciudadanos.

**civil rights/derechos civiles** Derechos de todos los ciudadanos de ser tratados con igualdad ante la ley.

**civil war/guerra civil** Guerra entre grupos de personas dentro de un mismo país.

**claim/reclamar** Decir que un territorio pertenece a un país.

**climate/clima** El estado del tiempo en un lugar a lo largo del tiempo.

**common/común** Que no es raro ni inusual.

**community/comunidad** Lugar donde viven personas.

**compass rose/rosa de los vientos** Símbolo de los mapas que muestra los puntos cardinales norte, sur, este y oeste; también puede mostrar el noroeste, suroeste, noreste y sureste.

**conditions/condiciones** Circunstancias existentes.

**conflict/conflicto** Desacuerdo.

**Congress/Congreso** El cuerpo legislativo de los Estados Unidos, que crea las leyes.

**consequence/consecuencia** Resultado o efecto de una acción.

**conserve/conservar** Proteger un recurso.

**constitution/constitución** Plan o conjunto de reglas que explica cómo funcionará un país.

**consumer/consumidor** Usuario de productos y servicios.

**contribute/contribuir** Dar o ayudar.

**convert/convertirse** Cambiar; adoptar una religión, opinión o idea política diferente.

**cost/costo** El precio necesario para obtener una cosa.

**council/consejo** Grupo de líderes locales.

**culture/cultura** Artes, creencias y conductas de un grupo de personas.

**custom/costumbre** Una manera de hacer algo

**cyberbullying/ciberacoso** Acción de enviar mensajes agresivos por Internet.

# D

**decade/década** Período de 10 años.

**deed/obra** Acción.

**delegate/delegado** Persona elegida para actuar en nombre de otros.

**desert/desierto** Zona de tierra muy seca donde crecen pocas plantas.

**despite/a pesar** Sin ser afectado por algo.

**develop/desarrollar** Crear.

**discover/descubrir** Hallar.

**discrimination/discriminación** Tratar a las personas de un modo diferente por su raza, género, edad u otra característica.

**display/exhibir** Mostrar.

**diverse/diverso** Formado por diferentes grupos de personas.

**document/documento** Registro escrito.

# E

**earthquake/terremoto** Movimiento repentino de la capa superior de la Tierra.

**ecosystem/ecosistema** Todos los seres vivientes y cosas no vivientes que interactúan en un lugar determinado.

**elder/anciano** Un líder mayor.

**electricity/electricidad** Un tipo de energía usado para encender focos y hacer funcionar máquinas.

**element/elemento** Una parte de algo mayor.

**elevation/elevación** La altura de la tierra por encima del nivel del mar.

**emergency/emergencia** Un problema inesperado y urgente.

**energy/energía** Potencia que puede usarse.

**enforce/hacer cumplir** Asegurarse de que las personas obedezcan las leyes y reglas.

**entrepreneur/empresario** Alguien que crea una empresa.

**environment/medio ambiente** El mundo natural donde viven las personas, las plantas y los animales.

**equator/ecuador** Una línea imaginaria que se extiende alrededor del centro de la Tierra.

**ethnicity/etnia** Personas que tienen antecedentes o una cultura en común.

**executive/ejecutivo** El poder del gobierno que hace cumplir las leyes.

**explorer/explorador** Persona que va a una zona desconocida para aprender sobre ella.

**export/exportar** Enviar bienes a otro país.

**eyewitness/testigo presencial** Persona que estuvo cuando ocurrió un suceso.

**F**

**feature/característica** Parte importante o interesante de algo.

**federal/federal** Nacional.

**fine/multa** Dinero pagado como consecuencia de algo.

**folklore/folklore** Todas las tradiciones, costumbres, creencias y cuentos de un grupo de personas que se transmiten por medio de la palabra.

**founded/fundado** Creado.

**fund/financiar** Pagar algo.

**future/futuro** El tiempo después de ahora.

**G**

**generation/generación** El período de tiempo entre el nacimiento de los padres y el nacimiento de sus hijos.

**globe/globo terráqueo** Un modelo de la Tierra.

**good/bien** Un artículo que se puede ver, como un lápiz o un carro.

**governor/gobernador** Líder del poder ejecutivo del gobierno de un estado.

**H**

**hemisphere/hemisferio** Una mitad de la Tierra.

**heritage/herencia** Tradiciones que son transmitidas de padres a hijos.

**hero/héroe** Alguien que hizo actos especiales y es un modelo para otros.

**high-tech/de alta tecnología** Que usa tecnología y computadoras avanzadas.

**human capital/capital humano** Destrezas, conocimientos y experiencia de las personas.

**human geography/geografía humana** Estudio de cómo las personas influyen en la superficie de la Tierra.

**human resource/recursos humanos** Talentos y destrezas de las personas.

**hunter-gatherer/cazador-recolector**
Personas de la antigüedad que sobrevivían cazando animales y recolectando nueces y plantas para comer.

## I

**ideals/ideales** Ideas que esperamos que se vuelvan realidad.

**identity/identidad** Todas las cosas que hacen a las personas ser quienes son.

**immigrant/inmigrante** Persona que deja un país para establecerse en otro país.

**import/importar** Hacer entrar bienes desde otro país.

**independence/independencia** Libertad respecto del control o gobierno de otros.

**influence/influencia** Cuando algo afecta a otra cosa.

**interact/interactuar** Actuar juntos.

**invest/invertir** Gastar dinero en algo ahora con la idea de obtener una ganancia en el futuro.

**irrigate/irrigar** Llevar agua a un área.

**issue/asunto** Un tema público importante.

## J

**job/empleo** Lo que una persona debe hacer; su deber.

**judicial/judicial** El poder del gobierno que se asegura de que las leyes sigan lo que dice en la Constitución de los Estados Unidos.

## L

**landform/accidente geográfico** Parte natural de la superficie de la Tierra.

**landmark/sitio de interés** Un edificio o monumento importante.

**latitude/latitud** Líneas en un mapa o globo terráqueo que miden las distancias al norte y al sur del ecuador.

**law/ley** Una regla oficial.

**legacy/legado** Algo que es transmitido desde el pasado.

**legislative/legislativo** El poder del gobierno que crea las leyes.

**legislature/cuerpo legislativo** El poder del gobierno que crea las leyes.

**local/local** Cercano.

**longitude/longitud** Líneas en un mapa o globo terráqueo que miden las distancias al este y al oeste del primer meridiano.

## M

**map key/leyenda de un mapa** Recuadro que explica el significado de los símbolos en el mapa.

**map legend/leyenda de un mapa** Recuadro que explica el significado de los símbolos en el mapa.

**mayor/alcalde** Líder de un gobierno local, generalmente una ciudad.

**mineral/mineral** Recurso que proviene de abajo de la tierra.

**mission/misión** Un asentamiento español construido por la iglesia católica.

**modify/modificar** Cambiar.

**movement/movimiento** Una serie de acciones llevadas a cabo para lograr una meta.

**mudslide/avalancha de lodo** El movimiento en forma de caída de una gran cantidad de lodo, que suele ser causado por inundación o lluvia.

## N

**natural resource/recurso natural** Un elemento que se halla en la naturaleza y la gente usa.

**need/necesidad** Algo que uno debe tener para poder vivir.

**nonrenewable resource/recurso no renovable** Recurso que no puede ser reemplazado.

## O

**obey/obedecer** Cumplir una regla o ley.

**obsidian/obsidiana** Material negro similar al vidrio usado por los indígenas norteamericanos para hacer herramientas.

**obtain/obtener** Adquirir, conseguir.

**occupation/ocupación** Empleo.

**official/oficial** Aprobado o reconocido para su uso.

**opportunity cost/costo de oportunidad** Algo a lo que renuncias para tener otra cosa.

**option/opción** Elección.

**oral/oral** Hablado.

**oral history/historia oral** Relatos o canciones transmitidos dentro de una familia.

**original/original** El primero.

## P

**participate/participar** Ser parte de algo, involucrarse.

**past/pasado** El tiempo antes de ahora.

**physical geography/geografía física** La tierra, el agua y otras características naturales de un lugar.

**physical map/mapa físico** Mapa que muestra los accidentes geográficos y las masas de agua que hay en un lugar.

**political map/mapa político** Mapa que muestra información como las fronteras nacionales y estatales y las ciudades.

**pop culture/cultura pop** Actividades y productos que se dirigen a una audiencia amplia.

**population map/mapa de población** Mapa que muestra dónde viven las personas.

**prepare/preparar** Dejar algo listo.

**present/presente** Ahora.

**preserve/preservar** Guardar o mantener.

**presidio/presidio** Fuerte que protegía una misión.

**primary/primario** Más importante.

**primary source/fuente primaria** Una fuente escrita o hecha por una persona que estuvo presente en un suceso.

**prime meridian/primer meridiano** La línea de longitud marcada como 0°.

**process/procesar** Cambiar algo y hacer que tenga otra forma.

**produce/producir** Hacer o crear.

**producer/productor** Creador de bienes o servicios.

**promote/promover** Alentar o ayudar.

**property/propiedad** Algo que le pertenece a alguien.

**public virtue/virtud pública** El bien que hay en todos los ciudadanos y la voluntad de trabajar por el bien de una comunidad o una nación.

**pueblo/pueblo** Un asentamiento usado sobre todo para agricultura y ganadería.

**purchase/adquirir** Comprar con dinero.

## R

**rancho/rancho** Una granja grande.

**range/cordillera** Grupo de montañas.

**refine/refinar** Quitar las partes no deseadas de algo.

**region/región** Una gran área de tierra con características similares que es diferente de otras áreas.

**relative location/ubicación relativa** Dónde está un lugar en relación con otro lugar.

**rely/confiar** Depender, tener confianza.

**renewable resource/recurso renovable** Recurso que puede ser reemplazado.

**require/requerir** Necesitar.

**reservation/reserva** Área de tierra controlada por un grupo de indígenas norteamericanos.

**responsibility/responsabilidad** Un deber que una persona tiene que cumplir.

**responsible/responsable** Persona en quien se puede confiar que haga lo correcto.

**right/derecho** Idea o verdad básica que las personas valoran.

**risk/riesgo** Posibilidad peligrosa.

**role model/modelo** Alguien que tiene un buen comportamiento y es un ejemplo para los demás.

## S

**scale/escala** Símbolo que representa la distancia en un mapa.

**seal/sello** Símbolo oficial de un lugar, un grupo o una oficina.

**secondary source/fuente secundaria** Fuente que fue escrita o hecha por alguien que no fue testigo de un suceso.

**secure/asegurar** Hacer que algo sea seguro y no falle.

**series/serie** Un grupo de cosas similares, una junto a la otra.

**service/servicio** Trabajo que hacen las personas.

**settle/establecerse** Organizarse y vivir en un lugar.

**settlement/asentamiento** Lugar donde las personas construyen una comunidad.

**slavery/esclavismo** La práctica de comprar y vender personas.

**sovereign/soberano** Que recibió el poder de gobernarse a sí mismo.

**state seal/sello del estado** El símbolo oficial de California.

**stereotype/estereotipo** Una idea injusta y demasiado simple acerca de un grupo de personas.

**strike/huelga** Acción de trabajadores que deciden no hacer su trabajo hasta que mejoren las condiciones de trabajo.

**structure/estructura** Un edificio.

**sufficient/suficiente** Bastante cantidad.

**support/apoyar** Ayudar con dinero.

**symbol/símbolo** Algo que representa otra cosa; marca o color que representa otra cosa en un mapa.

## T

**tax/impuesto** Dinero que el gobierno recauda.

**technology/tecnología** El uso de la ciencia para resolver problemas y hacer que las cosas funcionen mejor.

**title/título** Línea de texto que dice lo que muestra un mapa.

**tourism/turismo** La actividad de ofrecer hoteles, restaurantes y entretenimiento a las personas que visitan un lugar.

**tourist/turista** Persona que viaja por placer.

**trade-off/intercambio** Renunciar a una cosa para obtener otra.

**tradition/tradición** Forma de vida que se transmite a lo largo de muchos años.

**translate/traducir** Poner palabras en otro idioma.

**treaty/tratado** Acuerdo escrito.

**tribal government/gobierno tribal** Gobierno indígena.

## U

**union/sindicato** Grupo de trabajadores que se unen para conseguir más derechos.

## V

**valley/valle** Área de tierra baja entre montañas y colinas.

**value/valorar** Considerar que algo es importante.

**violate/transgredir** Romper o no cumplir una regla.

**volunteer/voluntario** Persona que trabaja o colabora sin recibir un pago.

**voyage/travesía** Viaje.

## W

**want/deseo** Algo que a uno le gustaría tener pero no necesita para vivir.

**wealth/riqueza** Cantidad grande de dinero u otros artículos de valor.

**weir/presa** Represa construida por los indígenas norteamericanos para atrapar peces.

**White House/Casa Blanca** El lugar donde el Presidente de los Estados Unidos vive y trabaja.

# Index

This index lists the pages on which topics appear in this book. Page numbers followed by *m* refer to maps. Page numbers followed by *p* refer to photographs. Page numbers followed by *c* refer to charts or graphs. Page numbers followed by *t* refer to timelines. The terms *See* and *See also* direct the reader to alternate entries.

## A

**Y**

# Credits

## Text Acknowledgments

### The Cabrillo National Monument Foundation
An Account of the Voyage of Juan Rodríguez Cabrillo. Copyright © The Cabrillo National Monument Foundation.

### David Kupfer
The Final Interview with David R Brower by David Kupfer. Copyright © David Kupfer.

### Simon & Schuster
Mine Eyes Have Seen: A First-Person History of the Events That Shaped America by Richard Goldstein. Copyright © Simon & Schuster.

### Torch Press
Adobe Days: A Book of California Memories by Sarah Bixby-Smith. Copyright © Torch Press.

## Images

CVR: Craig Tuttle/Getty Images; CVR: Dee Jolie/Alamy Stock Photo; CA001B: Michael E Halstead/Shutterstock; CA001T: Mitch Diamond/Photodisc/Getty Images; CA002: Cbies/Shutterstock; CA003B: Ian Dagnall/Alamy Stock Photo; CA003T: 7505811966/Shutterstock; CA004B: Photo Researchers/Science Source/Getty Images; CA004T: Judy Bellah/Alamy Stock Photo; CA005B: David Sherman/National Basketball Association/Getty Images; CA005T: Anthony Harvey/Getty Images; CA008: Stephen Oliver/Dorling Kindersley ltd.; CA017: MyTopShelf/Fotolia; CA018: Roy H. Anderson/National Geographic/Getty Images; CA020: Bst2012/Fotolia; CA021: Paul Marcus/Shutterstock; CA022: SuperStock/Alamy Stock Photo; CA023: Jan Hakan Dahlstrom/Photographer's Choice/Getty Images; Copyright Page: Rachid Dahnoun/Aurora Open RF/Alamy Stock Photo; i: Sumiko Scott/Alamy Stock Photo; iii: Camarillo Dr. Albert M.; iii: Dr. James B. Kracht; iii: Dr. Kathy Swan; iii: Dr. Linda B. Bennett; iii: Elfrieda H. Hiebert; iii: Jim Cummins; iii: Kathy Tuchman Glass; iii: Paul Apodaca; iii: Steven Hackel; iii: Warren J. Blumenfeld; iii: Xiaojian Zhao; xii: California State Library; xivT: Bryant Anderson / Del Norte Triplicate; xivB: Michael Ochs Archives/Getty Images; xxiii: Jamie Grill/JGI//Blend Images/Getty Images; xxiiL: Sierrarat/E+/Getty Images; xxiiR: PureStock/Alamy Stock Photo; xxiv: Irina Mos/Shutterstock; xxv: California State Library; CO-001: Jon Bilous/Shutterstock; 003: Jamie Grill/JGI//Blend Images/Getty Images; 004: Sierrarat/E+/Getty Images; 005: PureStock/Alamy Stock Photo; 007: Chad Ehlers/Alamy Stock Photo; 008: David Litman/Shutterstock; 009: Tom Reichner/Shutterstock; 010: Irina Mos/Shutterstock; 012: Dancestrokes/Shutterstock; 018L: Thomas Stankiewicz/Look Die Bildagentur Der Fotografen GmbH/Alamy Stock Photo; 018R: Kropic I/Shutterstock; 019L: David Litman/Shutterstock; 019R: Corey Jenkins/Imago Source/Alamy Stock Photo; 023: Inga Spence/Alamy Stock Photo; 024: Anthony Dunn/Alamy Stock Photo; 025: Zuma Press, Inc./Alamy Stock Photo; 026: Raphael Gaillarde/Gamma-Rapho/Getty Images; 029: California State Library; 030B: Zack Frank/Shutterstock; 030T: USDA Forest Service; 032: Tracie Cone/AP Images; 036-037: Ian G Dagnall/Alamy Stock Photo; 039: Scholastic Studio 10/Photolibrary/Getty Images; 040: Roy H. Anderson/National Geographic/Getty Images; 043B: Basketry vessel, Nevada, early 20th century (willow, bracken fern, red bud), Dat So La Lee (Louisa Keyser) (c.1829-1925)/Brooklyn Museum of Art, New York, USA / by exchange/Bridgeman Art Library; 043T: The Protected Art Archive/Alamy Stock Photo; 044: Sumikophoto/Shutterstock; 045: Ric Francis/AP Images; 047: Buyenlarge/Archive Photos/Getty Images; 048: William Greene/Smithsonian - National Museum of the American Indian; 050: Library of Congress Prints and Photographs Division; 052B: Mark Dufrene/KRT/Newscom; 052T: Buyenlarge/Archive Photos/Getty Images; 054B: The Protected Art Archive/Alamy Stock Photo; 054T: Gary Crabbe/Enlightened Images/Alamy Stock Photo; 056B: Daderot/Wikimedia Commons; 056T: Bobbi Onia/Underwood Archives/Archive Photos/Getty Images; 059: Richard Wong/Alamy Stock Photo; 061: Yaacov Dagan/Alamy Stock Photo; 062: Edward S. Curtis/Library of Congress Prints and Photographs Division[LC-USZ62-101260]; 063: Damian Dovarganes/AP Images; 064L: David Carbo/Shutterstock; 064R: Steve Byland/Shutterstock; 065: Inga Spence/Alamy Stock Photo; 066: M.Sobreira/Alamy Stock Photo; 069: Timothy Hearsum/Stockbyte/Getty Images; 070B: PureStock/Alamy Stock Photo; 070T: Bryant Anderson / Del Norte Triplicate; 072: Gary Crabbe/Enlightened Images/Alamy Stock Photo; 076-077: Archive Images/Alamy Stock Photo; 080: Underwood Archives/Archive Photos/Getty Images; 082: Richard Cummins/Robertharding/Alamy Stock Photo; 090: Richard Wong/Alamy Stock Photo; 091: UC Berkeley, Bancroft Library; 092B: Photo Researchers, Inc/Alamy Stock Photo; 092T: Brian Hendricks/Shutterstock; 093B: Oleksandr Lysenko/Shutterstock; 093T: MyTopShelf/Fotolia; 094: Bettmann/Getty Images; 095: LAMB/Alamy Stock Photo; 096T: Smith Collection/Gado/Archive Photos/Getty Images; 96B: Stock Montage/Getty Images; 097L: Richard Wong/Alamy Stock Photo; 097R: Julia Reschke/Shutterstock; 098-099: North Wind Picture Archives/Alamy Stock Photo; 100: Tomacco/Shutterstock; 101: Charles Phelps Cushing/ClassicStock/Alamy Stock Photo; 102: Carleton E. Watkins/Library of Congress Prints and Photographs Division[LC-USZ62-53892]; 104: Lynn Y/Shutterstock; 106: Eddie J. Rodriguez/Shutterstock; 107: David Litman/Shutterstock; 108L: Classic Image/Alamy Stock Photo; 108R: Lyudmila Suvorova/Shutterstock; 110: Anthony Dunn/Alamy Stock Photo; 112: Carl Simon/United Archives GmbH/Alamy Stock Photo; 114B: Tony Hertz/Alamy Stock Photo; 114T: Vintage Images/Alamy Stock Photo; 115: Ian Paterson/Alamy Stock